MIGHT VALOR – WITH CHARLEY COMPANY ON HILL 714

VIETNAM 1970

JOHN G. ROBERTS

ISBN: 9781549892615

Other books by John G. Roberts

A Damn Big Fight—Crazy Horse, Custer and Sitting Bull at the Little Bighorn

Operation Texas Star—The Last American Battles of the Vietnam War

THE INFANTRY

And the Angel of the Lord appeared to him and said, "Mighty warrior, the LORD is with you."
-From the *Book of Judges, Chapter 6, verse 12*

No one has greater love than this—that one lays down his life for his friends.
- From the *Book of John, Chapter 15, verse 13*

There is many a boy here today who looks on war as all glory; but, boys, it is all hell.
-General William Tecumseh Sherman

*-The Infantry's primary role is close combat, which may occur in any type of mission, in any theatre or environment. Characterized by extreme violence and physiological shock, close combat is callous and unforgiving. Its dimensions are measured in minutes and meters, and its consequences are **final**. Close combat stresses every aspect of the physical, mental and spiritual features of the human dimension. To this end, Infantrymen are specially selected, trained and led-*
-From a US Army Infantry Training Manual
Courtesy Mike Lucky, Alpha Company 2nd/502nd Infantry. Veteran of Hill 882

PREFACE

This is the history of an infantry battalion serving in the Republic of Vietnam during the year 1970. More specifically, it's about a single rifle company within that battalion and the events that over took them during an operation called Texas Star. Some of the memories from my tour with the 101st Airborne Division in Vietnam have become dim, shrouded by the passage of many years. Others still burn bright and pop unwanted into my mind, like a trip flare suddenly igniting in the middle of the night. The Veterans Affairs doctors say I have post-traumatic stress disorder (PTSD), something I had never heard of until about ten years ago.

The beginnings of this book were first put on paper in 1982. I'd been home about twelve years and the urge to write about my time in 'the 'Nam' was becoming strong. I worked on my notes sporadically over the next eighteen years or so, using only my memory, until the summer of 2001. Some of my memories are not consistent with the official documents, so, whenever possible, I have attempted to verify my recollections with statements from fellow veterans who served with me.

Shortly before my mother passed away, I learned that she had saved every one of the letters I had written home during my time in the service. These are a gold mine of information and, after reading them, the memories came flooding back. I have used information from these letters to fill in any gaps left by the official documents. I hope my letters will give a more personal touch to this manuscript.

I had been trying for about six months to locate old army buddies using the newfangled (to me) Internet. I was looking specifically for info on Mike Lucky, whom I had not seen for thirty-one years. In fact, I thought he was dead, killed on Hill 882. I found two men named Mike Lucky, with phone numbers, in his home state of Texas. I called the first number and hit the jackpot: when I heard Mike's Texas drawl again, it was as if the preceding thirty-one years had never passed. We talked as if we'd seen each other only last week.

It turned out that Mike was a career employee at Veterans Affairs. His knowledge helped me considerably while I navigated the VA's maze of rules and regulations, and I finally got help for my service-related injuries. I'm very grateful for his willing help.

Through Mike, I learned what official, declassified records were available to the public from the National Archives. I ordered copies of after action reports, unit histories, and the all-important daily journals. Using these resources, I began to put this work together.

I have included portions of tactical maps that will help to illustrate the movements of the various units in their areas of operations around the different firebases. Remember, when reading a tactical map, find the gridline, and look "to the right and up." I have also included a glossary of terms for those who may not be familiar with military terminology. All glossary terms appear in boldface on their first use.

The personal memories of the veterans who were there add an eyewitness reality to what I've tried to say. Some of them had to reach into long-suppressed and hidden recollections and re-open Pandora's Box. It must have been tough, and I'm glad they were able to do it.

As time passed and I located more of the veterans I served with, the thought of perhaps publishing a book began to take shape. A few years back, a wonderful book was published called *West of Hue: Down the Yellow Brick Road.* The author is a veteran named James P. Brinker who served in the Recon Platoon in my battalion while I was serving in Charlie Company. His book helped to clarify some memories of those traumatic months in the spring of 1970. It was Brinker who, in an e-mail, suggested I write about my unit. Since my wife had been urging me for quite some time to write a book, Brinker's nudge was all I needed to dive in head first.

I have many people to thank: first and foremost is Shari, my beautiful wife and partner of many years, who allowed me to bounce ideas off her like a human basketball backboard. I also want to thank my three children, Amie, Mike, and Rick, for putting up with my PTSD-induced faults while growing up and for listening patiently without rolling their eyes while I told the same 'war stories' over and over.

Also deserving of thanks are my fellow veterans James "Jimbo" Brinker, Harold Carstens, Daniel Kulm (Gerry Kulm's nephew), Larry Kuss, Terry Lowe, Eraldo Lucero, Mike Lucky, Robert "Noff" Noffsinger, Bruce Scott and Terry Williams. All but Dan belonged to the "O-Deuce," the 2nd Battalion 502nd Infantry, 101st Airborne Division. They were right in the middle of the actions I describe in this book.

These men are survivors, and, thanks to God, my wonderful family and the professionals at Kaiser Permanente and Veterans Affairs, so am I.

CONTENTS

Authors Photo Album

Chapter 1

The Beginning: An Opportunity Lost

I was just your normal, spoiled, red-blooded American boy when I dropped out of college in June of 1968. I was bored with my classes, bored with my professors, and, especially, bored with my fellow students. I got a job as a meat cutter/sales clerk in the meat shop (I still have the scars) at a small mom-and-pop grocery store in Montclair, California. I thought I could save some money, travel a bit, and go back to school when I felt like it. Of course, that's not the way it turned out.

In April of 1968, I received a letter from the Selective Service System (Draft Board) ordering me to report to the Armed Forces Induction Center in Los Angeles for a pre-induction physical examination. I drove into LA and submitted myself into the clutches of the Selective Service clerks and doctors. I filled out paperwork, peed into a bottle, gave blood, had my eyes checked for color blindness, and had a hearing test. The final indignity came when I had to stand in a circle with 15 or 20 other naked men while we were examined by a doctor; he peered into our eyes, nose, ears and throats, checked for hernias and flat feet. Then he ordered us to face outward from the circle, had us bend at the waist and spread our butt cheeks apart.

About a month after that, I received my draft card in the mail; the classification box on the card said I was '**I-A**' meaning I was eligible for immediate induction into the armed forces. I was required to carry this card on my person all the time.

Having a classification of I-A in the Selective Service System should have been a warning that I would be immediately drafted if I gave up my student deferment status. However, I chose to ignore this, dropped out of school and paid the price for my indifference.

While I was in school, I usually ate lunch in the student cafeteria. After a while, I noticed a group of men who had taken over a couple of tables in one corner of the room. It was the same group of men every day; they were very quiet, talking among themselves in low voices. I saw that most of them habitually wore parts of military fatigue uniforms; they didn't smile or laugh very often. I asked some people who they were and was told that they were Vietnam War veterans and that I shouldn't bother them.

Little did I know that, three years later, I would be back in that same cafeteria with much the same feelings that those men must have had.

So, when, late in 1968, I lost my job in the meat shop, I went to the local unemployment office to apply for benefits. As I was standing in line, I happened to look toward the entrance and saw my father walk in with a tan envelope clutched in his hand. He walked up to me and said, "Son, you're not going to need unemployment. It looks like you've been drafted."

I grabbed the envelope from his hand and ripped it open. He was right! I had been drafted by local draft board #94 in Pasadena, California, and ordered to report at 8:00 a.m. on January 15, 1969.

While growing up in the small town of Covina, California, I'd had no experience with things military, although two of my uncles had served in WWII, one in the invasion of Normandy and the other in the invasion of Leyte in the Pacific. The only thing I knew about war was gleaned from watching episodes of *Combat* on television and the series *Victory at Sea*.

It was Uncle James, my father's older brother who, serving with the 803rd Tank Destroyer Battalion, went ashore driving an M-18 tank destroyer on June 6, 1944. He fought all the way across France, losing several tanks in the process. His tank, armed with a 3-inch (76mm) gun, was destroyed by a German Tiger Tank (armed with an 88mm gun) during the Battle of the Bulge, not far from Bastogne, Belgium. Thrown clear by the explosion, he lay wounded in the snow for over twenty-four hours, playing dead when the Germans came around, until he was rescued by American **medic**s.

I believe my uncle had PTSD all his life. No one had ever heard of the disease then, much less given any thought to treatment. After I came home from Vietnam, he would talk to me about combat, sometimes breaking into tears as he told me about the things that had happened to him during "his" war.

Family legend has it that I also had an uncle, three or four greats ago, who had died at the Battle of Pea Ridge while serving with the 15th Arkansas Volunteer Infantry Regiment during the Civil War.

I didn't know what to expect in the modern army, but I knew I would find out soon enough.

Chapter 2

Like It Or Not: You're In The Army Now

After an emotional good-bye breakfast with my family at Clifton's Cafeteria in downtown Los Angeles, I duly reported to the Armed Forces Induction Center at 1033 S. Broadway, Los Angeles. As I reached for the glass door of the induction center, someone grabbed my arm. I looked around and found myself looking in to the glaring eyes of a scruffy-looking young man. He urgently began speaking to me: "You don't have to go, man! Don't go! Come with me and we can have you in Canada in three or four days! You don't have to go!" But I jerked my arm free and went inside, sealing my fate.

After a couple of hours of filling out forms, I took the oath and that was it—I was in the army. I sat and waited in a small waiting room. While I was there, four or five frightened young men entered the room, escorted by a Marine gunnery sergeant. They all had little red signs hanging around their necks with 'USMC' in yellow letters printed on them. I remember thinking, "Those poor guys. I'm glad that's not me." The brutality of Marine Corps boot camp was legendary.

Eventually I found myself on a bus, clutching a sack lunch and a pocket-sized New Testament. The bus drove north out of Los Angeles along US Highway 101, California's coastal highway. Our destination was Fort Ord, California, just north of the city of Monterey. The ride north was long and slow, with very little conversation. It appeared that everyone preferred to keep his own counsel.

Incidentally, on the southbound side of US Highway 101 just below Santa Barbara, there is now a huge sign depicting the division logo and the words "The Screaming Eagles Highway–101st Airborne Division." Every time I pass that sign, I get a tingle.

Late that afternoon, the bus pulled off the highway in San Luis Obispo so we could take a break. There was a Denny's restaurant there and some of the men rushed inside attempting to get some civilian food, the last they would eat for some time. Interestingly, that Denny's is still there after more than forty-eight years.

At about 9:00 p.m., the bus pulled through the gates of Fort Ord and we stepped off the bus into a damp, foggy night. We were greeted by cadre personnel who, yelling and cursing, forced us into a rough formation. A big E-7 (sergeant first class; see Army Ranks: Enlisted, Warrant, and Commissioned Officers) stepped in front of the group and glared at us. Dressed in stiffly starched, sharply creased fatigues and a shiny black helmet, he growled, "Welcome to the United States Army Infantry Training Center and Fort Ord." He gave the standard speech about obeying orders, no fighting, no booze, no dope, and no weapons allowed on the post. We were offered the chance to get rid of any contraband we might have by dumping it into an 'amnesty box,' conveniently located to the sergeant's right. No one moved, so we were led into a building where we, guess what, filled out more forms. We were finally allowed to go to bed after about three hours, but only after we received a lesson from a pissed-off PFC in how to make up a bunk to military specifications.

After waking very early the next morning, we walked through the thick fog to the mess hall where I had my first army meal, '**SOS**', the breakfast food of champions.

Then we began the week-long ordeal of aptitude tests, fingerprinting and photographs, haircuts, uniform and equipment issue, and, finally, shots. We had to pay the barber a dollar after he shaved our heads down to the scalp in about 30 seconds.

The experience of receiving inoculations army-style was interesting because the shots were administered by army medics using pneumatic needles. The serum was injected by shooting a blast of air through the skin and into the muscle. We got four shots simultaneously, two in each arm. A couple of men passed out and the rest of us were given the opportunity to 'work the soreness out' by doing pushups.

While I was waiting at the reception center, I was given the opportunity to take the test for helicopter flight school. I passed the test, but when they told me I'd have to enlist for an additional two years, I opted out. If I flunked out of flight school, I would have had to do the additional time plus my initial obligation of two years; at that point, I was not prepared to give the army that much time from my life. I was also offered the chance to attend officer's candidate school, but that also required additional time in the army. I had to turn that down, too, and take my chances with the army classification system.

Chapter 3

Going Up The Hill: Basic Training and AIT

Soon after that, I was sent up the hill to my basic training company. It was called 'up the hill' because the basic training barracks were built on a high slope while the rest of Fort Ord was down at sea level. I endured, along with everybody else, the tough physical training and harassment that went with learning to be a soldier and, after about eight weeks, I had learned the basics.

We were taken to the basic training area of the fort in big open trailers called 'cattle cars' because the trainees, along with all their gear, were packed onto the trailers like cattle on the way to the slaughter house.

As soon as we arrived, the DI's began screaming at us. I remember that I didn't move fast enough while climbing the stairs to my platoon bay on the top floor of the three-story barracks. I was grabbed out of the line of huffing, puffing trainees and ordered to lie on my back. I had to wriggle my arms and legs back and forth and scream at the top of my voice "I am a dying cockroach; I am a dying cockroach!"

Each trainee had to wear a white rectangular piece of cloth sewn above the name tag over the right pocket of the uniform shirt and jacket. Known as a 'maggot patch,' the trainees' platoon, company, battalion and brigade was written on the patch. Mine read 4-D-1-3 and stood for 4th platoon, Delta Company, 1st Battalion, 3rd Brigade. This was used so basic trainees could be instantly identified should they wander away from the restricted area of the basic training barracks.

A few weeks into the training cycle a couple of enterprising trainees figured out a way to remove the maggot patches and, for a fee, would sneak out of the barracks after lights out and bring back candy and potato chips for any half-starved trainee who had the money to pay them.

We were constantly hungry, so they did a thriving business. Food, outside of the mess hall, was forbidden in the barracks. We ate at 5:30 AM, 12:00 PM and the last meal at 5:00 PM. The twelve hours between dinner and breakfast meant that many of us woke in the middle of the night with loudly growling stomachs. This strict regimen caused us to lose our civilian fat quickly and replace it with muscle which, of course, was the whole idea.

Another necessary but unpleasant aspect of barracks life was 'meningitis control.' Spinal meningitis is a disease that thrives in warm, poorly ventilated areas among large groups of people living in close quarters. There had been an outbreak of the disease at Fort Ord several years earlier; many trainees became ill and several died.

To counter the threat, the post surgeon had decreed that all windows in the barracks must remain open, even in the coldest, wettest weather. The barracks were very cold, and we were miserable, but it greatly reduced the threat of another outbreak of spinal meningitis.

Several other things have stuck in my mind about basic training. One is a big DI (drill instructor) named SSG Salmon with a Clark Gable-style mustache who called himself Sgt. Fish and an E-7 named Fletcher. Sgt. Fletcher's favorite thing was calling us out in the middle of the night, especially when it was raining, to perform the manual of arms with our footlockers while wearing only our underwear. He'd repeat, in a strong Brooklyn accent, *"It's good trainin' for you'se trainees, good trainin'. If it ain't rainin', you'se ain't trainin."* I failed to see the need for special training to learn how to get wet. This harassment stopped after the word somehow got back to the battalion commander.

The company's first sergeant was a man named McNerney. He was a no-nonsense guy who was awarded the Medal of Honor for actions around Pleiku, Vietnam, in March 1967. As a good first sergeant will, he kept things running smoothly.

Physical training, known by its initials **"PT"**, was used by the army to develop trainees into physically fit soldiers. Many of us were in poor shape physically, so the rugged daily routine of calisthenics, performed by the numbers in unison was hard on us. Some of the exercises were: side-straddle hops (jumping jacks), toe-touches, sit-ups, leg lifts and everybody's favorite, the push-up. There was even an "8-count push-up" which was a real instrument of torture.

Tear gas training is something that all recruits go through and I recall my exposure to the gas very clearly. We were issued and taught how to use and maintain a gas mask. We marched to the chemical weapons training area and were told to put on our gas masks. Then, in groups of ten or twelve men, we entered a small shed where a type of tear gas had been released to fill the interior of the building. When everyone was inside, and the door secured, we were ordered to take off our masks. We did so reluctantly; almost immediately, the gas took effect. My eyes began to burn, and tears poured down my face. My nose filled with snot and I began to cough. We were nearly blind, and the instructors turned us to the right and made us march in a circle around the device that was producing the gas fumes.

When they were sure we'd all had a good dose of the gas, we marched to the door where we had to recite our name, rank and serial number before we could exit the gas-filled building. The poor guys at the end of the line were desperate to reach the clean air outside the hut. Fresh air didn't help much and rubbing our eyes only made the irritation worse.

Another unpleasant part of basic training was pulling **KP** (kitchen police) duty. It was the policy in D/1/3 that recruits who were members of the regular (volunteer) army would not be assigned to KP. This onerous task fell exclusively to draftees, reservists and national guardsmen doing their 6-months active duty.

The first time I pulled KP was memorable. We were rousted from our bunks at 3 AM by the CQ (charge of quarters) and escorted to the company mess hall. We were put to work preparing the ingredients for breakfast which was served at 5:30 AM. I remember cracking several hundred fresh eggs and dumping them into a huge aluminum pot. When a trainee asked for eggs, the cook would reach into the pot with a Styrofoam cup and scoop up two egg yolks which he'd then cook anyway the trainee wanted.

After the egg-cracking duty, I was assigned as the 'pot man.' This meant I had to stand in front of a huge sink full of hot soapy water and scrub, to military specifications of cleanliness, every pot and pan used by the cooks in the preparation of all three meals that day. It was back-breaking, exhausting work and my fingers were raw by the end of the day.

Finally, about 8 PM that evening, we finished cleaning the mess hall to the satisfaction of the mess sergeant. But then one of the cooks noticed a trainee had taken a couple of small boxes of cereal and stuffed them inside his fatigue shirt. Everyone was immediately punished for this major transgression. We had to do push-ups until we collapsed in a quivering heap on the floor. We were forced to do the low crawl around the tables and chairs while shouting "I am a maggot worm; I am a maggot worm." Finally, the cooks got tired of the harassment and we were allowed to return, completely exhausted, to our bunks.

I graduated from basic on March 21, 1969, as a private E-2 making about $88.00 a month (before taxes) with an **MOS** of 11B10 (light infantry). I was immediately ordered to Charlie Company, 2nd Battalion, 2nd Training Brigade, an **AIT** training company. Proudly wearing my single stripes (called 'mosquito wings'), I climbed aboard a truck for the trip down the hill to the AIT barracks. Usually, a new graduate of basic training was given a two-week furlough, but those of us designated 11B10 did not get the leave.

Charlie 2/2 was in the older part of Fort Ord and the company was housed in old wooden World War II-era barracks. Because the barracks were very flammable, we each had to pull hour-long turns at 'fire guard' duty. We were required to pace slowly up and down the aisles between the rows of bunks, alert for a fire, ready to sound the alarm should a fire start.

Anyway, I got through my advanced infantry training with flying colors. We didn't do any more close-order drill or the manual of arms. We set about learning the tactics used in Vietnam and how to use and maintain the deadly weapons of modern war. During the Vietnam era, emphasis was given to small unit tactics. We learned how to operate in elements as small as a fire team, three to five men.

One Saturday in April, after training, Jerry Dyer and I took a Fort Ord taxi to his sister's house in San Jose, California, just to get away from the army for a while. While we were sitting around talking about what to do for entertainment that evening, Jerry's brother-in-law suggested we go to a newly opened topless bar. Jerry was already twenty-one, but I would not reach twenty-one for another two weeks. The brother-in-law said I could use his ID to get into the bar, but the only resemblance between the two of us was that we both had brown hair. When I ordered a beer at the bar, the bartender asked for my ID, looked at me, and frowned. I told him I was on the way to Vietnam and just wanted a beer, and he served me.

The topless part was kind of a disappointment. The waitresses were older women and not the exciting young girls we had been expecting. We drank our beers, hailed a taxi, and called it a night.

In another episode brought on by boredom, two or three friends and I decided to go to Stillwell Hall, the big enlisted men's club built on the sand dunes overlooking Monterey Bay (see photo on page 31). The club was named after General Joseph "Vinegar Joe" Stillwell of WWII fame. You could buy a pitcher of beer for about two bucks and there was plenty of it. There was a local rock 'n' roll band playing the latest hits at full, earsplitting volume.

We listened to the music and drank beer for a while. I didn't notice that one of my friends was gulping down more than his share of the brew. Late in the afternoon, we decided to go back to the barracks to get ready for the next week's training. Then I noticed that the big drinker was so drunk he couldn't sit up in his chair. We dragged him to his feet, but he could not stand up on his own. Since it was at least a mile walk back to the company, we decided to pool our money and call a taxi. Fort Ord had its own taxi service and they were there quickly.

We had managed to get him outside by now, and when the driver pulled up and stopped, he took one look then rolled his eyes and shook his head. Having seen hundreds of inebriated GIs, he made no effort to help us. We managed to pour the guy into the backseat, I climbed in to help him, and we arrived at the barracks.

When we got there, I saw a couple of guys sitting on the barrack steps. I enlisted their help and we got him inside. Unfortunately, our bunks were on the second floor. I can't remember how we got him upstairs, but it must have been quite a show. We laid him on his bunk and he passed out right away.

Not more than fifteen minutes later, the DI decided to do a head count. When a DI or other enlisted cadre member entered the platoon bay, the first person to see him was supposed to yell, "At ease," and everyone would jump to their feet and assume the position of at ease. With help, I managed to get my inebriated friend on his feet and keep him reasonably upright by propping his elbows on the top of the bunk on either side of him.

As the DI walked down the rows of bunks, he immediately walked up to my buddy, stared, and asked me, "What's wrong with him?" The only thing I could think to say was, "He's really sick, Drill Sergeant." He grinned a little, and then told me, "Make sure he's sober in the morning." I said, "Yes, Drill Sergeant," and gently placed him back in his bunk; luckily, he had a lower bunk.

One of the other things that come to mind about basic and AIT training are the songs we sang while marching. One of them went something like this: *"There ain't no use in looking down, ain't no discharge on the ground. Ain't no use in looking back, Jody's got your Cadillac. Sound off 1-2; sound off 3-4; bring it on down 1-2-3-4, 1-2, **three-four**,"* the last two words shouted out. The name Jody referred to the men who remained at home, dating your girlfriend and driving your car.

Toward the end of AIT, I was called to the orderly room by the training sergeant and offered the chance to attend the Non-Commissioned Officers Candidate course at the US Army Infantry School at Fort Benning, Georgia. Since there was no additional enlistment required to get the school, I accepted, as did my friend Jerry Dyer.

By this time, I knew I was headed for Vietnam, so I figured, "Why not go to the 'Nam as an E-5 (sergeant) and be paid more for getting shot at?" Plus, I would be receiving corporal's pay while at the school.

Chapter 4

Non-Commissioned Officer Candidate

75th   **Company**

Harmony Church, Fort Benning

I reported to Fort Benning, Georgia, in early June 1969. I was assigned to the 7th Candidate Battalion, 75th Company, in class number 47-69 at NCOC School. As the taxi driver let me out in front of the 75th Company orderly room, he gave me some advice: "You better get rid of that 'bus driver' hat. This is Airborne country." He was referring to the stiff-crowned hat (see Chapter 6) usually worn with the class-A green uniform. It seems that parachute-qualified troops took exception to the wearing of that hat. Airborne troops wore the overseas cap with the "glider patch" sewn on the left side. This identified them as paratroopers, one of the army's elite. Wearing the bus driver hat identified you as a **straight leg**, a non-jumper. Soldiers who were **jump qualified** received **jump pay**, at that time an extra $55.00 per month.

The 7th Candidate Battalion was in an area of the post called Harmony Church. The wooden two-story barracks had been built for General Patton's troops prior to the invasion of North Africa during WWII. They were of single-wall construction with no insulation. The latrines were added on to the barracks later and were at least two feet lower than the barrack itself. Every time the platoon showered, the latrine would flood to a depth of three or four inches of soapy water. We had a special mop-and-bucket detail to soak up the water.

The only good thing about these old barracks was that we had a coin-operated Coca Cola dispensing machine and an ice water drinking fountain on the first floor. These were a blessing after a day of training in the hot, humid weather of western   Georgia.

Another privilege peculiar to Fort Benning were the 'pogey-bait' trucks. These were mobile canteens operated by civilians that traveled to the different training sites around the Fort Benning reservation dispensing cold sodas, ice cream, candy bars (pogey-bait) and other goodies to quench the thirst and craving for sweets of the young NCO candidates. We could be out in the middle of the woods, seemingly far from civilization and these trucks would appear like magic. My favorite treat was an ice-cold Royal Crown cola and an ice cream sandwich.

At the time I was there, the assistant commandant of the infantry school was Brigadier General Sidney M. Berry. He went on to become the assistant division commander of the 101st Airborne in 1970, when I was serving with C 2nd/502nd Infantry.

I had reported in several days early (which I quickly learned was a big mistake) and I was looking forward to a few days off, but I had no such luck. The first sergeant had looked at my personnel file and had seen that I had two years of college and that I knew how to type. He sent a runner who told me to report to the orderly room ASAP. When I arrived, he had my file open on his desk. He asked me, "It says here you can type; is that so?" I replied "Yes, first sergeant." He ordered, "After noon chow, report back here." I did, and he put me to work filling out requisition forms. I worked in the orderly room until the new 12-week training cycle started a few days later.

NCOC School was designed to teach a soldier how to be an infantry small-unit leader at the squad or fire team level. We had more basic infantry weapons training but, in addition, we were taught how to call in and adjust artillery and mortar fire as well as medical evacuation and supply helicopters. We were taught map reading and land navigation, field sanitation, how to treat wounds in the field, patrol and ambush techniques, and the correct way to dig a foxhole and how to place weapons around a perimeter for maximum defensive fire.

One of the ways they taught leadership was to choose a student first sergeant, usually at random, and put him in charge of the company under the direction of the cadre, some of them newly-promoted E-5s themselves. This direction was most often given directly into the student's ear at the top of the cadre members voice, often causing mass confusion as the student first sergeant tried to make his orders heard over the yelling, screaming cadre members.

That's what happened to me when I was appointed to be the first student first sergeant of the training cycle. By reporting in early, I had come to the attention of the cadre and they had decided to appoint me to that exalted position.

The company was formed in platoons on the first day of classes. While I waited for the order to move out, I heard the command, "Candidate Roberts, front and center." I was very surprised, but I managed to report to the cadre in the prescribed manner to receive my orders: "You are appointed student first sergeant. March the company to class." It took a few seconds for this to penetrate my brain, and I must have looked stupid standing there with my mouth hanging open. When I didn't immediately take charge, they started in on me: "Are you stupid, Candidate? Didn't you hear your orders, Candidate? What are you waiting for, Candidate?"

A soldier attending NCOCS was a candidate for the rank of sergeant E-5 and was referred to as 'Candidate.' When addressing a cadre member, the soldier referred to himself in the third person, such as, "Sir, Candidate Roberts requests permission to speak to the tactical sergeant, sir." At NCOCS, even the tactical sergeants were called sir.

Anyway, I managed to perform an about-face, surrounded by two or three yelling cadre. Shouting at the top of my voice, I tried to get the company to do what I wanted them to do. The poor guys must have been as confused as I was, but I managed to get them to "right, face" and then "forward, march."

There was another barrack at the end of the parade ground and the company was marching straight toward it. I had to command the company to "half-right, march" and then "half-left, march" to get them on the road and headed in the right direction. With the cadre screaming in my face, I became confused and gave the opposite orders from the correct ones. When I saw my men marching in the wrong direction, I gave up and yelled "company, halt." Mercifully, they did.

This drove the cadre crazy and they yelled even louder, if that was even possible. I just stood there at attention, gazing over their heads until they ran out of energy and quit yelling; screaming at someone is hard work. One of the real sergeants took charge and got the troops properly started. They told me to rejoin the company, which I thankfully did.

After some intense, one-on-one instruction, the rest of my week as student first sergeant went much more smoothly, as if they had decided to give me a break. I managed, with luck, to do an acceptable job and soon it was someone else's turn.

As with most advanced army schools of that era, especially infantry schools, there was considerable physical and mental harassment of candidates. We were even harassed while we tried to eat our meals in the mess hall. We had to eat a 'square meal.' This meant that you sat rigidly at attention on the forward one-third of your chair, staring straight ahead. You could briefly glance at the plate to place the food on the fork/spoon. The food-laden utensil was then brought vertically up to a position directly in front of your mouth, and then moved horizontally into your mouth. The utensil was returned to the plate in reverse of the above movement. Then your hand was placed into your lap where it remained until time for the next bite.

While I was at Harmony Church, several companies of ROTC cadets were also there undergoing their summer training. When we passed them while marching, we always yelled out in derision, "ROT-Cee Rangers, ROT-Cee Rangers." We considered them privileged college boys on summer vacation and we looked down on them.

The 75th Company used a marching song that went something like this: "Late at night while you're sleepin', Charlie Cong comes a-creepin' around. Vi-et Na-a-am, Vi-et Na-a-am. Late at night while you're sleepin', Charlie Cong comes a creepin' around." This was sung to the tune of the pop song "Poison Ivy."

We got up every week-day morning at four a.m. and underwent a series of vigorous exercises from one of the army physical training drills. Each drill was a group of twelve different exercises, all performed to the shouted cadence of one or more of the tactical sergeants. My 'favorite' was the eight-count push up. After we were 'warmed up' by an army drill, we ran in formation for one to two miles, depending on how much time we had before classes began.

It wasn't a full-out run: we used something called the 'airborne shuffle.' This was a shuffling run that covered distance very quickly and the pace could be maintained for long periods of time, sometimes an hour or more.

As we ran we sang songs to help us keep in step. One of the songs went like this: *"I wanna be an Airborne Ranger; I wanna live a life of danger; I wanna go to Vi-et Na-am; I wanna kill a Char-lie Co-ong; here we go, all the way, every day, all the way."*

In my mind, I can still hear of 200 pairs of combat boots slapping the pavement in unison as we ran through the pre-dawn darkness.

Sometimes the company did not perform to the satisfaction of the tactical sergeant in charge of the morning run. He would halt the company and order us to 'assume the Chinese thinking position.' This was a push-up position but instead of supporting your body with your hands, arms and toes, you had to support your body on your toes and elbows with your chin resting in your cupped hands. After a few seconds, this became quite painful and very effective at changing your attitude into one of cooperation.

All of this was done before morning chow and before classes began for the day. It was no wonder that many of us had trouble staying conscious during class room instruction. I will say this: when I graduated from NCOC School, I was in the best physical shape of my entire life.

One Sunday afternoon, bored out of my mind, I walked to the Harmony Church PX and bought a combination record player and radio for about $30.00. The only record they had that I thought worth listening to was the Four Seasons' Greatest Hits. I made the purchase and lugged everything back to the barrack.

Everyone on the first floor of my two-story platoon barrack soon grew tired of the Four Seasons album. Luckily, I could tune in a local radio station broadcasting from Columbus that played a variety of music. We listened to that station nearly every morning while getting dressed and cleaning the barrack.

We spent a lot of time in the thick woods of the Fort Benning reservation, learning to use a map and compass and practicing patrol and ambush tactics.

I was amazed on one occasion when, after we had sprung an ambush on another squad of NCOC candidates, to hear children's voices coming from the woods around us. We had special 'blank adapters' fitted to the muzzles of our weapons that allowed them to be fired on full automatic, ejecting the spent brass cartridges onto the ground. Suddenly we were surrounded by kids carrying sacks; they began scooping up the spent brass cartridges and stuffing them into the sacks. Almost as soon as they arrived, they were gone, and all the brass had been harvested. A cadre sergeant said they were 'brass pickers' who sold the used cartridges to metal salvagers to eventually make their way back into the army's inventory. We could have taken lessons from those kids about moving undetected through heavy brush!

In the middle of the night on July 20, 1969 the men in my barracks were awakened and marched to the 'day room' (company recreation room) where the small black and white television was playing. As we gathered around the TV, I realized that the first moon landing had been made and that one of the astronauts was about to be the first human to set foot on the surface of the moon. There was some grumbling about losing sleep after an exhausting training day, but that soon died away as we became caught up in the drama of that historic moment. The TV picture was very fuzzy, but I could make out the shape of a man dressed in a bulky white pressure suit slowly climbing down a ladder and making that last little hop onto the soil of the moon. I don't remember anyone cheering or making any comments but I, for one, was proud of what our country had accomplished.

We usually had Sundays off, so early one Sunday morning I hitched a ride with another candidate who was going into Columbus. We parked and walked down the sidewalk looking for a café to get some breakfast. I noticed a family walking towards us, Mom, Dad, sister, and brother, all wearing their Sunday best. Before they had to pass us, they crossed over to the other side of the street. We walked a little farther and, curious, I looked behind us and saw that the family had crossed back to our side of the street after they had passed us. You can imagine how this made us feel; we were getting ready to go to Vietnam and fight for our country, yet the good citizens of Columbus, Georgia, wouldn't even walk by us on the same sidewalk.

In another instance of Southern xenophobia, I went into Columbus on a Saturday night with a friend named Robert Wills who was from Maine. He had a strong down-east accent which was apparent every time he spoke. Anyway, we found a bar that catered to people our age and went in. We got drinks and stood around checking out the action. I saw a pair of pretty, blonde girls, real 'Georgia Peaches,' who had looked at us a couple of times. Gathering my courage, I asked them if they would like to have a drink with us. They agreed, and I called my friend over. We tried to start a conversation, but as soon as they heard Robert speak, they looked at each other and one of them said:" Oh, *a God damn Yankee!"* Without another word, they turned and just walked away from us. Wills was later killed in action while serving with the 25th Infantry Division.

The rest of the NCOC training went smoothly, and I graduated on September 2, 1969, with the rank of sergeant E-5. I had orders to report to an AIT company at Fort Ord to complete the OJT (on-the-job-training) portion of the NCOC course. Jerry Dyer was on the same set of orders, as was William 'Mike' Lucky from Sulphur Springs, Texas, a new buddy I had met while at Fort Benning.

Chapter 5

Back to Fort Ord: Leadership Learned The Hard Way

I reported back to Fort Ord in mid-September 1969 after a few days at my parents' home in Upland, California. I checked into the transient **NCO** barracks and the next day I was assigned to E Company, 3rd Battalion 2nd Training Brigade as a student squad leader for the OJT portion of my NCOC training. I was placed in charge of a squad of AIT trainees under the supervision of the platoon's DI.

It was the first time I had been responsible for real troops, even though they were only trainees; it was like my AIT all over again. But, because of my exalted status as a brand-new E-5, I did not have to get as down and dirty as I had before. We did not have private rooms as most sergeants did; we lived with the troops in the squad bay. We did have some "privacy," behind a line of lockers that separated our bunks from the squads' bunks.

My first bad experience as a squad leader came after I spoke to a trainee about polishing his boots and wearing a clean uniform. A large, heavy-set man well over six feet tall, he was a Pacific Islander and had a heavy accent. He looked me right in the eye then turned and walked away. I was a little nervous because of his bad attitude.

A few days later, after the training day was over, another student sergeant named Tim Smith and I went into the upstairs latrine to clean up. As I was getting out my shaving gear, the latrine door slammed open and in walked the big trainee. When the door had shut, he pulled out a pocket knife, opened it and said, _"I'm going to kill you!"_ Shocked, I asked him why he wanted to kill me, and he replied, _"You shamed me, made me_ lose face in front of my friends, so now I've got to kill you." I looked over at Smith and the expression on his face plainly said, _"You're on your own, Roberts."_

I began talking as I'd never talked before and finally he put away his knife. I remember telling him *"If you kill me, you'll have to kill Sgt. Smith, too. He's a witness!"* I apologized for embarrassing him and told him it was my job to keep trainees looking good; he looked at me for a long time and then turned and walked out the door. I never had any more trouble with him. I learned how to better deal with troops because of that incident.

The rest of the training cycle went smoothly for the most part. A bad incident occurred during hand grenade training: a trainee somehow dropped a live grenade and blew himself up. The cadre member with him managed to scramble out of the pit before the grenade went off.

One Sunday afternoon, a group of us went to the nearby town of Carmel to get away from Army life for a few hours. We wandered around for a while and, as we approached a small city park on the southwest corner of 6th Avenue and Juniper Street in downtown Carmel, we saw a crowd of people in the street. It was an anti-war demonstration. Some of the people were carrying home-made signs denouncing the war and we saw at least two National Liberation Front (Viet Cong) flags in the group. These flags had wide red and blue horizontal stripes with a big yellow star in the center. I experienced conflicting emotions; I believed they had a right to protest the war, but at the same time, the people who owed allegiance to that flag would be trying to kill me in just a few months.

We were attracting stares from some of the demonstrators because of our GI haircuts and conservative civilian clothing, so we decided to leave the area of the park. We drove down to the city beach at the end of Ocean Avenue and enjoyed the warm sun and cool sea breezes until time to return to Fort Ord.

I had another incident brought on by my own stupidity. One weekend after Saturday morning training was finished, I got a thirty-six-hour pass. I decided to fly home to see my girlfriend even though we had been expressly warned not to do that. I was flying standby and, of course, when it came time to fly back to the post, there were no seats available and it was the last flight to San Jose.

My father drove me to the local bus station where I caught a Greyhound to Los Angeles. I had to wait a couple of hours in LA before the bus that would take me directly to Fort Ord left. I arrived at the base early in the morning and went to bed to try and get some sleep. The company was leaving later that morning for a weeklong stay in the field.

The next morning, the first sergeant (known as Top) called me to the orderly room for a little chat. Top said that the captain wanted to give me an Article 15 and bust me to **PFC**, but Top had talked him into only giving me a fine. Apparently, the army badly needed sergeants, even brand-new **shake-n-bakes**, to send to Vietnam.

Top asked for a $60.00 fine and I gladly handed it over. I left with my squad for the field and never heard another thing about it. And I never flew home to visit my girlfriend again.

Toward the end of the training cycle the company mail clerk was caught opening incoming letters to the trainees from home; he would remove any cash and whatever else caught his eye. I don't remember how they caught him, but he was given a court-martial, convicted and sentenced to the stockade for theft from the mail.

The day after the court-martial, I was called to the orderly room and told that I was detailed to escort the newly sentenced prisoner to the Fort Ord stockade to await transport to the military prison at Fort Leavenworth, Kansas. Top told me to wear my Class-A green uniform and to make sure my shoes were highly spit shined and that all the brass accoutrements on the uniform were brightly polished.

Following orders, I reported to the orderly room the next morning and picked up the prisoner. He was not handcuffed, and I was given a pistol belt with an empty .45 pistol in the holster. They did give me a loaded magazine, which I stuffed in my trouser pocket.

We had to walk from E Company 3rd/2nd across the main post to the stockade. I ordered the guy to walk in front of me and told him, "Please don't do anything stupid because I don't want to shoot you." He promised to obey my orders because he didn't want another charge added for trying to escape.

After about a ten-minute walk, we arrived at the stockade and a guard let us into a fenced area through a chain link gate. A big door opened in the solid cement wall of the building and another guard motioned us toward him. I have never forgotten the look of fear and despair on the clerk's face as he stepped through that door. I hurried back to E 3rd/2nd, glad to be finished with such a rotten detail.

E Company 3rd/2nd Infantry completed its training cycle in mid-November and I was graduated from OJT with the permanent rank of sergeant E-5 and an MOS of 11B40. I got my orders sending me to Vietnam, but I also got some good news. I was given a forty-five-day leave because I had not gotten a leave after basic training. I did not have to report to Oakland Army Terminal for shipment overseas until January 2, 1970. That meant that I would get to spend Thanksgiving, Christmas, and the New Year holidays with my family. I left Fort Ord as happy as a man could be who was headed straight for Vietnam.

Chapter 6

Oakland Army Terminal: Gateway to Vietnam

After a tearful farewell with my family at Ontario Airport, I boarded an Air California Boeing 737 jet and took off for Oakland, California. It was Friday, January 2, 1970. Jerry Dyer, traveling from his home in Somis, California, was to meet me at the Oakland Airport. When I landed and got off the plane, Jerry was waiting. We shook hands then went outside and got aboard the usual green army bus for the short trip to the terminal. We headed north on the I-880 freeway and as we passed the Oakland Coliseum, I saw a big banner advertising "Super Bowl IV," but I don't remember what teams were playing.

We arrived at the army terminal, entered the huge building and presented our orders to a clerk at a desk inside the door. There was a large group reporting in, so we were lead to a room with a set of bleachers inside. As we sat there, a PFC counted us and divided us into two groups. From there, we were issued two sets of jungle fatigues and two pairs of jungle boots. We packed our dress greens into a box for shipment home, filled out a bunch of forms, and then waited.

Formations were announced two or three times a day when men's names were called, and they were sent off to their fate. Finally, late in the afternoon of Sunday, January 4, my name and Jerry's were called. I got onto a bus for the trip to Travis AFB in Fairfield, California. The seat behind me was occupied by two WOJGs (warrant officer, junior grade) who said they were helicopter pilots on their way to the 1st Air Cavalry Division in the Central Highlands, wherever that was.

The bus filled up and we took off for Travis Air Force Base, an hour or so drive north of Oakland. I remember conversation in the bus being very quiet as we approached Travis.

We pulled into a parking area near the passenger terminal and parked. Walking into the waiting room, I noticed how modern it was. Through the large windows at the front of the terminal, I could see a big civilian airliner waiting on the tarmac. It was a Douglas DC-8 'stretch 8,' an extra section of fuselage having been added to accommodate more passengers. It was marked 'Flying Tiger Lines.'

After a short wait, we boarded the aircraft and took off, heading north into the darkness. It was quiet in the cabin, no one being in a talkative mood. I recall reading a book by Agatha Christie, an Hercule Poirot mystery. The flight attendants served dinner, but I didn't eat much.

After several hours, we began our approach into the civilian airport at Anchorage, Alaska. A half-moon shone on the snow-capped mountains surrounding the city and it looked cold and frosty. The aircraft parked about one hundred yards in front of the terminal and we all got off so the airliner could be serviced and refueled. As I walked across the tarmac, I felt the hair on my arms stand up and I began to shiver. It was Sunday, January 4, 1970, the middle of winter in Alaska, and I was wearing only cotton jungle fatigues.

Pretty soon, we took off again for the long flight to Japan. Somewhere over the North Pacific, I fell asleep and the plane crossed the International Date Line and it became January 5, 1970.

The sound of the landing gear coming down woke me up and I looked out the window at the city of Tokyo, Japan. One thing I remember about Japan was the thick smog hanging over the city like a grey-brown fog. We made a long, slow approach to the airfield, and I could see the commuter trains and the jammed-up freeways passing underneath. As I got off the aircraft, I saw a sign: 'Welcome to Yokota AFB.' The base had a great **PX**, but I couldn't afford to buy anything, not having been paid since November.

After waiting a couple of hours, we re-boarded the plane and took off for the mysterious and dangerous land of Vietnam.

VIETNAM

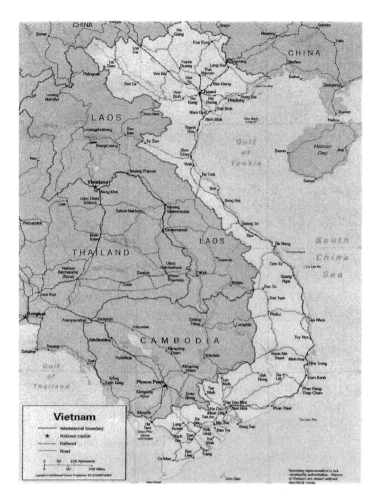

The Jewel of the Orient

Chapter 7

The 90th Replacement Battalion

January 6, 1970

As the aircraft made a steep, plunging approach to the runway at Bien Hoa AFB just outside Saigon, the capitol city of the Republic of (South) Vietnam, I could see several big flares hanging in the dark sky beyond the airfield. The plane made a short taxi and stopped. After traveling over 8,000 air miles, it was a relief when the doors opened, and warm, moist air flooded into the cabin. The cabin crew stood at the exit and wished us good luck and told us they'd see us in a year for the trip home. I've never forgotten the sad looks on their faces. They knew that some of us wouldn't be going home on an airliner.

I guess every GI who served in Vietnam remembers his first lungful of Vietnamese air. It was hot and humid and the smell of feces, garbage, and something unidentifiable hung in the air. As we came off the stairs, we were pointed toward a big open-air shed for processing.

We received short lectures on how to behave around Vietnamese civilians: don't touch them on the head, don't drink untreated water, don't eat native food, and don't trust any Vietnamese. One of the lecturers told us that there were a hundred species of snake in Vietnam; 99 percent of them were venomous, and it was up to us to figure out the safe 1 percent.

We stood in line to exchange our greenbacks for MPC (military payment certificates). The bills were a little bigger than Monopoly money and came in various colors. There were no coins; paper money took the place of nickels, dimes, and quarters.

After that, we boarded the inevitable green army buses for the short drive to Long Binh Military Post and the 90th Replacement Battalion. There was wire mesh fastened to each window frame to keep the friendly local peasants from heaving hand grenades into the bus. I looked in amazement at the primitive huts made from C-ration cartons, pieces of wood and galvanized roofing sheets. The street was filled with trash, and there was a pungent smell in the air.

We arrived at the 90th Replacement Battalion soon after sunup. I turned in my orders and was told to pick a barrack and get some sleep. There would be an assignment formation two or three times a day and we were expected to attend every one. I started toward the nearest barrack and saw Jerry Dyer approaching. After a handshake, we found empty bunks and tried to sleep in the hot, humid air.

That afternoon, after a few hours' sleep, Jerry and I walked around a little and ran into Mike Lucky, our buddy from NCOCS and OJT at Fort Ord. He was waiting for orders, too. I also met the knife-wielding trainee, sitting against the side of a building. He recognized me, stared for a few seconds, and then looked away. I wished him good luck, but he didn't reply. I never saw him again.

January 7

That morning after chow, I decided to look around the place. I wandered over by the battalion headquarters and saw a jeep parked in front of the building with what appeared to be bodies sprawled in the back seat. As I got closer, I could see that the bodies were dressed in the black 'pajamas' habitually worn by peasants and the Viet Cong. They had obviously been killed by gunfire. After asking around, I learned that they had been killed by a security patrol while attempting to breach the wire perimeter surrounding the 90th.

Later that day, at an assignment formation, Jerry Dyer received orders to the 199th Light Infantry Brigade. Known as the "Red Catchers," they were currently operating in the Iron Triangle area west of Saigon (now called Ho Chi Minh City). Jerry left immediately, and I didn't see him again until March 1971, when he was an usher at my wedding Unfortunately that marriage did not survive.

Chapter 8

On Our Way To The War

January 8, 1970

At the morning assignment formation, both Mike Lucky and I received orders to the 101st Airborne Division, known as the 'Screaming Eagles.' They were operating from a place called Camp Eagle located near the city of Hue (pronounced 'way') in Thua Thien Province, Republic of Vietnam, in the I Corps (pronounced eye-core) tactical zone near the **DMZ**. The 101st wears a distinctive shoulder insignia, the head of a bald eagle.

Above: the 101st Airborne Division shoulder patch. A representation of "Old Abe", the Screaming Eagle. Author's collection.

The division was a famous one, best known for their midnight parachute drop into the French countryside just before the Normandy landings on June 6, 1944 and for their courageous stand while surrounded by Germans at Bastogne, Belgium, during the Battle of the Bulge in December 1944. When the acting division commander, Brigadier General Anthony McAuliffe, replied, *"Nuts"* to the German demand that he surrender the division, he went down in history. One of the sayings credited to the Division while they were at Bastogne is, "They've got us surrounded, the poor bastards," which only added to the 101st's fame.

The original Old Abe was a live bald eagle who served as the mascot for the 8th Wisconsin Volunteer Infantry Regiment during the American Civil War. Old Abe was present at the siege and the surrender of Vicksburg, Mississippi in 1863 and at several more battles. The 101st Airborne traces its mascots' lineage directly to Old Abe, the 8th Wisconsin's bald eagle mascot.

Chapter 9

'Phu Bai Is Alright' – But Camp Evans Is Better

Mike and I left immediately. We boarded an Air Force C-130 at Bien Hoa and flew north to Phu Bai (pronounced 'phoo bye') AFB just south of the city of Hue. As we got off the aircraft, I noticed a large sign hanging from the control tower proclaiming '**Phu Bai Is All Right.**' The weather was cool and cloudy with drizzling rain, so I wasn't sure at that time if Phu Bai was all right or not.

After waiting in the musty lobby of the terminal, we were told to board a canvas-covered **deuce and a half**, a two-and-a-half-ton truck with all-wheel drive that could go virtually anywhere without bogging down. We boarded the truck, and the driver drove north on QL-1 at high speed. QL stands for **Quoc Lo**, Vietnamese for 'highway,' and QL-1 is the Vietnamese national highway, running from the Hanoi-Haiphong area in the north to Saigon in the south. Heavily traveled, it was in very poor condition.

Driving into Hue (pronounced 'Way') we became stalled in civilian and military traffic in the Hue marketplace. Looking out the back of the truck, I could see destroyed and heavily damaged buildings left over from the 1968 Tet Offensive. Viet **Cong** and **NVA** forces had captured Hue in February 1968 and had to be pushed back out in heavy house-to-house fighting by the Marine Corps and the army's 1st Air Cavalry Division.

As we came to a stop, we were immediately surrounded by 'soda boys' selling soft drinks kept in an aluminum container and cooled with dry ice. The containers could also conceal a bomb, so we kept a close eye on the soda boys. Smaller children with hands held out approached the truck, calling, "Hey GI, you souvenir me chop-chop?" and "GI, GI, you souvenir me Salem?" They were asking for food (chop-chop) and menthol cigarettes. The Vietnamese were crazy about menthol cigarettes, and a pack of Salem could be used as money.

We finally cleared the marketplace, crossed the Song Huong (Perfume River), and continued north. We passed Camp Sally, base camp for the 2nd Brigade, and drove into a rural area. Finally, we arrived at Camp Evans, the base camp for the 3rd Brigade and the home of the Screaming Eagle Replacement Training School, known as SERTS (pronounced "certs").

SERTS training turned out to be an abbreviated rehash of AIT. There were also classes about the history of the 101st and instruction on the way the 101st operated, and, of course, we filled out more forms.

It was cold and raining, the tail end of the northern monsoon and Camp Evans was a sea of ankle-deep mud. Part of the training was pulling guard duty on the Camp Evans **bunker line**. One night, three other men and I were escorted to the perimeter and assigned a **bunker**. The bunker was a massive sandbagged structure, some of it above grade and some below. It had openings to allow the guards to fire if the base was attacked. The interior was muddy and had a strong moldy smell.

Since there were four of us, we each had a two-hour turn at guard; my turn came in the dark hours before dawn. One of the cadre had checked on us sometime in the middle of the night and told us to stay calm, no trouble was expected. Even though it was unlikely we would be attacked, I was still nervous. After all, I **was** on guard in the Vietnam War Zone. It was weird the way that sounds you wouldn't pay any attention to during daylight took on a sinister meaning in the darkness. Well, we had all survived our turn on bunker line duty, and with the dawn, the training went on. Later, the sounds I heard that night would take on a new meaning.

Chapter 10

Life Among the REMF's

January 16-24, 1970

On the sixteenth, Mike Lucky and I were trucked back down QL-1 to Camp Eagle, built on rolling hills west of the village of Phu Bai. Eagle was the headquarters base camp for the 101st Airborne, and it held all the supporting units as well as the combat battalions of the 1st Brigade. The 1st Brigade had been in Vietnam since July 1965, and consisted of the 1st/327th, 2nd/327th, and 2nd/502nd. The rest of the division did not join the 1st Brigade until late 1967.

Lucky and I were assigned to the 2nd/502nd Infantry, a highly motivated unit with lots of *esprit de corps.* Known as 'The Eagles Claw', 'Widow Makers' and the 'Strike Force,' the 1st, 2nd, and 3rd Battalions 502nd Infantry had fought at Normandy, in Operation Market-Garden and at the Battle of Bastogne, all mentioned above.

The Second Battalion was called the Strike Force and in January 1970, it was commanded by LTC (Lieutenant Colonel) Roy J. Young, call sign "Cajun Tiger." Members of the battalion refer to it as the "O-Deuce" or the "Five-O-Deuce."

The O-Deuce was organized into a Headquarters and Headquarters Company (HHC), and four line companies (Alpha, Bravo, Charlie, and Delta), with Echo Company acting as a heavy weapons company (81mm mortars, 90mm recoilless rifles, and .50 caliber machine guns). Echo Company also controlled the Recon Platoon, which acted as scouts for the battalion.

We reported to battalion headquarters and got our company assignments. Mike was assigned to Alpha Company and I went to Charlie Company. I did not see Mike Lucky again until 2002 when we had a reunion with Jerry Dyer at old Fort Ord. I thought Mike had been killed in action on Hill 882 for over thirty years.

After drawing all my field gear, I was collected by the 'top' sergeant for Charlie Company, First Sergeant Ira C. Stanley and driven across a small stream that divided the main battalion area from the line companies to the Charlie Company orderly room.

There were several of us reporting in, and Top Stanley told us to bunk where we could find the space to lie down. Sergeants Frank R. Poole and Arnold D. Shaw reported to Charlie Company at the same time.

It rained off and on all night and the roof leaked. Early in the morning, we were awakened by loud booms that we thought were incoming rounds. 'Top' Stanley heard us rustling around and came to tell us it was OK because all we'd heard had been outgoing rounds fired from an eight-inch self-propelled howitzer battery located near the O-Deuce. After that, I quickly learned to tell the difference between outgoing and incoming rounds.

The next morning, I was walking toward Alpha Company to see how Lucky was doing when I met a stocky, tough-looking man. He asked me where I was going and my rank. I hadn't yet had time to buy the subdued stripes worn by NCOs in Vietnam. I explained that I was an E-5 and I was headed to Alpha Company to visit a friend. I then noticed the insignia of a command sergeant major on his collar, and I thought, *"Aw, shit. I'm already in trouble, and I just got here!"* Pointing to a detail of men working in a ditch alongside the battalion mess hall, he ordered, *"Get over there and take charge of that detail and I don't mean standing around watching. Get down in the ditch and help them."* Coming to the position of parade rest, I barked, *"Yes, Sergeant Major,"* and did what I was told.

Later that day, I learned that I had encountered Command Sergeant Major Walter J. Sabalauski, the highest-ranking NCO in the O-Deuce. Called "Sabo" by the troops (but not to his face), he had two stars on his CIB (combat infantry badge), meaning he had served in WWII, Korea, and now Vietnam. He had been with the O-Deuce since 1965. He was first sergeant of Charlie Company at Tou Morong when Captain Bill Carpenter was forced to call in a napalm strike on his own positions to prevent the enemy from over running the company. Some of the Charlie Company veterans from that time refer to themselves as "crispy critters."

Sabo had been a two-time Golden Gloves champion in his youth, and he had somehow scrounged the materials needed to build a boxing ring at the O-Deuce area. He was serious about it and usually organized several bouts and boxing tournaments when the troops came in from the field for a stand-down.

Incidentally, the modern-day 101st Airborne Division's Air Assault School at Fort Campbell, Kentucky, is named in honor of Command Sergeant Major Walter J. Sabalauski.

The rest of my time in the rear was taken up by guard duty and getting my gear ready to go to the field. Luckily, there were some men from Charlie Company in the rear for various reasons friendly enough to show me how to properly pack my rucksack, so it would ride easier when I carried it in the field.

One afternoon, Frank Poole and I were both picked for guard duty. Learning that they only needed one NCO, Poole and I flipped, and he lost. That night, I got to watch the movie in the outdoor theatre and drink beer. I don't remember what movie was shown, but it was better than staring at the wall of the tent where I was sleeping.

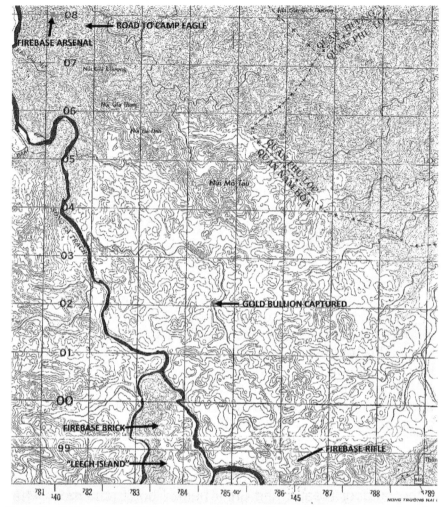

Detail of Firebase Rifle area of operations from map series L-7014, sheet 6541-IV. Author's collection.

Chapter 11

My Introduction To The Jungle

January 25–February 14, 1970

Finally, Charlie Company came into Camp Eagle for a brief resupply. I remember being a little surprised as I saw the wet, dirty, ragged men jump off the helicopters and thinking, "Damn, that'll be me in a few days."

I had been assigned to the 1st Platoon and Top Stanley took me to the platoon and introduced me to SSG (staff sergeant) Phillip Gibbons, the platoon sergeant. Gibbons was an older-looking man with a heavy five o'clock shadow and a strong New England accent. Known as "Gibby," he sent me to the 3rd Squad, 1st Platoon.

Shortly after that, Charlie Company boarded helicopters and took off. I was in the middle of the cabin, so I couldn't see the terrain passing under us. Not being able to see the ground was disorienting, and I made it a habit to sit in the door from then on. In a few minutes, I felt the helicopter slow and the pilot pull the nose up, and then we touched down with a little bump. Scrambling off the helicopter with the others, I found myself standing on the landing zone (**LZ**) at a **firebase** called Rifle. LTC Young had his field headquarters there, and the battalion was operating in the hilly jungle surrounding the firebase.

We were told to get off the LZ because another flight of **slicks** (so-called because they did not have any rocket or gun pods attached to the outside of the fuselage) was coming in to take us to the area where we would start our patrol. After a short flight, the slicks set us down on a small, one-ship LZ surrounded by tall trees. It was getting dark and we quickly got off the LZ, moving about two hundred meters into the surrounding jungle.

The platoon began to set up an **NDP** (night defensive position) and someone showed me where to put down my rucksack and said that would be my position for the night. I pulled my turn at guard and, like every other **FNG** ever assigned to the infantry, I was sure I heard battalions of the enemy crawling through the jungle to attack us. It was eerie; the sky was completely overcast but the trees and vines were silhouetted, even in the darkness. I recall thinking, "I'm never gonna get used to this shit." But, of course, I eventually did.

We only moved short distances during the days that followed. We set up ambushes and observation posts, but we had no contact with the enemy. It seemed I had gotten lucky; it was a quiet AO (area of operations), and I had time to settle in and get used to the routine of living in the jungle.

Things were not always quiet. In a 2012 telephone conversation, Harold Carstens, a veteran of 2nd Platoon, told me about an interesting experience occurring on January 28. In summary, Carstens told me the following: The platoon was walking in a streambed because the vegetation was too thick to walk through without making a lot of noise. The stream made a sharp bend, and Carstens could see the point man, Brian Fletcher, as he suddenly opened fire. They had surprised about eight NVA in their campsite. As they came under fire, the enemy fled in all directions, leaving behind most of their equipment and one previously wounded NVA soldier. When they searched the enemy rucksacks, the point man found a K54 pistol that he kept for a souvenir. They also found several small, thin sheets of gold bullion and some paper money. They carried the wounded enemy soldier to an LZ, where he was evacuated to the rear. Some members of the point squad kept pieces of the gold, but Carstens does not remember what happened to the rest of the bullion.

Bruce Scott, who was on the same patrol, says: "I remember that the **gook** had paper-thin type sheets...they were only about an inch wide and three inches long, but they were in[a] pack probably an inch deep...the gold was imprinted with some kind of design or oriental writing. Who knows who ended up with it? I don't know how many packs there were."

During a personal interview with SGT Jesse "Go-Go" Gomez, I had some gaps in the above story filled in for me. Go-Go told me that his squad was the point squad for the 2nd Platoon of Charlie Company. They were following a small creek down to the big river. They came around a sharp bend in the creek and the point man suddenly opened fire. A group of NVA soldiers fled from a small campsite on the banks of the creek. Gomez immediately reorganized his squad and went after the enemy. They suddenly came under heavy automatic weapons fire and he   could see that the fire was coming from a cave washed out of the creek bank. His squad overpowered the enemy with heavy **M-16**, **M-60**, and **M-79** fire. The surviving NVA ran off into a heavily wooded area, and, not knowing the strength of the enemy, Gomez led the squad back to the original contact site. Jesse Gomez was awarded the Bronze Star with "V" Device for his leadership during that action.

Jesse says he remembers the gold being in a duffle bag, contained in a box about the size of a domino box. He also says that the sheets of gold had a map of Vietnam stamped on one side. This map depicted the whole country and was labeled Haiphong, Da Nang, and another seaport. He kept one of the sheets as a souvenir and took it home with him.

Life soon became very simple: when it rained, you got wet; when it was hot, you perspired and fought off clouds of mosquitoes and battalions of little land leeches, all seeking your blood; when resupply didn't come on time, you went hungry.

One of the things we did on a regular basis was something called a "leech check." While walking through bamboo thickets and certain other types of jungle vegetation, land leeches would attach themselves to your body by dropping on you when you passed under an overhanging branch or when you brushed against vegetation. Most of the time, you were not aware that a leech had attached itself to you. Leeches secrete a natural anesthetic in their saliva that numbs the skin in the area where they bite. You only become aware you've been bitten when the leech drinks its fill, drops off and you continue to bleed or when you do a leech check and find the little bastard. They also have an anti-coagulant in their saliva which keeps the blood flowing while they drink their fill.

Leeches like warm, dark places on your body: around your collar and waistline, in and behind your ears, under your arms, behind your knees or even in the crevice between your buttocks. That's why it's necessary to check for them every so often. A leech bite, like every other injury which breaks the skin, can become infected very quickly in the filthy environment of the jungle.

The only safe way to remove a leech from your body while it's still feeding is to squirt it with GI '**bug juice**' or by burning its abdomen with a lit cigarette. Pulling it off may cause the head to break off inside the wound, causing a nasty infection.

I had the time to get acquainted with some of my fellow squad members. I met big James "Bear" Pando, the squad's point man; Chuck Swenson, a smiling Swede from Wisconsin; Bob Noffsinger, (Noff for short), a tall mountain man from West 'By God' Virginia; Gerry Kulm, the machine gunner; and his **A-gunner**, Vern Okland.

Later, I would meet and become friends with Frank Carvajal, a shy Hispanic from New York City, "Ace" Marler from Arkansas, and Billy Ray 'Kentucky' Lucas, another point man. Carvajal's nickname was '**Green Beanie**'; apparently, he had left Special Forces for some reason he would not talk about. He and three other members of 1st platoon would die in combat three months later during the battle for Hill 714.

We heard the helicopter as it neared, and someone threw out a smoke grenade, so the pilot could find us in the dense thicket. There were five colors of smoke grenades: green, red, purple, white, and yellow. Red smoke was never used except to warn a helicopter away from danger, as in a landing zone under fire, called a 'hot LZ.'

The heavily loaded log bird came in to land, and I immediately saw a bright red mail bag called 'Pony Express' next to the stacked cases of **C rations** (aka Charlie rats). When it was safe to approach, several men swarmed around the bird and began tossing the cases of Charlie rats to the ground on either side of the helicopter. It reminded me of something I had seen as a kid: a dead grasshopper being attacked by a swarm of ants. The rations were passed out to the different squads; I got a can of warm Coke that exploded all over me when I opened it and my first mail from home.

I remember that a few times, when we were in a **DDP** sending out small patrols and waiting for movement orders, Vern Okland, Frank Carvajal, and I would practice throwing our bayonets at tree trunks. Gerry Kulm was usually busy writing letters and did not participate in this nonsensical activity. I was still an FNG and did not yet realize how dangerous it was to make noise, yet none of the more experienced men ever said anything to us. I guess everybody, even the old-timers, let themselves be lulled by the lack of contact with the enemy. I got pretty good but, thankfully, did not have to throw my bayonet at anybody.

One misty, drizzly night, I was pulling my turn at guard duty when I thought I heard soft rustling sounds coming from in front of me. I was starting to get drowsy, but these sounds immediately brought me to attention. I listened hard and heard them again. I was on the point of waking up the other men at my position when I heard a voice, softly but distinctly say, *"Fuck you, fuck you."*

I was amazed and thought I was hearing things; then I heard it again, clearly, *"fuck you, fuck you."*

Suddenly, my mind flashed back to the days in training at Fort Ord and Fort Benning. I remembered hearing the stories told by training cadre who'd served in Vietnam about the famous 'fuck you lizards' who lived in the jungles of that country.

The sergeant, who had served in the 101st Airborne, told us, "*Just wait 'til some dark night when you're pullin' guard in the jungle and you hear someone telling you to get fucked. You'll think that it's Charlie trying to piss you off so you'll fire your weapon, but it'll be the 'fuck you lizard.'*"

At the time I'd thought he was just a telling a bullshit story to impress green trainees, but now I realized he'd been telling the truth.

It seems that the 'fuck you lizard' was a species of gecko whose mating cry sounded, to GI ears, just like that epithet. Apparently, it was a male gecko trying to attract a female of his species. I wished him luck and ignored the sounds thereafter.

One afternoon in late January or early February, Charlie Company received an intelligence report that an enemy unit was thought to be moving along a certain route through the Firebase Rifle area. At dusk, the 1st platoon moved into place to act as a blocking force; other units moved into position trying to force the enemy unit to move toward the 1st platoon.

The platoon was spread in a long line across a grassy hillside with two men to a position. As it grew fully dark, the 81mm mortars on Firebase Rifle began to fire parachute flares over 1st platoon's position to illuminate any enemy passing through the area. The flares burst high overhead and sank slowly toward the earth, the burning flares swaying beneath their parachutes. The swaying motion caused flickering shadows to move over the ground, giving the illusion of movement where there was none.

As the flares burst open overhead with a sharp **POP,** the open end of the mortar shell fell toward the ground; as it fell, the shell tumbled end-over-end. The air passing across the open end of the shell made a strange *'whoo-whoo-whoo'* sound until the shell hit the ground with a thump. Some of these shells were landing very close to our positions as we lay in the grass along the hillside. Finally, one of these shells hit a man, causing him to cry out sharply in pain and surprise.

The platoon leader called the mortar battery on Rifle and shifted the fire so that no more shells landed near us. The mortar flares were fired for quite a while, but we saw nothing. If an enemy unit had really been in the area, they had managed to slip by us without detection.

Things continued in this quiet way until early on the morning of February 11, 1970. I woke up right at daylight and heard an unusual amount of radio traffic at the platoon **CP.** Word soon filtered down that Firebase Rifle had been partially overrun early that morning. The firebase was defended by men from the Recon platoon of the O-Deuce and elements of the 4th Battalion, 54th ARVN (Army of the Republic of Vietnam) Regiment.

I learned later that sappers (troops trained to penetrate wire barriers without being detected) had penetrated the perimeter wire during a 30-minute 60mm mortar barrage. It was also determined that the sappers' main objective was the COC (combined operations center). The breach in the wire occurred in the 4th-54th ARVN section of the perimeter. Rumor had it that Sabo had singlehandedly driven back the sappers from in front of the COC.

Some forty years later, while reviewing an after-action report about the attack dated March 2, 1970, I saw that credit had been given to Captain John O'Connor, the S-3 Air, for stopping the sapper attack on the TOC. O-Deuce casualties were nine **KIA**; NVA casualties were known to be at least twelve KIA. I don't know which version of the defense of the TOC is true, but both versions illustrate the type of men who were serving in the O-Deuce in 1970.

In coincidence two years after I came home, I met a man who had been inside the TOC during the February 11 attack. By that time, I was a deputy sheriff for San Bernardino County, California, as was this man. During casual conversation, he told me that he had served in the 101st Airborne in Vietnam and was with Headquarters Company of the O-Deuce. He didn't want to talk much about it, but he did say that he was on duty in the COC during the February 11 attack. He told me there was absolute chaos inside the COC, with sappers throwing a barrage of satchel charges at the entrance, some of them landing inside the COC. The interior of the COC received a burst of **AK-47** fire, but no one was hit. He survived with no wounds except a ruptured eardrum. He credits his survival to an (unknown to him) officer who had stopped the sappers with M-16 rifle fire as they tried to enter the COC.

On that same day, Bravo Company's 2nd Platoon was attacked by an unknown sized NVA unit, probably the sappers withdrawing from Rifle, resulting in two more US KIA.

Chapter 12

Fun and Games With The REMF's

February 15–March 4, 1970

On the fifteenth, Alpha Co moved to Firebase Rifle and began closing the base. Bravo Co became **OPCON** to the 1st/327th Infantry. Charlie and Delta continued patrolling in the AO. On February 17, Charlie Co found five **booby trap**s (now known as 'IEDs') made from 60mm mortar rounds scattered along a well-used trail. The next day, 1st Platoon Charlie Co found another booby trap on an LZ. I was getting nervous; booby traps were hard to see and were very dangerous. It seemed that the enemy had taken the time to plant a lot of these devices in the new AO. Other than these incidents, the AO was very quiet.

During this time, the 5 O-Deuce was selected as the 101st Division's IRF (immediate reaction force). Charlie Company was appointed the battalion IRF with 1st Platoon designated to be the first to respond to a situation.

So, on February 20, 1st Platoon was combat assaulted from Firebase Arsenal to a designated LZ in the area. One of the LZs was near a big base camp (I can't remember which one) with a long bunker line. The slicks landed in tandem in a dusty field behind the bunkers, throwing up a huge cloud of dust. We were supposed to run quickly from the slicks and 'aggressively' man the bunkers.

Of course, this was considered a bullshit assignment by combat troops who had been in the field for months, so we acted accordingly. This pissed off the staff officer watching the rehearsal, so we had to do it again because we had not shown enough 'enthusiasm and aggression.' Not wanting to spend all day trying to please a **REMF** (rear-echelon motherfucker) staff officer, we decided to do what they wanted. This time, when the slicks landed, we quickly scrambled off and charged (it was not easy wearing an eighty-pound rucksack) to the bunkers and took up aggressive stances, looking as fierce as we could. This apparently satisfied the staff officer, who walked along the bunker line telling us, "Good job, men," and "You look good, men."

One day in late February 1st Platoon received orders to move to a nearby LZ and prepare for movement by air to an abandoned firebase. We were told to secure the old firebase because an artillery battery was being flown in by CH-47 "Chinook" helicopters to conduct an **artillery raid.**

Soon a flight of slicks came into the LZ and we scrambled aboard, six fully-loaded grunts to a helicopter. The day was cloudy and cool, and I shivered as I sat in the door in the 80-knot slip stream. We flew for what seemed a long time. Finally, I felt the slick slow down and take a nose-up attitude as the pilot brought us in for a landing on a bare hill top. The LT was there and directed us to positions around the **military crest** of the old firebase.

Finally, I could look around, I saw that we were on a bare red clay hill top surrounded by double and triple canopied jungle. Blackened stumps protruded at odd angles from the ground and fallen tree trunks were scattered over the slopes of the hill. We began digging defensive positions as we waited for the Chinooks to bring in the artillery battery.

Soon we heard the Chinooks approaching. As they came over the hilltop, I saw they were each carrying a 105mm howitzer on a sling dangling beneath. Slung under the howitzer was a net containing a basic load of artillery projectiles. Guided by a **pathfinder,** the huge birds first dropped the ammo load, moved over a few feet, and lowered the howitzer into place. The Chinook then landed and the artillery crew for that gun scrambled off. Manhandling the guns into position took only a few minutes and the guns were soon firing.

1st Platoon remained on the hill for several hours while the artillery blasted selected targets within the guns' 12,000 meter (about 7 miles).

Late that afternoon, the Chinooks returned and recovered the guns and their crews. A flight of slicks came for 1st Platoon and moved us to a different LZ than the one we'd left that morning. This process was a good example of the concept of air mobility as practiced by the 101st Airborne Division in 1970.

On the twenty-first, Alpha Company found seven graves containing the bodies of enemy soldiers killed in combat. Since the usual policy was to open the graves to try and determine what NVA unit the dead had come from, the poor guys assigned to this detail must have had a very bad time.

During this time, the 1st Platoon continued patrol in the rain-soaked jungle. One overcast, drizzly day, word came over the radio that Recon had encountered some gooks and had killed one. We were told to be extra cautious because NVA were in the area. Walking along a wide jungle trail, we came upon the dead gook. He had been stripped of his uniform for intelligence purposes and I was able to see the wounds that killed him. It appeared that the bullets had entered his upper torso from the side and had traveled under the skin and muscle across his chest, exiting on the opposite side and raising big welts. They were the strangest looking wounds I ever saw. I could not confirm when the incident occurred or who was involved in the shooting, but I remember the incident clearly.

No action of any significance occurred until March 1, when battalion ordered each company to practice river crossing techniques. There were a lot of rivers in the Firebase Arsenal AO, but I think the river we used was either the Khe Lau or the Khe Chon. I remember that the river ran through a wide plain covered with elephant grass and low scrub brush. The river was 40 or 50 meters wide but only about knee deep.

The method we used was to send two men across the river; one pulling a rope and the other for security. The two men would securely tie their end of the rope to a tree while we did the same on the other side of the river. The platoon would then cross the river holding on to the rope. It was easy because the river was low, but I saw how difficult it would have been if the river had been waist deep or higher. There were quite a few drowning casualties during the Vietnam War.

From March 4 to 13, the battalion moved to Camp Eagle for refresher training. I remember one of the classes I had to take was a lecture on how to deal with Vietnamese civilians and the very basics of the Vietnamese language. We received this training because Charlie Company was going to be under the OPCON of the 2nd-327th Infantry, one of our sister battalions in the First Brigade and we would be working in the lowlands, the populated areas along the coast.

March 5–April 6

The rest of the battalion, minus Charlie Company, moved to a new AO near the Roung-Roung Valley and opened Firebase Pistol. The action around Pistol was light until the twenty-first, when Bravo Company was attacked by an NVA squad resulting in one Bravo KIA and one WIA.

In one of my letters dated March 3, I wrote: "We are going to Camp Eagle tomorrow. We will be there for 10 days. Then we are supposed to go to Eagle Beach for 3 days. Eagle beach is an in-country R&R center. They have…a PX and you can swim in the China Sea."

The next day, 3rd Platoon Alpha Company was attacked while they were in their NDP by a sapper squad; Alpha lost one KIA and eight WIA. About thirty years later, I discovered that one of the wounded was my friend Sgt. Mike Lucky

March ended with no more action except that Alpha Company found some abandoned hospital bunkers, one of them containing three dead NVA.

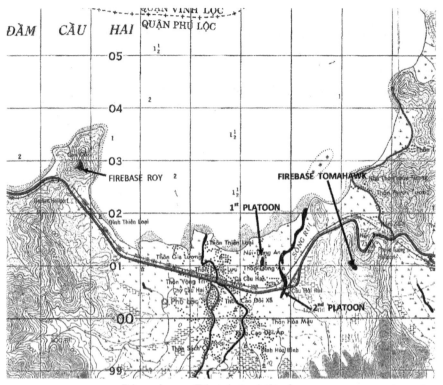

Phu Loc District AO from map series L-7014, sheet 6541-I. The dark line is QL-1, the main north-south highway of Vietnam with railroad line running alongside it. Authors' Collection.

Chapter 13

Life Among the Villagers: Duty in the Lowlands

Just before we left Camp Eagle, I told my folks, "We're going back to the field on the [March] fourteenth. We are supposed to guard a bridge in the lowlands for a couple weeks. Then we will go back into the hills. I'd rather be in the hills and mountains…it is much cooler up there."

One or two days before the company was to leave for the Phu Loc District, I was called to a meeting with Captain James Schoonover, the company commander, the 1st platoon leader and SSG. Phil Gibbons, the platoon sergeant. Gibbons said they had decided to appoint me to be the squad leader for the 3rd squad of 1st platoon.

I wasn't sure I wanted the position. Even though I had undergone quite a bit of extra training, I had only been in the field about a month and had yet to be exposed to an actual firefight. I didn't think I was qualified yet and I told them so. SSG. Gibbons told me they thought I could handle the job and wanted me to accept the position. So, reluctantly, I did accept.

I was issued a compass and the appropriate maps for the coming operation and that was it. I was now in charge of a ten-man squad of combat infantryman, all of them more experienced than me. Since I had been in the field since late January, I already knew the men I was now in charge of. My being made squad leader immediately changed any relationship I had developed with these men. It was possible that a decision I made could result in the wounding or death of one or all of them. It was an awkward situation and whether I was really in charge (or not) remained to be seen.

During this time Charlie Company was under the OPCON of the 2nd/327th Infantry. At Camp Eagle, we climbed aboard deuce and a half's for the trip south on QL-1 to the Phu Loc district for bridge security and patrol and ambush operations along QL-1 and the adjacent railroad line.

Since Charlie was OPCON to the 2nd/327th Infantry, I don't have any official documents to cover this period and I apparently did not write many details in my letters home about it—thus, what follows is written mostly from memory. I tried to locate documents from the 2nd-327th covering this period, but researchers at the National Archives could not locate any.

The trucks carrying 1st Platoon turned off QL-1 onto a dirt road and dropped us off near an abandoned and partially destroyed government building. We took up positions in and around the building and the Charlie Co CP group, along with 3rd platoon, took positions on a small hill (Hill 28) that rose steeply out of abandoned rice paddies about seventy-five meters behind the building. Our positions were halfway between Firebase Roy and Firebase Tomahawk and the northern approaches to the Deo Phouc Tuong, Deo being the Vietnamese word for a pass.

In one letter home, I described what the area was like: *"I am down in the lowlands near the South China Sea. There are a lot of rice paddies and [small] villages here…and kids! They appear out of nowhere selling cokes, bread and jackets made from GI poncho liners."*

They were friendly and mostly looking for handouts, but you had to watch them closely; they would steal anything you weren't sitting on. They especially liked to help themselves to our **frag** grenades, flares, and ammunition.

We did our ambushes at night, so we mostly had the daylight hours to ourselves. One day, we were all sitting around enjoying the warm sun, sleeping or just taking it easy. I was busy compiling a 'wish list' of items my squad needed brought out to us in the next re-supply when I noticed a group of villagers approaching with what looked like two Buddhist monks, playing a flute and banging on a little triangle.

There were several grave mounds close to our positions and the group headed directly to one of them. A lot of the Vietnamese were dressed completely in white, which I discovered later is the Vietnamese color of mourning. A couple of men began to open the grave mound while the monks and the others stood around chanting.

When they had opened the grave, they pulled out a long narrow coffin. The men pried the top open and put a smaller box next to the coffin. The men began to dig around in the coffin, pulling out bones and placing them in the smaller box.

By this time, they had everyone's interest, and I walked closer with several other men. The Vietnamese gave us dirty looks but did not interfere with us. We watched, fascinated, as the two men fished around in the decomposing flesh and dug out every bone, even the small finger and toe bones. Often, they would stop, and a villager would rub something onto their upper lips under their noses. I guess it was something to mask the horrible odor of death rising from the coffin.

Finally, they put a lid on the small box and the parade marched away. The two men who had dug out the bones reburied the casket and left. I have never seen anything like that before or since, and the memories are still very clear.

I did not know it at the time, but I had just witnessed an ancient Vietnamese religious ceremony known as **Cai Tang.** This practice usually occurred if the family had not been able to afford a proper burial or if the body was buried in a hurry, a common practice in Vietnam during the war years. Usually several years after the death, surviving members of the family would locate the bones, disinter them, wash them and re-bury them in a more suitable final resting place.

The area was quiet, with no contact except for the village kids who were almost always present; they were probably spies for the local Viet Cong.

Another incident that I recall with distaste occurred while we were working around a banana grove and some scattered gook **hooches**. The platoon stopped to take a break and some of the men dropped their rucksacks and wandered around. I heard a commotion and saw a few of the men in a group, looking at something on the ground. Curious, I wandered over to see what was going on. They had cornered a small cobra and were teasing it, making it strike at them. I didn't think that was such a good idea and kept my distance. Cobra venom, a nerve toxin, can stop your heart in just a few minutes.

Finally, the snake got tired and tried to crawl away. Some brave guy ran up and squirted the snake with lighter fluid and then threw a lighted match at it; predictably, it caught fire. Some of the men stood there laughing as the snake coiled and writhed, trying to get away. Finally, the cobra lay still, and someone smashed its head.

One day we were in positions very close to QL-1 when we got a radio call from First Lieutenant Wildes, the company **XO**, who said he was bringing a Red Cross girl out to meet us. Known as "Donut Dollies," they were always welcomed by troops in the field. Many times, we hadn't seen any women, much less an American Girl, for months at a time. Just hearing a soft female voice speaking American English made us feel better.

The area around our position was flooded ankle-deep, but when the XO pulled up in his jeep with the girl, I decided to go meet her.

She was very nice and was surprised that I'd wade through water just to meet her. I was wearing a **boonie** hat with 'California Dreamin'' embroidered on the brim. When she saw that, she told me she was a California girl and we had a little reunion. I don't remember what part of the state she was from, but it was nice to meet her. The XO then drove away, saying he wanted to take her to the other platoons for a visit.

Left: south bound QL-1 at Phu Loc. The small dark hill at left center was Charlie Company's position. Firebase Tomahawk was at left end of ridge just above small hill.

One cloudy, cool night 3rd Squad set up an ambush along the railroad tracks which ran beside QL-1. Our position was in some low bushes growing between QL-1 and the tracks. We set out trip flares and claymores to cover the kill zone. I had already pulled my turn at guard and was lying half asleep; as the squad leader, I didn't like to sleep too soundly while set up in an ambush position.

Suddenly I felt something crawling across my stomach and then my chest. My body reflexively jerked, and then I felt a burning sensation where whatever it was had crawled. It felt like someone was dragging a lit cigar across my flesh. The creature crawled out through the collar opening of my shirt and I saw it was a big centipede around six inches long. I'd seen the big insects crawling around in the brush, but I had no idea they could sting. It burned the rest of the night and I got no more sleep.

When I took off my shirt the next morning, I found a wide, red welt running from just above the waistband of my pants to my left shoulder. It didn't burn too much anymore, but it would itch like crazy for the next several days. In Vietnam, even the insects were out to get you!

Sometime during this period, 1st platoon had been issued a 'starlight scope', a battery-powered device that amplified the ambient light available at night allowing you to see in the dark in much more detail.

One night, 1st platoon was scheduled to set up a platoon-sized ambush some distance away from the building we occupied during the day. The LT told me to bring the starlight scope with my squad. I got the scope, packed in a sort of metal briefcase and gave it to a member of my squad to carry to the ambush site. When we arrived and began moving into position, the LT called for the scope. I asked the man I had tasked with carrying it where it was, and he said he'd left it in the building because he didn't want to carry the extra weight. He had not told me about leaving it behind because he did not want a confrontation with me.

I told the LT what had happened, and he became very upset. He radioed the CO who told him to send me back to the building to recover the scope. I was horrified; it meant that I would have to travel several hundred meters through hostile territory by myself, hopefully find the scope still there, and then return to the ambush site. I immediately asked the LT to order the man who'd left the scope behind to go with me and he did so. I knew it had been my sole responsibility to take care of the scope, so I led the way, slowly and cautiously back to the building. To my amazement, the case containing the scope was still in the corner of the room where the man had left it. Wondering if it had been booby trapped, I carefully tied a length of rope I had to the handle, retreated around a corner of the building and gave the rope a good yank! Nothing happened.

Retrieving the scope, we made our way, by a slightly different route to avoid a possible ambush, back to the platoon. Taking advantage of clumps of vegetation to hide in, I used the scope several times on the way back to scout the path we were taking but I didn't see anything suspicious.

I was very angry at the man who'd left the scope behind, but I had to be careful how I handled the situation. He had placed me, and himself, in danger un-necessarily. I suspected he had disobeyed my order to test my reaction. He was popular with the other men of my squad and I thought they might have put him up to it.

After we got back to the platoon, I made sure he was at my guard position on the ambush perimeter. Very quietly, I told him that his actions had put not only himself but others in danger and that he should think twice about not following orders in the future. He said he felt badly about what he'd done and that it wouldn't happen again, so I left it at that.

Just before dawn the next morning, 1st platoon received orders to move to a small hamlet called Thon Thien Loai built among sand dunes at the mouth of a tidal river where it emptied into the Dam Cau Hai lagoon. Moving through the pre-dawn darkness across abandoned rice paddies, we soon arrived at the hamlet and set up a loose cordon around the edges of the village. Then we waited.

Nothing happened until well after dawn. I had a good view of the hamlet from my position in the cordon; it appeared to be uninhabited. There was no smoke from cooking fires, and no dogs or pigs wandering among the hooch's as was usual around a Vietnamese village.

I heard the peculiar buzzing rotor noise of an approaching LOH. The pilot circled the hamlet twice then dropped down and hovered over one of the hooch's. Because the doors had been removed, I could see a crewman in the back seat with what appeared to be a case of hand grenades between his feet.

As I watched, I saw him pull the pin on a frag and drop it through the palm frond roof of the hooch. The frag exploded with a dull thud but nothing else happened. The LOH then moved over to another hut and dropped another frag with same result. After dropping frags into each of the huts in the hamlet with no reaction, the LOH gained altitude and flew away.

My squad then moved into the hamlet and searched the huts for contraband; we found nothing. It looked as if the hooches had been empty for several months.

After the incident with the starlight scope, the company commander relieved me of my duties as squad leader for the time being, but no further action was taken. I guess the CO figured making me walk two or three klicks at night through enemy territory with only one other man was punishment enough. It was one of the longest nights of my tour in Vietnam. I learned another valuable lesson in leadership; never give an order without checking to see if it is being carried out.

On March 13, I wrote: *"Two Days ago, we found some air vents to an NVA tunnel complex. Yesterday we tried to blast our way into the tunnels, but they are too deep...they are bringing in a 'Mighty Mite'...a compressor that forces colored smoke into the tunnel and you can [see]the[tunnel]entrances when the smoke comes out."* I don't remember the outcome of this venture, but we worked at it for two or three days.

On March 30, I wrote about an Easter service at Camp Eagle: "Yesterday I went to Camp Eagle for a big Easter service. They brought out helicopters to take us back. The service was real nice. They had a big choir from Saigon and the speaker was Dr. Halverson from a big church in Washington DC."

Toward the end of our stay in the Phu Loc area, my squad ran a RIF around the base of Hill 28. As we came around the eastern slope of the hill, I saw five or six figures suddenly appear out of the brush on the hillside. They were looking right at us and walking steadily toward us. We got ready to fire but then I saw that they were probably a patrol from the local villages' security forces, known as Popular Forces, so I told the squad to let them get closer.

When they got close enough to talk to us, the leader stopped, held up his hand and said "**Chou Ong,**" roughly meaning "hello, sir" in Vietnamese. I replied, and he came closer. I saw that he was in an old French army fatigue shirt, filthy shorts and carrying a disreputable looking M-2 carbine of WWII vintage. His eyes were fixed on my collar where I was wearing the black metal chevrons of my rank.

He said something like *"Me trung si, me trung si. You souvenir me,"* pointing at the stripes. I knew *'trung si'* meant 'sergeant' in Vietnamese and that he wanted me to give him my metal sergeant stripes. I shook my head, but he kept insisting, his voice getting louder. The squad moved closer and he backed off, probably realizing he was coming on too strong. I told him *"di di mau"* (to leave quickly) and pointed back toward the way he and his patrol had come. They moved away, giving us dirty looks over their shoulders as they went. We watched them until they moved out of sight and then continued our patrol. We didn't see them again.

On one occasion, the 1st platoon was moved by truck north a couple of klicks along QL-1 from Phu Loc. They dropped us off near the site of Firebase Roy and we were to patrol on foot along QL-1 back to Phu Loc. As we rode in the trucks, I noticed what looked like a platoon of ARVN soldiers dressed in camouflage fatigues standing along the west side of the highway. I then saw a row of dead bodies lying side by side near the group of ARVN. The bodies were dressed in the black cotton 'pajamas' habitually worn by Vietnamese peasants and the Viet Cong. There was a pile of weapons near the row of bodies. It appeared that the ARVN had pulled off a successful ambush and were displaying the dead VC and captured weapons for the benefit of the local villagers who were standing in a tight group on the other side of the highway. Some of the villagers may have had relatives in the group of dead VC.

We didn't have any contact with the enemy in Phu Loc, and we were picked up by CH-47 Chinook helicopters and taken back to Camp Eagle. As the Chinook lifted off, I remember hearing Simon and Garfunkel's new hit, "*Bridge Over Troubled Water*," coming from someone's transistor radio. We weren't supposed to have radios out in the field, but the rule wasn't strictly enforced when we were in a 'safe' area. However, it was strictly enforced at night while we were in our NDP or in a place where we knew there were a lot of NVA.

From Camp Eagle, we were airlifted by slicks to join the rest of the company on Firebase Jack, near Camp Evans and the city of Quang Tri.

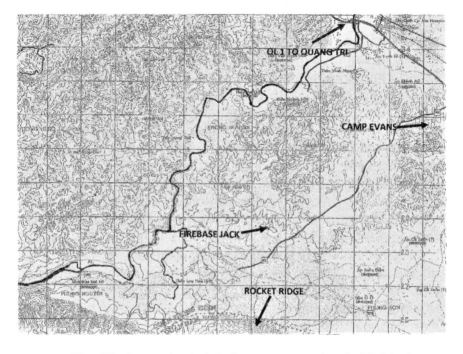

The Firebase Jack AO from map series L-7014 sheet 6442-II, Hai Lang District of Thua Thien Province and a portion of Quang Tri Province.

The Firebase Strike Area of Operations from map series L-

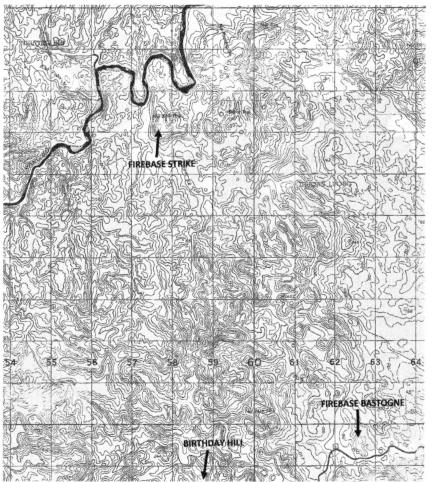

7014 sheet 6441-I Ap Lai Bang District of Thua Thien Province. Author's collection

Chapter 14

Skulls and Bones: Firebase Jack and Firebase Strike

April 7–April 24, 1970

While 1st Platoon was on Firebase Jack, we were **CA**'d several **klicks** out from the firebase with orders to patrol back towards Jack. Sgt. Major Sabalauski came with us and, as luck would have it, when we separated into squads, the tough old soldier chose to come with my squad.

As we patrolled back toward Jack, we found nothing but heat, '**wait-a-minute bushes**,' and several streams we had to cross. At one of the deeper streams, I paused on the bank to make sure my cigarettes and letters from home would not get wet. I wasn't aware that Sabo had come up behind me until he barked, "Sergeant, get your ass across that stream and get on with it." That was my second close encounter with Sabo, and he must have thought I was an idiot by then.

We got back to the firebase OK and went to our guard positions on the perimeter to get ready for the night. There was no wire and no fighting holes or bunkers, so we relied on claymore mines and a lot of trip flares for security and to give us warning.

The 1st Air Cavalry had been involved in heavy fighting on and around Jack during Tet '68, and there were a lot of bones and skulls scattered through the low brush around the base. In the brush in front of my position, I saw a lot of femurs and sternums with some of the ribs still attached. Some of us found skulls and put them on poles that we stuck into the ground in front of our positions. The next day the LT, who had no sense of humor at all, made us take them down.

In an observation dated April 17, I wrote; "Right now I'm up around Camp Evans at Firebase Jack. The firebase is on a [low] hill right in the middle of a valley. It is beautiful, different shades of green and bright blue sky. But nothing beats the sight of old Mt. Baldy, covered with snow."

I was referring to Mt. San Antonio, which at 10,028 feet was the highest peak in the San Gabriel mountain range, just north of my home in Upland, California.

From Firebase Jack, I could see a long, dark green ridge about 150 meters high called Nui Bai Cay Tat by the Vietnamese and known as 'Rocket Ridge' by the GI's operating in the area. The Viet Cong used Nui Bai Cay Tat as a firing point for their 122mm tripod-launched rockets. The ridge was strategically located and allowed the enemy to launch their rockets at the 3rd Brigade base at Camp Evans and the 2nd Brigade base at Camp Sally. The 1st Brigade base at Camp Eagle was at the extreme end of the 11-klick range of the 122mm, but that did not stop the enemy from trying.

There was very little contact with the enemy around Firebase Jack and the battalion CA'd into the Firebase Strike AO on April 19, my birthday. I celebrated my twenty-second birthday on an elephant grass-covered hilltop overlooking a tributary of the Ngoc Ke Trai River a few klicks south of Firebase Strike. My birthday cake was a C-ration pound cake with a match for a candle and canned pears for dessert. I enjoyed it very much.

In a note to my folks on April 17, I described the makeup of 1st Platoon: *"A couple of days and I'll have reached the old age of 22. I'll be one of the oldest in the platoon. The oldest man is 25...most of them are only 18 or 19 years old."*

There was no contact with the enemy in the Firebase Strike AO, so the battalion was CA'd into the AO around Firebase Veghel. Many signs of recent enemy activity were found, but we had no idea of what was to come.

OPERATION TEXAS STAR

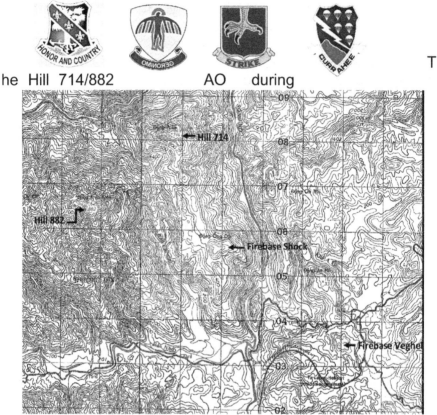

he Hill 714/882 AO during

Operation Texas Star from map series L-7014 sheet 6441-I, Ap Lai Bang District of Thua Thien Province. Authors' collection.

Author's Note

What follows is a detailed day-by-day account of the Veghel Operation, a part of Operation Texas Star. It included the battles for Hills 714 and 882, lasting from April 25 through May 24, 1970. I have attempted to present the story as accurately and completely as I can, using personal accounts, after action reports, unit histories, and daily journals from Headquarters, 2nd/502nd Infantry, written at the time the action occurred. Because a very good book, *Echoes of a Distant Past—Screaming Eagles-Vietnam, 1970* by Eraldo Lucero, has been recently published describing Alpha Company's ordeal on 882, and another great book, *West of Hue—Down the Yellow Brick Road* by James P. Brinker describing Recon's experiences on Hills 714 and 882, was published a few years ago, I will concentrate mostly on what happened to Charlie Company. I have tried to get the chronology and map grid locations down as correctly as possible. James Brinker, Harold Carstens, Terry Lowe, Robert Noffsinger, and Bruce Scott helped straighten it all out when things became confused. If there are any errors in the chronology or inaccuracies regarding dates, times, units involved, places or events, the fault is entirely mine.

Chapter 15

Firebase Veghel and Firebase Shock

April 7–April 24, 1970

April had begun quietly with the O-Deuce moving into a new AO. There was relatively little contact with the enemy and the 1st and 2nd Platoons of Charlie Company passed to the OPCON of the 1st/501st Infantry, part of the 2nd Brigade.

During this time, we made a lot of CAs, sometimes as many as two or three a day. During all of this, Bravo Company was busy building Firebase Falcon and having a hard time of it because of bad weather.

On April 7, the 1st Platoon was sent to Eagle Beach for some in-country **R&R**. Managed by the USO and the 101st Division, Eagle Beach was located on a barrier island near the village of Tan My on the South China Sea.

There were barracks with cots and blankets, picnic tables under the trees, a mess hall, a bar (twenty-five cents per drink) with a stage for what we called "floor shows."

Though barracks were available, a lot of troops preferred to sleep in the warm beach sand, usually after drinking too much and passing out.

When you woke up in the morning and looked around, there were bodies sprawled all over the sand as the guys slept off the effects of partying the night before. It was quite a sight.

I remember one night when we had a floor show. The band was from the Philippines, or maybe Taiwan and they weren't very good. But the girls wore miniskirts and the music was loud, and that's all that mattered to us. Sometimes we would get lucky and the performers would be from Australia with blond "round eye" (Caucasian) dancers.

One of the most popular songs, one we wanted to hear every time there was a show, was the song '*We Gotta Get Out of This Place*' originally performed by *Eric Burdon and the Animals*, a British rock group. The chorus of the song is the words: "*we gotta get out of this place if it's the last thing we ever do; we gotta get out of this place; girl, there's a better life for me and you.*" When the band sang this part, most of the GI's in the audience would join in, bellowing the words at the tops of their voices.

We really meant it; we wanted out of Vietnam and would do what we had to do to survive and go home.

In a message home dated April 10, I described my activities at Eagle Beach: "*We left Eagle Beach yesterday. It was real nice. They had a band and a movie every night...the mess hall has real good chow. I went swimming until I stubbed my toe on a rock and couldn't go in because the salt water stung like mad.*"

After surviving the perils of Eagle Beach and two days and two nights of partying, we were airlifted to the field to join the rest of Charlie Company.

The line companies were finding graves, abandoned bunkers, and ammunition caches all over the AO. We destroyed the bunkers if we could and blew up the ammo. During this time, Recon ran into and killed one NVA soldier. This was typical of small-unit action in Vietnam. Most of the contacts with the NVA were what is known as 'meeting engagements.' This meant that you literally bumped into the enemy while walking on a trail. A good deal of the time, the NVA just seemed to be strolling down the trail with their AKs carried at sling arms. A US point man, however, always carried his M-16 in firing position with the selector switch set on full auto. Most of the time, the NVA were on the losing end of the exchange.

Chapter 16

Things Become Serious

April 24–May 2, 1970

The 2nd/502nd Infantry began operations in a new area west of the Song Bo River by inserting Recon onto the top of Hill 714 at YD508082. The Vietnamese name for Hill 714 is Dong A La ('dong' is the Vietnamese word for mountain or hill). As the lift ships approached the LZ on the peak of Dong A La, flying along a north-south ridge, they began taking fire.

That statement is based on information obtained from the "Daily Journal Situation Report" for April 24, 1970. However, Sgt. Jim "Jimbo" Brinker from Recon was aboard one of those helicopters; he recalls that they were **not** fired on as they approached Hill 714 on that day.

Recon was dropped, and they scouted the area around the peak of the mountain. When the Recon Platoon was extracted that afternoon, the lift ships received fire from the same ridge mentioned above. Companies A, B, C, and D from the O-Deuce were told to move close to landing zones in the jungle-covered hills near Firebase Veghel, alerted for possible action the next day.

Bob Noffsinger tells an unusual story about the number 714. In an e-mail written to his family and forwarded to me in May 2012, he relates: *"You have all heard me tell about my premonition of [Hill] 714. How, after hearing a ghost story on a Boy Scouts camping trip that had Room 714 in it, the number always stuck out when I saw it long after I had forgotten the ghost story. I was near the LT when the radio call came in that we were moving to a new area . . . turned out to be west of the Song Bo. Since I happened to be standing there for some reason, I got involved in decoding the coordinates, something I had never done before. When they were decoded and plotted on the LT's map, I saw Hill 714. I immediately had a bad feeling about the place, [that it was a bad place]."* Bob Noffsinger's premonition about Hill 714 being a bad place turned out to be accurate as the following chapters will illustrate.

April 26

Early on the morning of April 26, Recon was again landed on the LZ at the summit of Hill 714. They immediately came under fire while still on the LZ. One platoon from Bravo Company was brought in to support Recon. As both units moved down the well-used trail from the summit, they began to meet scattered resistance from NVA troops in bunkers. It became clear that the NVA was occupying Dong A La in strength and they were willing to fight.

On the night of April 26–27, Charlie Company was in an overnight position near an LZ at YD551050. We were only about thirteen hundred meters to the northeast of the newly reopened FSB Veghel at YD549036. We had a clear view of the firebase and could see the artillery and mortar positions.

At about 1915 hours in the evening of April 26, we were all awakened by a lot of explosions. From my sleeping position, I could see FSB Veghel and I realized they were receiving mortar or rocket fire. I counted more than fifteen explosions, most of them landing inside the barbed-wire perimeter of Veghel. The mortar barrage ended at about 1935 hours.

Company A had been moved by air to FSB Veghel shortly before the mortar barrage began. According to Eraldo Lucero, a member of Alpha One, ". . .*mortar rounds were coming in like raindrops. They were slamming all over the place, really close to out foxhole. This was an awful feeling, as you can't defend yourself against incoming mortars; all you can do is hope and pray that a mortar round doesn't make a direct hit on your position. . .*" Eraldo Lucero, *Echoes of a Distant Past,* page 89.

In case you're wondering why we were already asleep at 7:15 p.m. when the mortar barrage began, it's because combat infantrymen in the field go to sleep as soon as it's fully dark. They're up and down all night long and need as much rest as they can get.

I knew we would be going after the NVA troops who had launched the mortar attack on Veghel. The stage was now set for the Battle of Dong A La, Hill 714.

April 27

Thudding rotors and the rush of wind through the open cargo doors made normal conversation impossible. We communicated with hand gestures and exaggerated facial expressions. It had started out as a helicopter lift of Charlie Company, 2nd/502nd Infantry (Ambl), in support of Bravo Company, and Recon, already heavily engaged attempting to destroy an enemy bunker complex on Hill 714. But we had been circling the tall, bald-topped mountain for a lot longer than usual, so I knew something was wrong.

Because I was sitting in the door, I had the best view of the ground passing beneath. The helicopter banked steeply, and I saw explosions from artillery or mortars hitting around the top of the hill. I tapped the knee of the door gunner next to me. When he looked at me, I raised my eyebrows and pointed at the explosions on the hilltop below. He moved the microphone away from his mouth, leaned over and yelled that the first helicopters that had tried to land on our intended LZ had been fire on and one had been shot down, blocking the LZ. They were prepping an alternate LZ with artillery fire before we tried to land.

Later, I found out that we had been scheduled to land at an LZ near a hill called Dong Ong Doi about five hundred meters high at the southern end of the 714 ridge, down the ridge line from the place where Bravo Company was engaged with the NVA. We were to have attacked back up the ridgeline in support of Bravo Company. When the first helicopter attempted to land, the NVA hit it with so many rounds of small arms fire that it crashed directly onto the LZ, preventing any other helicopters from using it.

According to Bob Noffsinger: "I was in the third or fourth chopper headed in to the LZ south of Hill 714 when the first one in was hit and crashed [on the LZ], we circled for a while since we could not land and then headed to the LZ directly on top of Hill 714."

We circled for what seemed like hours. It was not a good situation. We were very vulnerable inside the thin-skinned helicopters; I knew the aluminum deck we sat on would stop a bullet about as well as a beer can. I wanted to be on the ground where we would have some cover.

The next day, the downed helicopter was recovered. A platoon of Combat Engineers from Alpha Company, 326th Engineers was sent in to build FSB Shock on the site of the crash (YD518056), to be used to support the fight to take Hills 714 and 882.

Company B and Recon had been inserted the day before (April 26, 1970) on the peak of Hill 714. While working their way south along the ridge from the summit, they had discovered several enemy bunker complexes.

We finally stopped circling and headed toward the hilltop landing zone. As we got closer, I could see old fighting holes forming a circle around the peak. A well-used trail led from the peak down a long ridge toward a lower hill about three hundred meters away. As the helicopter touched down, we jumped out and ran down the slope toward the fighting holes. The strong smell of high explosives and helicopter exhaust hung heavily in the air.

Looking around, I could see that we were on the highest hill in the immediate area. The side I was on sloped steeply to the east into a narrow valley with the Song Bo River flowing at the bottom. I could see a lot of double and triple **canopy** jungle on the hills surrounding us, and I knew it would be difficult terrain to work in.

Farther around to the right, I spotted the bare ocher-colored patch of earth that was Fire Support Base Veghel. I saw puffs of gray smoke as the battery of 105s based there fired.

Someone sat down behind me. I turned and saw the '**Kit Carson Scout'** (KCS) attached to 1st Platoon. KCS' were former VC/NVA soldiers who had surrendered under the 'Chieu Hoi' (open arms) program and agreed to serve as scouts for American units. The name tag on his shirt read "Hahn." He looked scared, so I asked him, "What's wrong, Hahn?" Pointing to the jungle-covered hills below us, he said "Beaucoup NVA, beaucoup. Number ten, very bad, very bad." Many Vietnamese spoke a strange kind of barely understandable 'pidgin' English made up of French, English, and Vietnamese words.

Then, as if on a cue, I heard explosions and rapid M-16 fire answered by the distinctive clack-clack sound of AK-47s coming from the direction of the trail I had seen as we landed. It sounded far away, but it was hard to tell.

Staff Sergeant Gibbons came by and told us to get ready to move. Bravo Company and Recon were three hundred meters down the trail in heavy contact with an NVA unit occupying a bunker complex.

Forming a single file, we automatically moved into our usual places in the file. We walked around the side of the hill to the trailhead. We started off at a quick walk. The trail led along the edge of the ridgeline, with a steep slope on the left and huge trees and underbrush on the right. I could see down into the river valley where the Song (river) Bo broke into rapids over rocks. More gunfire and explosions sounded off to our right front.

We began to pass bloody, bandaged walking wounded from B Company making their way up to the hilltop for evacuation to the rear. I thought, "Oh fuck, what the hell am I getting into?" Then I saw four men struggling to carry a body bag up the steep trail. I edged over to the inside of the trail, so they could pass. A wet, sloshing sound came from the heavy bag as if it were full of liquid. Bob Noffsinger told me he had helped carry that body bag, but I don't remember seeing him. My stomach got queasy and the skin on the back of my neck tightened. I heard more gunfire in front of us, much closer than before.

A knoll rose to our front, the trail turning sharply to the right at the base of the knoll. Passing two men from Bravo Company guarding the trail, we entered a little clearing (YD509079) in a saddle between two knolls. Moving across the clearing to the far side, we began to take up positions to form a perimeter. The squad machine gun was placed overlooking the trail where it left the clearing and descended steeply down the slope to the west. I stayed with the machine gun, watching down the trail.

It was now late afternoon, and it began to rain hard. I was told that Bravo Company had broken off contact with the enemy because of the falling darkness and the rain. A platoon from Bravo Company plus Recon would shortly be coming up the trail into the perimeter.

We watched intently to make sure it really was Bravo Company coming up the trail and not the NVA. The rain began to slack off and visibility improved. Two mud-covered men appeared from around a bend in the trail. They stopped, looked up at us, and waved, and I could see they were Americans. The machine gunner gestured for them to come in and they began to struggle up the slick, muddy trail.

The rest of the platoon slowly followed. As they passed, I saw exhaustion and fear on their faces, the look of men who have been in hard combat. Some of them were carrying extra rifles and rucksacks. The last man, a second lieutenant, said that nobody else was behind him but the gooks. The men from Bravo Company and Recon silently passed through our positions and set up their own perimeter about two hundred meters farther down the ridge to the south of us.

By then, it was almost dark. I took two other men and went about ten meters down the trail to set up some trip flares and **claymore** antipersonnel mines. We hurried up the trail into the perimeter just as it got fully dark. We were all nervous and fully alert. We didn't know how badly the enemy had been hurt. I expected them to probe the perimeter of our NDP to try to discover our positions and test our strength.

That evening, the squad leaders met with the platoon sergeant and the platoon leader for a briefing. We were told that Alpha Company had located the NVA mortar site from which FSB Veghel had been mortared the night before. There was a position for a forward observer with a phone line running to the mortar pit five hundred meters away. I knew that if the NVA were using phone lines and forward observers to coordinate mortar fire, then we were dealing with at least a battalion or possibly a regiment.

I began to hear artillery rounds passing overhead and bursting in the valley below. It was called **H & I** (harassing and interdicting) fire, and it was meant to make it difficult for the NVA to move around at night. I don't know if it worked; it was annoying at first, but I soon got used to it and took comfort from it. Any NVA killed or wounded by artillery fire was one less we had to fight the next day. For Charlie Company, the night passed quietly.

April 28

It rained off and on all night and the day dawned cloudy, cold, and damp. About 0500 hours, the 2nd Platoon, Bravo Company at a separate NDP at YD510072 was attacked. Twelve NVA were killed. Bravo Company had one KIA (PFC Michael T. Sears) and six WIA who required a **dust off**. In the 101st, medical evacuation helicopters used the radio call sign "Eagle Dust Off," soon shortened to dust off. There were other wounded that did not require a dust off and remained in the field.

The rain stopped, and just after daybreak a helicopter landed in the small clearing; it brought extra ammunition and a couple of B Company men who had gone to the battalion aid station on Firebase Veghel for treatment of minor wounds. We loaded the rifles and rucksacks left behind by the wounded and killed from the battle of the day before. Loading the rifles, I counted more than twenty. I caught a glance from the door gunner on the right side of the ship. He looked at the pile of muddy equipment and sadly shook his head.

The pilot increased power, pulled up on the collective and the loaded **Huey** lifted off. I looked wistfully at the dirty green helicopter as it cleared the trees. I wanted to be on board, headed back to the "safety" of the firebase.

Pretty soon, word came down that Bravo Company was going to head back to the scene of yesterday's fight and attempt to contact the NVA again. Charlie Company would follow as their reserve.

I grabbed a can of C rats as a quick breakfast and got ready to move. Everybody gave their weapons a thorough check.

The overhead artillery fire had stopped during the night, but it began again as the platoon from Bravo Company moved down the steep, muddy trail. In a few minutes, the lead squad of our company started down. It was treacherous going because the passage of so many men had churned the wet trail into a slick, muddy mess. Quite a few men lost their footing and went down in the ankle-deep muck.

We followed the trail for about a hundred and fifty meters. Huge trees and thick clumps of bamboo met over our heads to form a dark, dank-smelling tunnel. Everyone was tense, and we were careful to maintain our intervals of three to five meters between each man.

Ahead, I heard the ring of axes on wood and then the sound of men's voices. We broke into a clearing and I saw soldiers from Bravo Company clearing trees and brush to build a landing zone.

My platoon moved into the trees on the far side of the clearing to act as security while the landing zone was being cleared. Word passed that the bunker complex Bravo Company had attacked the day before had been found abandoned. Recon and Bravo Company searched the abandoned bunkers and found fifty dead NVA hidden in some of the bunkers.

We were still a little nervous even though we'd been told that the NVA had withdrawn. You never knew what they'd do; it was not unusual for them to sneak up and fire a burst from their AKs hoping to cause casualties.

Soon, heavily loaded Hueys came into the landing zone. Cases of C rations were off-loaded and passed out to the different platoons.

April 29

Bravo Company continued its sweep down the ridge line from the peak of Hill 714 while Charlie Company remained in position awaiting orders.

That afternoon, Bravo Company found an occupied bunker complex at YD509077 and became involved in a hard fight attempting to dislodge the NVA. We were ordered to reinforce them as quickly as possible. 1st Platoon left immediately, almost running down a wide trail toward the sounds of the fight.

The ridge began to level out, and we stopped and dropped our rucksacks in a small clearing; some men were left behind to guard them. The rest of us continued down the trail at a quick walk. My heart was pounding, I felt increasingly anxious and my senses were fully alert; my vision appeared sharper and clearer than before. I was scared, but at the same time, I wanted to get there and help.

We suddenly broke out of the bamboo thicket and into a clearing. It was chaotic. Over to the right, I saw a bunch of men sitting hunched over or lying on ponchos, some with bloodstained bandages. Their bare torsos shone in the sun, white against the dark green vegetation. A group of medics were working on several of the men and I thought, "They must be the worst wounded."

Gunfire and explosions sounded from the trees in front of us. Bullets buzzed and whirred as they passed through the trees, knocking leaves and branches to the ground and thudding into tree trunks. The peculiar sound of the bullets buzzing and whining past made me want to fall to the ground; I felt like a big, fat target standing erect as I was. It was my first time directly under fire and it was a very weird feeling.

A call came down for all M-79 (a 40mm grenade launcher resembling a big shotgun) gunners to form a line at the edge of the clearing. Soon, seven or eight men had lined up and were furiously firing their high-explosive grenades into the enemy positions ahead of the Bravo, Recon, and Charlie Company skirmish line. Used as small mortars, the rounds were going over the heads of the advancing troops and exploding in the enemy positions in front of them.

My squad was placed on the right side of the skirmish line, along the edge of a deep, brush-filled gully, guarding against a flanking maneuver by the NVA. The rest of 1st Platoon joined Bravo Company's skirmish line. The firing was mostly M-16s now, but we could still hear sporadic **RPD** machine gun and AK-47 fire.

I warned the men in my squad to be especially alert because the NVA on Hill 714 were very aggressive. A few minutes later, one of the men in my squad shouted that he had seen movement in front of us, down in the gully. I couldn't see anything, but I directed the squad to fire a few shots (called recon-by-fire) into the brush in front of us to see if anyone returned fire. No one shot back, but we remained alert in case the NVA decided to attack Bravo Company's right flank.

We stayed on the right flank for another half hour or so. The firing slowed and finally died out altogether. I heard muffled explosions every so often as Bravo Company men threw grenades into bunkers and spider holes to clear out any NVA who might have remained behind when their comrades withdrew. Bravo Company took a lot of casualties, but they got the job done.

My squad was recalled from the flank and we joined up with the rest of the platoon. We were sent forward to the far edge of the bunker complex to act as security while a battered B Company reorganized. As we passed through the area so recently fought over, I saw pools of drying blood spotting the ground. A fatigue shirt, stained crimson with blood, hung from the branch of a small tree near a pile of bloody bandages. Empty rifle magazines and brass cartridges littered the ground.

We checked the area closely and found fifteen dead NVA as well as several weapons. Seven of the dead NVA were bandaged from previous wounds. We found US weapons, including an M-60 machine gun, an M-79 grenade launcher, and a PRC-25 radio that the NVA had captured somewhere and used against us. Bravo and Charlie Companies had lost twenty-six men wounded and a Scout Dog had been killed when he tripped a booby trap.

It began to get dark and we set out plenty of trip flares and claymore mines as defense against a night attack. Our packs were brought up and I gobbled down a much-needed can of C ration. I was lucky not to draw first guard and I went right to sleep.

When I was awakened for my turn at guard, I saw that the moon was about half full. The clearing was bathed in a soft white light. I was amazed at how bright it was and how far I could see. I was still very tired and to stay alert, I sang popular songs to myself. My favorites were Simon and Garfunkel's "The Sounds of Silence", "Homeward Bound" and "I Am a Rock." There were others, but I can't recall them after so many years.

A little after 2200 hours, I heard mortar rounds impacting somewhere to the south of us. Bravo Company and Recon were in a position about two hundred meters south of us, so I assumed they were under attack. I counted at least twenty explosions which, from the sound, were 82mm. No rounds fell near our positions.

April 30

The Big Cache

My final turn on guard covered the last two hours before daylight. I felt better, and I was fully alert. I knew that the NVA's favorite time for a surprise attack was just before dawn. They would use the night hours to recon the target and decide how to attack. After the mortar attack on B Company and Recon the night before, I knew there were still NVA in the area and I expected further contact with them. As the sky turned pink, I heard the company command post begin to stir. I woke up the other men at my position and we got ready for the new day.

Two patrols were sent out immediately to check for enemy movement and to try and locate the positions from which the mortars had been fired the night before. One of the patrols stumbled across an enemy patrol and a brief firefight occurred. Our patrol began to break contact and withdraw. I overheard the company **RTO** calling for **Cobra** gunships to support the patrol as they tried to get back to the perimeter.

In just a few minutes, a pair of Cobras appeared and began to circle overhead. The Cobra was the first helicopter designed solely as a gunship for the support of ground troops and for use against armored vehicles. They carried a two-man crew sitting one behind the other in a fuselage only thirty-six inches wide. Looking up, I could see these two were armed with rockets, mini guns, and an automatic grenade launcher.

I heard the RTO telling the Cobras where to fire. They made their diving approach directly over our position. The rockets left the launcher with a loud WHOOSH, almost immediately followed by a CRA-A-ACK as the rockets accelerated through the speed of sound. The rockets zoomed out and exploded in the trees about seventy-five meters in front of our perimeter line. The noise was awesome, and I could feel the earth jump against my chest and belly as I hugged the ground. Dust, smoke, and chunks of trees flew into the air.

The deadly Cobras made two or three passes, launching rockets each time. After expending their rockets, they circled our perimeter until the patrol made it back and the RTO dismissed them.

Immediately, we packed up and moved out in platoon-sized elements. 1st Platoon moved down a wide ridge that sloped gradually downhill toward Dong Ong Doi where Firebase Shock was being built. At about 1400 hours, we suddenly stopped. Told to form a hasty perimeter, we waited. After half an hour or so, word filtered down that the point man, Billy Lucas, and his slack man, Bob Noffsinger, had discovered an NVA rucksack and several bunkers just off the trail. This bunker complex was located at YD512076 on the east side of the main north-south ridge running from the peak of Dong A La.

While the point team checked the bunkers for enemy troops and booby traps, I ate a quick can of C ration for lunch. Beans and franks, my favorite! Never knowing when we would have a chance to eat, troops quickly learned to take advantage of breaks to grab a can of C ration. When I finished, I crushed the can with my boot to prevent the NVA from using it.

The reason I crushed the can was that C-ration cans were just the right size to hold a grenade. The NVA would fasten the can to a tree and then insert a grenade with the pin removed. The sides of the can would prevent the "spoon" from flying off and arming the grenade. A trip wire would be fastened to the head of the grenade and secured to a tree or bush on the opposite side of the trail. Anyone hitting the trip wire would drag the grenade out of the can and arm it, causing an explosion three to five seconds after the grenade was pulled from the can.

We moved off the trail around the bunkers and took up positions. It turned out the bunkers held a cache of weapons and ammunition, some of it captured from the French Army nearly twenty years before.

The rucksack contained an American PRC-25 radio, two antennas; an American poncho liner with an NVA poncho, AK-47 ammunition, a 100cc can of albumin, and bandages.

Sergeant Gibbons came by our position and told us to set out claymore mines and to leave one man at each position as guard.

In a letter dated May 2, I told the folks at home: "The other day we found another [big] cache. This one had rifles, machine guns, and mortars, along with [the] ammo for everything. The weapons were in real good shape; I'm glad we found them. That means the NVA will have less to use against us."

I remember watching as men dragged a variety of weapons from the cache. There were cases of rifle ammunition, French MAT-49 9mm submachine guns, fourteen Russian sniper rifles, and a Czech SKS assault rifle with a folding bayonet. The guys in the next bunker found a Czech-made RPD 7.62mm light machine gun and several crates of belted ammunition for it, as well as four complete 60mm mortars—tube, bipod, base plate, and aiming mechanism.

According to Bob Noffsinger: *"Billy and I got to pick a souvenir from the cache. I chose a sniper rifle rather than an AK since it was in excellent shape."*

By that time, the sky overhead was buzzing with helicopters. Five other men and I were sent to guard a clearing about fifty meters down the trail, so the battalion commander could land. The Huey came in quickly, thoroughly coating us with dirt and debris from the rotor wash. The battalion commander jumped out of the Huey and strode purposefully up the hill. His spit-shined boots and starched jungle fatigues looked very out of place compared to the dirty, ragged field grunts, sometimes called **boonie rat**s.

Cajun Tiger's Huey lifted off to make room for another, this one carrying the 1st Brigade Commander, Colonel White, and his entourage. This bunch of starched, spit-shined rear echelon troopers looked like models for recruiting posters as they marched up the dusty trail to the bunkers. Though I felt the usual disdain of the boonie rat for the rear echelon, I was secretly jealous of their clean clothes and their clean, well-groomed, and well-fed bodies.

The Colonel's Huey took off and we were called back to man the perimeter and help ensure the safety of the brass.

WHUMP! I was peppered by pieces of bark and dirt. Stunned by the sudden blast, I stopped dead in my tracks. My face began to sting so I ran my hands over my face and jaw, but there was no blood. As I stood there in total confusion, Colonel White crashed through the brush and came up to me. He asked if I was all right but all I could do was look at him and numbly nod my head.

It turned out that one of the troops returning to his position on the perimeter had stepped on the "clacker," the firing mechanism for the claymore mine, accidently setting it off. A claymore mine firing mechanism was usually covered by a steel helmet to prevent such accidents. Luckily, the mine was aimed away from me or I wouldn't be writing this. Caught in the back blast of the exploding mine, I had a severe headache and my ears rang for hours afterward.

It was decided to load all the captured weapons on the two colonels' Hueys and take them back to Camp Eagle. The ammunition was to be packed into the largest bunker and destroyed by an explosive charge the next day. All the brass finally left, and we settled in for a quiet night.

Early the next morning, Staff Sergeant Gibbons set a demolition charge with a half-hour fuse to destroy the captured ammo. We got ready to move and Gibbons lit the fuse as the last of the platoon left the bunkers. There was a wide, gently sloping trail leading away from the bunkers, so we made good time. About thirty minutes later, the charge detonated with a loud roar, but we were so far down the ridge that the blast was concealed from view by the jungle. We found a good place to set up a patrol base at YD514063 and stopped there.

We remained there, near where we had found the weapons cache, for the next two days. We ran squad-sized patrols all over the area looking for evidence of the NVA. We knew they were there in force, but for some reason they had chosen not to engage us. We received resupply by air, and the XO, 1st Lt. Wildes, and 1st Sgt. Ira Stanley came out on one of the log birds and brought our pay.

As an E-5 drawing combat pay and overseas pay, I was paid a whopping $356.40 monthly. Since we were in the field almost constantly, I had no place to spend the money. I kept about $50 for myself and sent the rest back to the rear where the money was kept in the company safe. When we returned to base camp, we could send money home in the form of a money order, leave it in the safe, or put it into a savings account.

Chapter 17

The Bunkers: First Day

When first under fire and you're wishful to duck,
Don't look or take heed at the man that is struck.
Be thankful you're living and trust to your luck,
And march to your front like a soldier.

--Rudyard Kipling, "The Young British Soldier"

May 3, 1970

Bob Noffsinger remembers: "*The morning of May third, before we started moving, Jerry Kulm, Vernon Okland, Frank Carvajal, and I had been sent down the jungle trail as an outpost...We did not usually talk about such things...but I guess it was on everybody's mind, so we were talking and someone said 'I wonder if all four of us will make it out of here.' We joked and passed it off, hoping we all would.*"

That morning we found a wide, smooth trail and followed it across the ridge and down the other side. We called this kind of trail a 'high-speed' trail or a '**freeway**.' This meant that the trail was used frequently by large numbers of NVA and that there were probably large NVA units in the area. We moved very slowly and with great caution, the point man stopping every few meters to scan the trail ahead. We knew there would probably be NVA trail watchers on the trail.

We began to pass a lot of tree stumps. Many of the trees appeared recently cut, possibly for use as the roof of a bunker. We knew there had to be a lot of NVA in the area because we found a place where the NVA had built a rock dam in a small stream to create a pool, probably for use as a laundry and bathing area.

By now it was late morning, and we began looking for a good place to set up a defensive position so recon patrols could be sent out. We found a small knoll at YD511062 that had good fields of fire, so we stopped.

My squad (3rd Squad, 1st Platoon) went out on the first **RIF** of that day led by Staff Sergeant Gibbons, his RTO (radiotelephone operator), and the platoon medic. We descended into a little stream bed and followed it downstream about one hundred to two hundred meters until we came to a well-used trail that led up a slope. I could smell traces of wood smoke in the air as well as the odor of human waste. As we climbed the slope, we suddenly stopped. The point man, Sgt. Terry Lowe, had found a couple of lean-tos sheltering a latrine site. This position was at approximately YD511063.

We continued up the slope, moving very slowly and quietly. As we crested the slope, a single shot rang out and Platoon Sergeant Gibbons went down. Instantly, the machine gun team (PFC Vernon Okland and **Sp4** Jerry Kulm) and Terry Lowe began to fire long bursts into the brush in front of us.

In a telephone conversation in August of 2012, Lowe told me that he was amazed to see Sgt. Gibbons walking nonchalantly right up the middle of the trail and he was not surprised when Gibbons was shot.

The rest of us hit the ground and looked around for targets. There was a loud BOOM, and the machine gun stopped firing for several long seconds but then began firing again. The NVA had thrown a grenade, a satchel charge or fired an **RPG** at the gun team, but Okland and Kulm were uninjured.

We began to withdraw back down the slope into the streambed. As Gibby came back down the trail, I noticed blood on the front of his shirt. He told us to get on line facing up the slope to give us a wider base of fire. I found a large rock and crouched behind it. I looked up the slope and saw figures moving through the brush on the slope of the hill. At the same instant, the man next to me shouted, *"I see gooks"* and fired into the brush. We all began to fire; I fired a magazine on semi-auto, as fast as I could pull the trigger and the movement stopped. I don't know if we hit anybody but they didn't fire back. Gibbons radioed for the rest of the platoon and they began moving toward us.

We couldn't see any more movement and we were not receiving fire, so Gibby had us move another twenty meters or so upstream to wait for the rest of the platoon. The medic started to treat Sgt. Gibbons' wound, and I saw that he had been hit by a single bullet in the upper left chest. The round had entered from the front, passed under his collar bone and exited his back just above the shoulder blade. The exit wound in his back was large, the bullet blowing out a wound more than an inch square.

About that time, the rest of the platoon caught up with us. The RTO called for a dust-off helicopter to evacuate Gibbons and for Cobra gunships to attack the hill where we had found the NVA camp. The platoon leader formed us into a perimeter with a couple of men about thirty meters out in front to act as lookouts.

We waited, watching the surrounding jungle intently for any sign of enemy movement. Finally, we heard the dust-off helicopter approaching. The RTO threw out a purple smoke grenade to mark our position and the pilot correctly identified the color.

It was not unusual for the NVA to throw out smoke grenades of the same color attempting to draw helicopters to the wrong location so they could be fired on. The NVA habitually tried to shoot down dust offs even though they carried no weapons and were clearly marked with large red crosses on the doors and nose of the aircraft.

In this case, the pilot located us and came to a hover about sixty feet overhead. There was no close landing zone, so the crew chief lowered the jungle penetrator down through the tree branches to the ground. The medic unfolded one of the seats from the side of the torpedo-shaped device and got Gibbons strapped in. As the **penetrator** started to rise through the treetops, I heard the distinctive "clack-clack-clack" of an AK-47 firing on full automatic at the helicopter. Anyone who has ever heard that sound will never forget it.

Most of the time, a helicopter crew can't hear gunfire coming from the ground and don't know they're being shot at unless the helicopter is hit. The RTO told the pilot they were taking fire; he replied, "Roger" but continued to hover. As Gibbons rose above the trees, the pilot lowered the nose and accelerated away with Gibbons still dangling beneath the ship. We learned later that they made it safely back to the 85th Evacuation Hospital at Phu Bai. I never saw Gibbons again.

Next to arrive were two Cobra gunships. We threw out yellow smoke to mark our forward positions and the Cobras began their firing runs. I remember the smell of that smoke as it drifted over my position, an acrid, sour smell. We all got as close to the ground as we could. We were very close to the enemy positions and there was real danger of us being struck by fragments from our own ordnance.

My position was down in a shallow gully, right where our line crossed the stream running at the foot of the NVA-held hill. As the rockets exploded in the trees to my front, I saw splashes as pieces of shrapnel hit the water next to my right leg. I curled up into a ball and got as close to a big tree root as I could. One of the firing passes was very close to my position, the rockets exploding with incredible force and noise. I felt a sharp sting in my upper left back. Reaching back, I felt a little lump on my back and saw a tiny bit of blood on my fingers. Apparently, I had been hit by a very small piece of shrapnel. The wound was just a scratch and I didn't bother to report it.

If I had reported it, the army would have notified my family that I had been wounded. I did not want to cause them any anxiety for such an insignificant injury.

Another pair of Cobras arrived and added their firepower to the attack. The noise was deafening, and I could feel the concussion in the pit of my stomach. I hoped the Cobras were blasting the hell out of the NVA positions.

After the Cobras had used all their ordnance, the platoon leader moved our platoon farther to the right so that our line now straddled the trail that led to the NVA positions. Because our platoon had found the NVA camp, we were given the job of advancing up the slope to locate the enemy bunkers and destroy them. The other two platoons that made up Charlie Company were too far away to be of immediate assistance.

The platoon leader,1st Lieutenant Gerald Dillon, put the platoons' machine guns and M-79 grenade launchers at either end of our line and they began to fire into the trees in front of us, trying to keep the enemy's heads down to prevent them from shooting at us while we advanced. The LT stood up, waved his arm in a 'follow me' gesture, and started up the hill.

At that instant, a ridiculous thought popped into my head: The LT's gesture reminded me of the 'Follow Me' statue in front of Infantry Hall at the infantry school at Fort Benning.

Anyway, we all followed, M-16s at the ready. We couldn't see anyone or spot any obvious enemy positions, but we knew they were there. I had placed my squad on the line about five meters apart but as we moved up the slope into the thick vegetation, we began to lose sight of one another. The men instinctively began to move closer together for mutual support; doing this made them better targets for the NVA concealed in their bunkers.

I had gone up the hill about ten meters when a shower of grenades and satchel charges came out of the trees above us. They exploded, showering us with smoke, dirt, and grenade fragments. Several men were hit and we all hit the ground. Enemy machine gun and rifle fire came in on us, but most of the rounds seemed to go over our heads.

We still could not see where the fire was coming from, so we crawled back down the hill, bringing the wounded with us. The LT radioed the situation to Captain Schoonover traveling with the 3rd Platoon, a little distance away. He told us to withdraw down to the streambed and take up positions there while he called in artillery fire on the enemy hill.

At around this time, 2nd Platoon joined us and took up positions at the base of the hill. Bruce Scott, an E-4 with 2nd Platoon has this to say: "On May 3, 1970, 2nd Platoon was assigned to search for the enemy. We went down a creek and dropped our rucksacks...I was in Glen Witycyak's squad. He was a shake-n-bake who came to the company in early January 1970 and he somehow got the name of 'Psychedelic.' *We proceeded up a ridge line...without any contact...We were not there long when someone, I assume [it] was the LT, called to Glen and we got up and followed him...The next thing I knew there was AK fire and explosions either grenades or RPG fire...all of a sudden, my position was fired up. The bullets were coming so close I [actually] thought I could see them...There was a call for a medic and a call for help to come up to the front of the line. I moved up and learned that the sergeant [Witycyak] had been hit. Doc [Kenneth] Fuller had gone to help him and was also hit.*"

Harold Carstens, another member of 2nd platoon, remembers how Witycyak got the nickname Psychedelic. Witycyak had received a very colorful scarf, like what 'hippies' wore, from a girl back in the world. He wore it all the time and was soon dubbed "Psychedelic" by the other troops in 2nd Platoon. In fact, Carstens did not know Psychedelic's real name until I told him during a telephone conversation in June 2012.

By now, air support had been called in with the bombs and napalm hitting all around Charlie Company's positions. Bruce Scott remembers: "Jets dropped napalm so close that it sucked the oxygen from where we were at. They dropped bombs so close I remember a piece of shrapnel come down that had to be six inches long."

After the bombing, artillery fire began to fall on the hill. Again, I waited in the streambed, huddling as close to the stream bank as I could. The big 105mm shells screamed overhead and burst on the hill above us. The noise was incredible, and the earth shook beneath us. Dirt, rocks, and pieces of shattered trees fell all around us. It's impossible to describe the violence of an artillery barrage unless you've had personal experience.

After the artillery stopped, men began to stand up and move into position for another advance back up the hill. A single rifle shot rang out. More shots sounded, and someone began screaming in pain and fear, calling for his mother and that he didn't want to die. It was unnerving as hell having to listen to the screams die down and finally stop. Frantically, I began searching the trees above us for targets, but I could see no one; no muzzle flashes, no gun smoke, no movement.

While we were talking on the telephone, Harold Carstens told me that Witycyak had the triceps blown off his left arm and was bleeding heavily. Carstens tried to help but couldn't get the bleeding under control. Soon the medic came up and, putting his body between the incoming fire and Witycyak, tried to stop the bleeding.

Carstens said that they had a '**cherry**' with them who threw a grenade at the place where most of the fire was coming from. The problem was that the cherry forgot to remove the safety clip from the grenade and the NVA threw it back at them. He believes that's how Doc Fuller was wounded.

By this time, Carstens himself had been hit under the left arm by AK fire. His friend Homer Hardy had had his right shoulder blown open, also by AK fire. They struggled to get back down the slope, trying to bring the dead Witycyak with them. They eventually got to a safer place where, later that day, they were evacuated to the hospital at Phu Bai.

Soon it became apparent that the NVA were firing down on us. We began to shoot into the treetops, trying to keep the snipers from firing down into our positions. Bruce Scott recalls: "I got down for cover and someone said something about snipers in the trees. I repeated that info and started firing into the trees."

Our fire was effective, because the sniper fire died out. We later discovered that the snipers had been firing from platforms constructed high in the trees that gave them a perfect view of us as we moved up the slope toward their positions.

According to James Brinker, before they moved onto Hill 714, the Recon Platoon had received a briefing on the possibility that the NVA had fighting platforms in the trees. Charlie Company leaders did not have this information, or, if they did, it was not passed down to the squad/fire team level. We found out about it the hard way: by taking casualties.

We stood up and tried to advance back up the hill hoping that the NVA would still be down in their holes, stunned by the artillery. We fired into the trees above us as we struggled through the brush. We got several meters farther up the hill before we were again showered with grenades. They burst all along our line and several men went down. I don't know if they were hit or just taking cover. I still couldn't see where the enemy positions were, and the grenades and satchel charges continued to fall on us.

I became entangled by a wait-a-minute bush, and, as I was struggling to free myself from the barbed thorns, two satchel charges came in on me and the guy next to me whose name I don't remember. I saw the charges, big yellow-orange chunks of TNT, tumble down the slope and stop about eight to ten feet in front of us. They both went off, but amazingly neither one of us was hit by shrapnel. I was stunned by the blast and it felt as if I'd been hit in my chest and abdomen with a baseball bat. I doubled over from the pain while my ears rang and my head roared. I was so dizzy I couldn't stay on my feet and I went to my knees and just fell over on my side. I lay there for a while. I don't know what happened to the man beside me.

I don't remember how long I lay there until I partially came to my senses. I was almost totally deaf, my abdomen hurt like hell, and I couldn't find my rifle or my helmet. I managed to get to a medic and tried to tell him what had happened. He looked me over and asked, *"Are you bleeding; do you have a wound?"* Barely able to understand him, I said *"no, I don't think so"* and he just shrugged and turned away to take care of others more seriously wounded. As a result, I was never tagged and was not sent to the rear for a medical exam.

At that time, the army did not know much about concussion injuries. I remember telling a medic that I was passing blood in my urine and my stool, but again, he put me off. Medical problems caused by the concussion from that satchel charge did not become apparent until more than ten years later.

After a while, I felt a little better; I went back up and managed to find my rifle and helmet but about that time, the LT decided to withdraw back to the streambed. Dragging the wounded, we scrambled back down the hill. Bullets tore through the brush and trees over our heads as we tumbled into the streambed. It was late in the afternoon as we tried to get reorganized. Captain Schoonover received permission to withdraw back to our original position at about YD511062.

Around the time that 1st Platoon started their withdrawal, 2nd Platoon began to do the same. Bruce Scott remembers: *"I know that Harold Carstens and Homer Hardy were wounded. Sgt Witycyak was killed. At that time, we thought he died from shock, but [I] [have] since learned that other than his bicep being split open he had a more serious wound to his back. We were unable to have choppers come in and get out the injured and [the] dead sergeant. So, we had to carry him out."*

Harold Carstens remembers lying on the ground waiting for the dust off. Homer Hardy, who had just returned from R&R with a brand new 8mm movie camera, asked Carstens to give the camera to the 1st Sergeant for safe keeping. Carstens did so, but when he returned to Charlie Company's rear from the hospital, no trace of the camera could be found.

Carstens told me that he felt guilty about the camera for more than thirty years until he finally found Hardy and apologized. Hardy said he had forgotten all about the camera until Carstens mentioned it.

Carstens remember that it was getting dark when it was his turn to be evacuated. The dust off lowered a wire gurney, the dead Witycyak was placed in first, and Carstens was laid on top of Witycyak.

As we moved back, it began to get dark, so the company commander ordered us to remain in our new position because it could be easily defended. We would spend the night there while artillery from Firebase Veghel (105s) and Firebase Bastogne (eight-inch howitzers) bombarded the hill all night.

After we moved, dust offs were called to evacuate the wounded. I don't remember if the NVA fired on the dust-off ships, but all the wounded were soon evacuated. I could hear the NVA shouting behind us. A few of us fired back up the hill to try to keep the NVA from coming after us as we withdrew.

We had lost thirteen wounded and one killed during the fierce fight that day. It was no consolation to learn that we had managed to kill at least twenty-seven of the enemy before we withdrew.

I remember some of the other wounded from that day. They are: Anthony Schweitzer, Alvin Nantz, and the medic Kenneth Fuller, who was wounded trying to treat Glen Witycyzk.

There was a small opening in the trees at our NDP and just before complete darkness a Huey log bird hovered over the clearing. The crew chief kicked out several boxes of ammo and grenades. We would need them in the morning because we had to go back up that hill.

I didn't sleep much that night. The continuous artillery fire kept me awake and so did worry about the next day. I had been very lucky so far. Even though several grenades had burst close to me, I hadn't even been scratched, except for the tiny piece of rocket fragment in my back. I still had a headache, my ears were ringing, and my guts hurt but I had recovered somewhat from the explosion of the satchel charge; I was still nauseated and in pain, though.

I knew the attack would be bad because we could not see the enemy positions. The only thing we could hope for was that the artillery would blow away enough of the screening vegetation for us to spot the enemy bunkers. Then we could maneuver against them with less chance of being fired on.

We spent the night on 50 percent alert, concerned that the NVA would probe our perimeter to try and inflict more casualties and further reduce our strength.

At some time during this part of the battle, Charlie Company had no medics in the field because they had all been wounded. James Brinker relates a story about Mike "Doc" Ackerman, who volunteered to rappel into Charlie's position to serve as our only medic. His offer was turned down, but when we heard of it, we very much appreciated his courage. According to Brinker, Ackerman had a serious death wish and was always volunteering for dangerous missions. It's a good thing he didn't make the attempt, because the NVA were all over the place and probably would have shot him as he slid down the rope.

Chapter 18

The Bunkers: Second Day

May 4, 1970

The long night finally ended, and those of us who weren't on guard duty started the day by stripping our weapons, giving them a thorough cleaning. I emptied all the bullets from the twenty-three magazines I carried and carefully reloaded them, replacing any of the rounds that looked dirty or corroded. I carried six fragmentation grenades and I checked to make sure that all of them were in good condition.

Right about then, word came down that we had been ordered to delay our assault on the enemy bunkers until the next day. I spent May 4 writing letters and listening to the artillery pound the enemy positions.

Also, on May 4, Firebase Veghel was closed and the battalion TOC (tactical operations center) was moved to the newly constructed Firebase Shock that had been built on Dong Ong Doi. The 326th Engineers had enlarged the LZ where the helicopter was shot down on April 27 and built a firebase.

Captains Schoonover and LT Dillon passed the word that the attack the next day would be a coordinated assault by 1st and 2nd Platoons. I went to the remaining members of my squad and checked to see if they had any equipment that needed to be replaced or if there were any wounds that hadn't been treated by the medics. Some of the men needed M-16 magazines and had used all their frag grenades, so I made a list and took it to the LT's RTO for transmission to the battalion TOC on the firebase.

I spent a good part of that night talking to Sgt. Frank Poole, one of the other men at my position. He was older than me and had been a high school math teacher in Oklahoma City before being drafted. He was married with a young son. He was worried about what would happen to his family if he were killed or wounded the next day. We both talked about what our lives had been like before the army and what we wanted to do if we got home. He told me that he wanted to go back to teaching. I told him I wanted to finish college and get married. We both knew that what we were going through would change us forever and we were worried about how we'd relate to our families back in 'the world.'

Frank was wounded the next day, but I don't know how badly he was hurt; I never saw him again.

Chapter 19

The Bunkers: Third Day

May 5, 1970

If your officer's dead and the sergeants look white,
Remember it's ruin to run from a fight;
So, take open order, lie down, and sit tight,
An' wait for supports like a soldier

--Rudyard Kipling, "The Young British Soldier"

.

At first light, word came down to pack up and move into position for the assault on the bunkers. I could still hear artillery bursting on the hill at YD509063. Both platoons moved out until we got to the streambed where we had fought the day before. The captain gave each of the two platoons a different sector of the hill to attack. He felt we had a better chance if we came at them from two different directions. Our platoon would go up the same way we had tried on May 3.

I have no personal memory of napalm strikes on the morning of May 5, but Bob Noffsinger remembers: "Then the Phantoms started prepping it at daylight. Right before we pulled out, a jet came in to napalm the hill we were headed back up, the napalm was dropped behind us rather than the hill we were to go back up...if they had been off just one hill rather than two we would have all been fried."

The area at the bunker complex was almost unrecognizable. Many of the leaves had been stripped from the trees by the concussion from exploding artillery shells that had pounded the area. There was a lot of light filtering down to the jungle floor, and I hoped it would help us find the concealed positions the enemy had fought from during our previous attempt to capture the bunkers. The only problem was that the NVA could also see us better.

I don't know why, but a part of my squad (including me) was detailed to guard the rucksacks and the company command post. The wounded would be assembled at our location for treatment and evacuation. Bear Pando, Terry Lowe, Noff, Gerry Kulm, Vern Okland, and Frank Carvajal were ordered to go up the hill. Except for Noffsinger, I never saw any of them again. I have guilt feelings even today about not going back up that hill with the rest of them.

The artillery barrage stopped and the platoon started up the steep slope. After moving ten to fifteen meters, they disappeared from my view. We heard no firing at first, but then we heard the whoosh of RPGs followed by several explosions. We then heard M-16s and AKs firing from above us and then from both sides. Bullets began passing through the trees overhead, knocking leaves and branches to the ground all around us. An RPG sailed over us like a big roman candle and exploded in the trees behind us.

I heard an M-60 machine gun firing long bursts until a sharp explosion abruptly silenced it. I could hear the wounded yelling and other people calling, "Medic, medic" and shouting directions about where to fire.

After what seemed like hours, the firing died down and finally stopped. I could hear the company radio man calling for dust offs to come pick up the wounded. Top Stanley and his radioman moved into a position very close to mine and I was able to hear his side of the conversation with the battalion TOC on Firebase Shock. I heard him say that we had three KIA (killed in action) and shock hit me like a bucketful of ice water when he radioed their names: Frank Carvajal, Gerald Kulm and Vernon Okland.

We received orders to carry as many of the rucksacks as we could up the hill to the rest of the platoon. Carrying my own rucksack and dragging two others, I struggled up the hill through the trees. I passed a shattered M-60 machine gun and saw two big pools of blood on the ground next to it. A little bit farther on, I found a dead NVA soldier lying on his back with his knees drawn up, dressed in a green, long-sleeved shirt, knee-length green shorts, and a pair of Ho Chi Minh sandals with green socks pulled up to his knees. He had been shot at the base of his throat and right between the eyes with what looked like a .45 caliber round. The back of his head was gone.

We had standing orders to search all enemy dead for any items that might help to identify their unit and rank; I stopped to search this man. He had no visible rank insignia, but I found several documents on him. When I checked his shirt pockets, I found a small black-and-white photo in a silver frame showing a young woman holding a small child. The woman was wearing the Ao Dai, the traditional dress for Vietnamese women. Thinking it was a photo of the dead man's' family, I returned the photo and frame to his shirt pocket but kept the documents. I wondered if his family would ever know what happened to him. I can see his dead face to this day, lying on the muddy ground. Later, I learned that this was the NVA who had killed Carvajal, Kulm and Okland. After hearing that, I didn't feel so sorry for his family.

I kept on up the hill and found a clearing with some GIs from another platoon on guard. I called out, "Strike Force," our battalion recognition signal. They saw me and waved for me to come on into the perimeter. I found First Sergeant Ira Stanley and asked him where my platoon was located. I saw two full body bags lying at the edge of the clearing, next to the helicopter landing zone, so I asked Top who they were. He told me the bags held the bodies of Gerry Kulm and his A-gunner, Vernon Okland. The shattered M-60 I had seen on my way up the hill had been theirs. Top told me that we had killed another five of the enemy that he knew of but that meant nothing to me.

I was still in shock. My squad had started the day with eleven men. By late morning we had three men killed. Top said Frank Carvajal had been severely wounded and had died in the dust off on the way to the 85th Evacuation Hospital. Bob Noffsinger, who was on the same dust-off helicopter as Carvajal, said Frank made it to the hospital but died later that day.

There were sixteen other wounded; some of the names I remember are Romey "Ace" Atkinson, Terry "Woodstock" Lowe, James "Bear" Pando, Frank Poole, and Bob Noffsinger.

Many years later, Bob Noffsinger has this to say about his personal ordeal on May 5: *"We were almost to the top when we heard grenades and fire behind us and heard one of the guys cry for help. I was almost to them and crawling over a log when I felt an AK round hit the side of my helmet. I dropped back behind the log and sprayed the area where the round came from, although I did not see whoever had shot at me."*

Completely unaware that he been wounded, Noff saw more of the enemy running from the hill, apparently trying to escape, and he opened fire on them; he does not believe he hit any of them. Right about then a sergeant named Gary Sands and a medic joined Noff.

Noffsinger continues his story: *"Kulm and Okland were dead, and it was weird that they looked so different. It was not just their wounds that made them look different, life was gone. Carvajal was alive, but barely, it seems, but he was Carvajal and looked like 'his self.'"*

The medic asked for some water to help him treat Carvajal, so Noff threw him a canteen. The medic told Noffsinger that the canteen was empty; Noff argued with the medic saying the canteen couldn't be empty because he had just filled it that morning. The medic threw the canteen back to Noffsinger and he noticed it had a bullet hole in it.

Noffsinger goes on to say: *"He threw it back to me, and as soon as I caught it I knew it was empty, it was so light; then I saw the hole in it and looked back at my hip and the canteen cover on my web belt. My hip and butt check was a bloody mess. It did not hurt at all; I guess the adrenaline was overpowering it."*

Eventually Carvajal and Noffsinger were evacuated to the hospital at Phu Bai along with many others. The NVA were still close by and took every opportunity to fire at the dust offs and log birds as they approached the LZ. They sprayed the perimeter several times, but their aim was off and no one else was hurt.

Says Noffsinger: *"As we were pulled up towards the chopper, it was not long before the AK rounds started flying by Frank and I, [sic] I prayed we would make it without being hit, it seemed a long time getting to the chopper and a very long time getting Frank and then me into it."*

I also heard that the platoon sergeant (SFC William Malcolm) from 2nd Platoon had been killed during a vicious firefight in front of a large bunker and that 2nd Platoon had been forced to withdraw and abandon his body. I asked Bruce Scott about this, but he has no memory of it.

The company moved fifty to a hundred meters west, and I joined what was left of my squad/platoon on the west side of the new company perimeter at YD510063. We were told to dig fighting holes, and, because of our losses, we would only have two men per position instead of the usual three.

I found a spot in front of a huge tree that had large roots spreading outward. I put my gear in between two of these roots because they sheltered me from the sides. I dug a foxhole large enough for two men in front of the sleeping position. It was hard work because I had to chop my way through the hard clay and a lot of roots from the big tree. I cut a shelf into the side of the hole and placed a few grenades and extra magazines for my M-16 on it.

Using my machete, I began to clear some of the bamboo and small saplings in front of the hole to give us a clear field of fire. As I cleared away the brush, the ridge line leading to the summit of Hill 882 came into view.

That afternoon, a Huey log bird coming into and out of the LZ with a load of C rations came under fire from an AK-47 somewhere down the slope in front of my position. Right after the log bird left, a dust off came in, and while they were hovering over the LZ loading two wounded men (this was probably Noffsinger and Carvajal) into the ship, the NVA opened up with two or three AK-47s, spraying the perimeter and the helicopter; thankfully, the dust off was able to get away undamaged. The NVA were still out there, close to our perimeter.

When it began to get dark, we set out some trip flares and claymore mines in front of our holes, expecting to be hit that night. However, the long dark hours passed quietly.

Chapter 20

The Bunkers: Fourth Day

One cannot answer for his courage when he has never been in danger.

-Francois, Duc de la Rochefoucauld, *Maxims,* 1665

May 6, 1970

The next morning, I woke up just as the sky was turning light. People were stirring all around the perimeter. I sat on the edge of my hole and wrapped myself in my poncho liner against the morning chill. The NVA chose that moment to spray the perimeter with AK-47 fire, RPGs, and satchel charges. I grabbed my M-16 as I rolled into my fighting hole. I heard the scream of an RPG coming in. Looking up from the bottom of my hole, I saw the rocket dart overhead with a whooshing sound trailing sparks and then explode with a bright flash in the tree above me. Most of the shrapnel blew another way but some it whined past my head, but again, I wasn't hit.

Grabbing a grenade, I pulled the pin, jumped up, and heaved it into the brush in front of my hole. Other men were throwing grenades, detonating claymores, and firing into the brush around the edges of our perimeter. Someone was screaming for a medic, so I knew there were wounded.

As suddenly as it had started, the AK-47 fire stopped. I heard the artillery forward observer frantically calling in a fire mission to the 81mm mortar battery on Firebase Shock. Within a minute, preplanned mortar fire began to drop around our perimeter.

There was no further incoming fire, and we saw no movement by the NVA toward our positions. It had simply been the enemy's way of telling us they were still out there. I checked all the men of my squad and found they were unhurt.

Unfortunately, one man (PFC Phillip Warfield) on the northern side of the perimeter had been killed by an RPG that burst in front of his position. Five other men were wounded and a dust off was called in, but the NVA did not fire at the ship this time.

Bruce Scott was in a position right next to the one occupied by Warfield. He remembers: *"Phillip Warfield was killed in the position next to mine. An RPG round hit the tree by him...there was a dead NVA soldier in the positions by where Warfield was killed. After a few days, we buried him. One of the guys I have talked to said he remembers that and [that] the guy's foot was still sticking out of the ground. He said he felt bad that his [the NVA's] parents did not know what happened to him."*

We spent most of that day improving our perimeter defenses. I took the time to deepen my fighting hole and clear more brush from in front of it. The NVA were obviously still in the area and we could be attacked at any time.

One of the small patrols we sent out to check for enemy movement around the perimeter found two dead NVA, killed during the early morning attack on our position. Later that day, Alpha Co found a huge trail running southeast to northwest, right through the area of the big bunker complex we had just destroyed. They found several bunkers and campsites with each location marked by three notches cut into a tree.

That afternoon, I was sitting on the edge of my hole when I heard the odd engine sound made by the Cessna aircraft flown by Air Force forward air controllers. This airplane had two engines, one in front to "pull" the aircraft and one behind the cockpit to "push." The pilots of these planes, called FACs, were the liaisons between ground troops and the jet fighters called in for air support.

I spotted the small Cessna circling around the summit of Hill 882. Suddenly, he dived down into the valley separating Hill 714 from Hill 882 and fired a rocket into the eastern slope of Hill 882. These small rockets contained white phosphorus that exploded into a brilliant white cloud that was easy for a jet fighter pilot to spot as he roared in on his bombing run at four hundred knots. The rocket burst in the trees and the Cessna pulled sharply up to get out of the way. The jets were right behind him, trying to drop their bombs as close to the white smoke as they could.

I could see the bombs as they dropped away from the fighters. They were two-hundred-fifty-pound "high drag" bombs with fins that popped open to slow the fall of the bombs. This gave the fighter time to pull out of his dive before the bombs exploded; otherwise, there was a good chance the jet could be hit by fragments from the bombs they had just dropped. The jets made several passes, causing huge, grey-brown clouds of smoke to boil up out of the trees on Hill 882.

The rest of the day passed quietly. The patrols we sent out to check the area around the perimeter found nothing. We were joined by elements of Delta Company and we received the mission of sweeping through the rest of the bunker complex located at YD508066 and YD509065 looking for enemy stragglers. We had a quiet night, although we heard gunfire and explosions echoing across the valley from the direction of Hill 882.

On a side note, I learned that day that a new battalion commander had relieved LTC Young. The new man's name was LTC Charles J. Shay, whose call sign was 'Shamrock.' LTC Shay was an Irishman and very proud of his heritage. He carried a kind of club with him, known as a 'shillelagh' (an Irish word meaning club), everywhere he went.

A boisterous, often profane man, Shamrock became a popular commander, admired by both the officers and grunts of the O-Deuce. According to Keith W. Nolan in his book *Ripcord-Screaming Eagles Under Siege, Vietnam 1970,* Shay was considered by many to be the "*best battalion commander in the division.*"

A New Yorker, Chuck Shay was only sixteen when he tried, unsuccessfully, to join the Marines in 1945 to fight in World War II. He later joined the army as the Korean War broke out and was sent to OCS. He was given command of a company in the 2nd 'Indianhead' Infantry Division where he was wounded by shrapnel. After being shot in both legs, he was finally evacuated. In 1960 and 1964-65, Shay was an advisor to the ARVN; after a brief period of staff duty with the 101st, he was given command of the O-Deuce, leading the battalion from May until December 1970.

Chapter 21

The Aftermath

May 7–May 10, 1970

Just before daylight the next morning, everyone went on 100 percent alert. We were told to be ready to fire a **mad minute** around the perimeter. A mad minute meant that each soldier would fire one magazine from his M-16. The purpose was to draw fire from any enemy who might have sneaked up on our perimeter during the night. The M-79s and M-60s would not fire unless we came under attack.

The captain roared, *"Fire"* and the perimeter erupted with gunfire. No one returned our fire. I threw a couple of extra grenades into a thick bamboo clump in front of my position, just to be safe. They exploded with bright flashes in the predawn darkness.

Later that morning, 2nd Platoon, who had been forced to abandon the body of their platoon sergeant on May 5, sent out a patrol to recover him. On the way back to the company position, they were fired on by several NVA but took no casualties.

We then received orders for a RIF down the western slope of the ridge we were on. We were to look for enemy base camps or supply caches.

We formed up in platoon-sized patrols, about fifteen men in 1st Platoon's case, little more than a squad. We moved down the slope and within fifteen minutes, found a small bunker complex being used as a supply cache. We checked the area carefully for booby traps and then searched the bunkers.

The one I searched was a pit about six feet by six feet and over four feet deep. It was roofed over with logs about six inches in diameter with two feet of earth piled on top of the logs. The trench leading into the bunker was dug in a zigzag, preventing direct fire into the bunkers interior. It would have taken a direct hit from a two-hundred-fifty-pound bomb to take it out.

We found a lot of NVA spare uniforms, food, salt, medical supplies, cooking utensils, ammunition, signal flares, and several documents, among them some personal diaries of NVA soldiers. Our KCS, Hanh, translated portions of the diaries and told us that the diaries documented the soldiers' journey down the Ho Chi Minh Trail into South Vietnam and how they prepared themselves for battle with the Americans. The diaries belonged to Tran Xuan Toi and Nguyen (pronounced 'when') Viet Dinh, and there was a pay record for Loung Dinh Hoc signed by his commanding officer, Pham Thonh Khaong.

Most of the items were placed in a pile and burned. The ammunition was destroyed with an explosive charge. We took the documents back to our perimeter for transfer to division intelligence at Camp Eagle.

May 8

The next day, Charlie Company was scheduled to be moved by air back up to the summit of Dong A La. However, one of Alpha Company's patrols was attacked by a squad of ten to twelve NVA, and the rest of A Company was moved by air to assist. Our move was rescheduled for May 9.

Charlie Company, along with elements of Delta Company, spent the day patrolling the long ridge line that ran south from the top of Hill 714. We made no contact with the enemy, although signs of his presence were found all over the area we searched.

That morning, we were moved by air back to the top of Hill 714 and resupplied with C rations and ammunition. We were moving out the next day on a sweep down the ridge line running west toward Hill 882 where Alpha Company had found more bunkers. I spent the afternoon going over my gear, cleaning my weapon, and writing letters home. I wrote nothing of what we had gone through during the last few days. I couldn't find the words to describe to my family what it felt like to be in combat and to lose friends. I did write something of what we'd been through to a female cousin, telling her that several of my friends had been killed but she did not reply and never wrote to me again.

After receiving the resupply, we moved off the top of 714 to a small knoll located at YD509083 on the northeast slope of the main hill. We set up a defensive perimeter and waited for further orders.

As we waited, I spent the time looking down into the deep, narrow valley where the Rao La River, a tributary of the Song Bo, ran. I could see a long stretch of the river with several wide sandbars visible. As I watched, I heard and then saw a UH-1 helicopter flying down the valley well below the height at which I sat. The Huey had to follow the curves of the river and canyon. As it flew along, it suddenly banked sharply to the right and came back around. I heard machine gun fire from the Huey and saw it come to a hover above one of the sandbars. Tracers from its door-mounted machine gun darted into the thick trees above the sandbar. I realized they must have spotted some NVA crossing the river.

A few minutes later, another Huey flew into the canyon and landed on the sandbar. I saw tiny figures jump from the helicopter and run into the trees. It looked as if a LRRP (long range recon patrol) team, or a **blue team**, from the 2/17 Cav had been dropped off to try to track the NVA back to their unit's position. I heard no more gunfire for the rest of that afternoon.

That afternoon, Battalion closed Firebase Shock, reopened Firebase Veghel, and moved the battalion TOC back to Veghel.

About forty years later, while I was researching some battalion daily journals for this memoir, I read an interesting Spot Report. It seems that John A. Mitchell, Alpha Company, 501st Signal Battalion, was bitten by a snake while helping close Firebase Shock and was evacuated to the 85th Evacuation Hospital at Phu Bai. I guess the snake was one from the 99 percent.

May 10

The night passed quietly, and the next morning we received orders to remain in position and run patrols and ambush operations in the area.

As I waited for the order to move out, I gazed down into the valley of the Song Bo and thought of my home in Upland, California. There is a thirteen- or fourteen-hour time difference between Vietnam and California. It was about 9:00 a.m. in Vietnam, so it was around 7:00 p.m. or 8:00 p.m. the night before in California. I wondered what my family and my girlfriend were doing and if they were thinking about me.

We ran several patrols around the summit and down some of the ridge fingers leading from the peak of Dong A La. We found no signs of recent enemy activity. The 1st and 2nd Platoons plus the company command post remained in defensive positions on the small knoll to the northeast of Dong A La peak. The area remained quiet and we had another good night.

Chapter 22

The Ones That Got Away

May 11–May 13, 1970

The next morning, we again received orders to remain near the peak of Dong A La and to prepare to receive replacements for the troops who had been wounded during the fight of May 3 to 6. I sat at my position thinking of home and wondering what was in store for us when we finally moved off Dong A La peak.

My thoughts were violently interrupted by gunfire. I grabbed my M-16 and hit the ground, looking for the enemy. I realized that all the gunfire was M-16; I heard no incoming fire. I learned that troops on the south side of our perimeter facing the summit of Hill 714 had seen two or three NVA soldiers scrounging around for any C ration cans we had discarded after our resupply. They had tried to shoot them, but the NVA had broken all speed records running from the bald top of the hill into the brush. The platoon sergeant asked for volunteers to check and see if any of the NVA had been hit. I volunteered and, along with two other men, cautiously approached the hilltop. We found no sign that any of the enemy soldiers had been hit. I did find fresh sandal prints leading from the LZ onto the trail down the ridge line.

We reported this to the company commander who passed it to the battalion commander. We received new orders to remain in place for the rest of that day and then on May 12, we would sweep back down the ridge we had fought over at the end of April attempting to find the unit the NVA had come from.

May 12

The next morning, we formed up and moved over the top of 714 back down the ridge line and through the area we had fought over with Bravo Company. That afternoon, the point element found (at YD502072) five 6-foot-by-6-foot bunkers with log and earth roofs. The bunkers were connected by tunnels reinforced with logs. We found evidence that the bunkers had been recently occupied.

While we were checking out the bunkers, a heavy thunderstorm moved into the area; rain and fog reduced visibility to just a few meters. We moved back up the ridge line and found a relatively level spot at YD505074 and began to set up a defensive perimeter to wait out the storm. Darkness began to fall, and the rain continued to pound down. The platoon leader decided we would spend the night there. We were all thoroughly soaked, and even though the temperature was probably in the 60s, we shivered with cold. The rain continued into the night with no let-up.

May 13

Sometime during the night, the rain stopped. Just after dawn, we received orders from battalion to build an LZ so that we could receive resupply that afternoon or the next day.

The shoulder of the ridge we had stopped on at YD505074 was a good place for the LZ; the log bird could approach and exit on a north-south axis. The hill dropped off steeply to the west, so the helicopter would not have to try and climb sharply immediately after a takeoff to clear the summit of Dong A La about eight hundred meters to the north.

We spent most of that day using machetes to clear the underbrush from the selected area. There were several large trees at the north edge of the LZ that had to be felled with some of the C-4 that just about everyone carried. C-4 was a plastic explosive issued in one-pound slabs wrapped in plastic. It looked like dirty white modeling clay and could be molded into any shape needed.

C-4 was very useful; not only could it blow things up, but it could be used to heat rations and water very quickly. A piece about the size of a man's thumb from the first joint to the tip of the nail would bring a canteen cup of water to a full boil within a minute.

The LZ was finished late in the afternoon. The weather again began to turn bad, so we were advised that the resupply would take place on May 14. Instead, we were directed to send out ambush patrols around the newly built LZ.

Since this was our second night in the same position and we had made a lot of noise building the LZ, we were positive that the NVA knew exactly where we were and in what strength. The ambush patrols would help ensure that the NVA could not move unnoticed into position for an attack.

Chapter 23

The Gully Fight

"I did not mean to be killed today."

-last words of the dying Vicomte De Turenne, during the Battle of Salzbach, 1675

May 14–May 16, 1970

Early the next morning, Battalion advised that we would not receive the resupply until late that afternoon. The captain had us move about two hundred meters south from the newly constructed LZ and set up a perimeter at YD504072 from which we could run RIFs in the area looking for NVA activity.

My position was on the west side of the new perimeter where the ridge curved from northwest to west and then dropped off into a steep, brush-choked ravine. A mountain stream with its head farther up the gully ran through the bottom of that ravine. There was a wide shelf on the edge of the gully where I dug a shallow fighting trench and placed what remained of my squad to the left and right of my position.

2nd Platoon sent out the first RIF of about twenty men. They passed through my position and began to move along the western edge of the ravine, and then they descended into the ravine and I lost sight of them.

Suddenly, they made contact (at YD504071) with ten to fifteen NVA who were moving up the ravine from the west. A sharp firefight developed, with the NVA firing at least five RPGs at the patrol. The patrol also reported receiving four 60mm mortar rounds from a position in the ravine about five hundred meters to the northwest. We received a lot of rounds fired by the NVA into our perimeter, but most of them passed through the trees way over our heads.

The patrol reported that they had one dead and four wounded and were attempting to disengage from the NVA. We learned that the NVA had lost four killed with an unknown number of wounded. During the disengagement, one of the members of the patrol became separated from his buddies. As the patrol moved back toward our perimeter, they realized they were one man short. They started back to the scene of the encounter with the NVA patrol to look for him.

They were only about thirty meters out from our perimeter line and we could hear the lost member of the patrol cursing and yelling at the top of his lungs. He was very angry because he thought the patrol had run off and left him. I saw the bushes shaking on the rim of the ravine and the lost patrol member came into view. He apparently saw me and others in our positions, for he called out, *"Strike Force, Strike Force,"* the battalion recognition signal. The patrol then caught up with him before the NVA did and escorted him back to the safety of our perimeter.

Bruce Scott from 2nd platoon recalls that the lost member of the patrol was the lieutenant who had been leading the patrol. Scott says that the LT was sent to the rear because of his poor performance but can't remember any more details.

After the patrol returned, we began to hear the NVA moving around down in the ravine in front of our positions. They were calling back and forth and seemed to be getting into position for an attack. Our M-79 gunners began dropping grenades into the area where we could hear the most activity and we called for Cobra gunship support. I waited tensely from behind my rucksack, the only cover I had. We hadn't had time to dig proper fox holes.

The returned RIF patrol began to carry their wounded through the perimeter and toward the LZ. One of the men carried past me was bleeding heavily. As they passed, I could see that he was already unconscious or dead, his skin an unusual yellowish color, apparently caused by blood loss and shock.

The company radio man called for a dust off, which arrived on station supported by two Cobras. The dead man (Sgt. Ronald E. Schmidt) and two of the wounded were flown to the 85th Evacuation Hospital at Phu Bai. The other two wounded were not seriously hurt, so they remained in the field.

We remained on alert for about two hours, waiting to receive the resupply scheduled for that day. Finally, at around four in the afternoon, we got word that the resupply helicopter was on the way and received orders to pop smoke so the pilot could identify the LZ.

In a few minutes we heard the thudding sound of the big rotors as the Huey log bird approached. Someone popped a yellow smoke and the pilot began his landing approach. He was forced to make a high, slow approach because of the tall trees around us. As he flared for landing over the ravine, still about one hundred feet above the ground, we heard an AK-47 on full automatic firing at him.

The pilot could not hear the gunfire, so the radio man told him he was under fire. He immediately lowered the nose of the ship and sped away. He circled and came around again, making his approach from a different angle. Both door gunners sprayed the trees under the approach path with machine gun fire as he came in.

As the helicopter made his second approach, the men on my side of the perimeter were directed to put out covering fire to try to keep the NVA's heads down and keep them from shooting at the log bird. 2nd Platoon's KCS, a man named Vinh, was wounded by a ricochet from the covering fire.

No more fire was directed at the helicopter and the pilot landed safely. The supplies of C rations and ammo were quickly off-loaded, the wounded scout was put on board, and the helicopter took off without incident.

By this time, the weather had turned bad again and it began to rain. Word then came down for us to get ready to move. The place where we were was not a good location to defend because the NVA knew exactly where our positions were, and the captain wanted to move to a better spot. It began to rain very hard as we started to move. I was tense because I knew that the NVA were all around us and there was a good chance of an ambush.

We began to move back up the steep ridge toward the summit of Dong A La. The rain and falling darkness screened our movement from the NVA. We moved about five hundred meters back up the steep ridge until we found an easily defended spot at YD508078. The area was close to the LZ B Company had built on April 28.

The rain was still pounding down and showed no signs of letting up. We were in an area of thick vegetation, so the captain allowed us to put up rain shelters using our rubber ponchos. We cut branches from the surrounding brush to place over the ponchos to break up their outline and make them harder to see by any NVA probing for our perimeter.

May 15

Very early the next morning, we were all awakened by an explosion. As I listened, I could hear the 'POP' of a mortar being fired. About twenty or thirty seconds later, I heard the explosion on the ridge north of our position. It seemed as if the NVA were trying their version of H&I fire with us as the target. Orders came down for us to pack up as quickly and silently as we could and move out of the area. As we packed up another shell came in, exploding much closer.

It had stopped raining, and there were scattered clouds backlit by a gibbous moon. We hurriedly packed and began to move back down the ridge onto the LZ built on April 28. As we moved, we heard the mortar rounds continue to explode. I estimated that six to ten rounds were fired, the explosions sounding like 60mm.

Crossing the cleared LZ in the moon light was eerie. A tropical moon is very bright, and we had excellent visibility, but so did the NVA if they happened to be waiting in the tree line. I waited nervously for daylight. It seemed as if a hundred pairs of eyes were staring at me from out of the dark tree line.

My fears were groundless, and at daylight, we received information from Battalion that Delta Company, in a position south of us, had also heard the mortar firing and estimated its position to be at YD504067. That was about twelve hundred meters to the south, the same position in the ravine from which 2nd Platoon had received mortar fire the day before.

That morning, we moved back into the area where we had spent the night and set up defensive positions. We ran small patrols in the area looking for signs of the enemy and the 60mm mortar position. Nothing was found, and it appeared we had driven the NVA from the high slopes of Dong A La down into the saddle between Dong A La and Hill 882.

We received orders to remain at that location and prepare to move toward Hill 882 in support of Alpha Company and the Recon Platoon, who were finding evidence of large NVA troop positions on and around the summit of Hill 882.

May 16

At about 0430 on the morning of May 16, while taking my turn on guard, I heard explosions and gunfire to the west of us. It seemed to be coming from somewhere on the slope of Hill 882 where Alpha Company was in its NDP. The gunfire continued for some time then died out.

At about 0515, I heard more gunfire and explosions coming from about the same area. This fight only lasted a few minutes.

Later that day, we received info that the first firefight had been an attack on Alpha Company in its NDP. It was a strong attack and Alpha lost five killed and twenty-two wounded. A man from Headquarters Company was also killed.

The second firefight had been a weaker attack on the Recon platoon in their NDP not far from A Company. Recon had repulsed the attacks with no losses and had killed three more NVA. James Brinker said the NVA soldiers, carrying RPGs, just kept walking into their perimeter, and they were killed.

About noon that day, we were directed to begin our move down the ridge. We were to find a good place to receive resupply on the seventeenth and then begin to move down into the bottom of the valley between Hill 714 and Hill 882 to support Alpha Company and Recon Platoon.

I was pleased to hear that we were moving to support Alpha Company because my friend Sgt. Mike Lucky was serving with Alpha Company's 3rd Platoon. I hadn't seen him since January, and I hoped he had survived everything we'd gone through since then.

We packed up and moved about seven hundred and fifty meters down the steeply sloping ridge to YD508072, which looked like a good place to take resupply on the seventeenth. We set up our NDP, sent out some observation posts and fire-team-sized patrols, and waited. I took the opportunity to write a couple of short letters home.

I said in a PS to a letter to my folks: "Sorry it's so short but there's nothing to write about." It was a lie, but I didn't want to worry them any more than they already were.

Chapter 24

A Gross Wound and Buddha's Birthday

"Those who do not do battle for their country do not know with what ease they accept their citizenship in America."

-Dean Brelis, _The Face of South Vietnam_

May 17–May 19, 1970

The next morning, we were directed to move back up toward the peak of Dong A La and find an LZ suitable to receive resupply. We packed up and began to move. As we moved back up the hill, the weather changed, and it began to cloud up.

We found a good LZ near YD506082 and the log bird came in, bringing a four-day supply of C rations, ammo, and, a nice surprise, clean fatigues for the whole company. The clean uniforms were not sorted by size but were stuffed into huge cloth bags that we dumped out onto the ground. Everyone had to root through the piles until they found a set of fatigues that were roughly their size.

I managed to find a pair of trousers and a shirt that fit well for a change. We stuffed all the dirty and torn fatigues back into the big bags and waited for word that the log bird was in-route to "back haul" the dirty fatigues and pick up outgoing mail. As we waited, a thunderstorm came up and it began to rain in torrents. Everything, including us, was soaking wet in minutes. My squad was detailed to act as security for the troops moving the soaked clothing bags up to the LZ for back-haul to Camp Eagle.

Struggling up the muddy trail, we made it to the LZ only to be told that the log birds had been forced by the storm to turn back and would not be able to make it in to pick up the back-haul until the next day.

We turned around and began to slip and slide back down the muddy trail, carrying the heavy, water-soaked clothing bags. As we passed through an area where the trail had been cut through a bamboo thicket, I heard someone fall to the ground and then a sharp cry of pain.

I turned around and saw a soldier sitting at the edge of the trail with a clothing bag in his lap. Thinking he had twisted his ankle or knee, I walked back to him and reached my hand out to help him get up, but he said, "*I can't get up, I think I'm hurt.*"

Another man and I pulled the clothing bag from his lap and were surprised to see a sharp bamboo stake sticking up through the crotch of his fatigue trousers. We cut away the ripped trousers and saw that the bamboo stake had penetrated the inside of his right thigh and then had skewered his scrotum. The sharp end of the bamboo stick was protruding from the top of his scrotum and he was bleeding heavily. Horrified, we frantically called for a medic who came running, slipping and sliding, up the muddy trail.

The medic took one look and told us we had to get him off the bamboo stake before he could do anything about the bleeding. We knew we couldn't just pull him up off the stake because it would only cause further injury. We decided to lift him as high as we could and hold him there as the medic used a knife to cut the stake where it entered the bottom of his thigh. We lifted him as gently as we could and, although it must have hurt him terribly, he made no sound.

We finally managed to get him loose and with the stick still impaling his thigh and scrotum, we carried him back down the trail to our NDP site. There we were told that the area around Hill 714 and Hill 882 was socked in by severe thunderstorms. The injured man would have to wait until the next day for evacuation. He was placed in the Company CP area and offered a shot of morphine to dull the pain and allow him to get a little sleep. The soldier refused the pain medication because he was afraid we would be attacked that night and he wanted to be fully aware of his surroundings.

As I had helped carry him down the trail, he told me that he had been scheduled to meet his wife in Honolulu for R&R in about a week. He knew he would be in no shape to go on R&R and was worried about what the army would tell his wife.

It rained off and on all night, but toward morning it began to clear up. The injured man had kept those of us not awake on guard duty from really sleeping most of the night, moaning in his sleep. We would be glad to get him on a dust off; that kind of wound was really demoralizing!

May 18

The next morning dawned reasonably clear with broken high clouds. We moved the injured man back up to the LZ and waited for the dust-off ship to arrive. It came in at about 0930. A log bird soon arrived to back-haul the clothing bags. We quickly packed up and waited for orders to move. While we were waiting, word came down from Division through Brigade and then Battalion that we were to observe a cease-fire in honor of the Buddha's birthday. The cease-fire would be in effect from 1200 hours on May 18 until 1200 hours on May 19. We were to take no offensive action unless directly attacked.

We all got a good laugh out of the latest political bullshit to filter down to the grunts from those on high. It didn't matter to us one way or the other. The NVA never honored cease-fires, so we knew it was business as usual for us.

We then moved east across the south slope of Dong A La to the ridge line overlooking the Song Bo at YD510072. We found a small knoll that was suitable for a company-sized NDP. There we set up defensive positions to wait out the cease-fire.

In another lie to my parents, I noted: "We have seen very little action, nothing to get excited about. It's just the same old boring routine of being a Boonie Rat."

May 19

The next morning, the captain told us that we'd been ordered to begin moving down into the saddle between Dong A La and Hill 882. Even though the cease-fire was still in effect, LTC Shay wanted us to check out the area where we'd been attacked back on May 14. 1st Platoon was on point for Charlie Company and my squad was told to walk point for the platoon. The point team for my squad was Billy 'Kentucky' Lucas, and his slack man was Charles 'Swede' Swenson. As squad leader, I walked right behind them.

The captain wanted us to move quickly, so he ordered us to follow a big trail leading along the southwest side of the ridgeline towards the saddle between the two peaks. It was not safe to move down a trail we had used before, but the captain was being pressured by Battalion to move quickly through the area.

So, we started back down that trail and soon walked into an ambush at YD507072. We had come to a big open area covered with elephant grass and scrub brush. Kentucky stopped and looked over his shoulder at me. I motioned for him to move to the right around the upper edge of the clearing. He scanned the area, took one or two steps, and then they hit us. The fire sounded like it came from an RPD, and, as I hit the ground, I saw Swede and Kentucky get hit. Bullets thudded into the ground and hit the trees all around me. The fire suddenly stopped and I realized I wasn't hit. A few of us fired bursts from our M-16s toward the ambush site but there was no return fire.

I stood up and dropped my rucksack. I saw Swede trying to crawl off the trail with blood on his shirt. I ran to check on him and saw he had a through-and-through gunshot wound to his right shoulder. He seemed OK, so I went down to check on Kentucky. He was lying face down in the mud with his rucksack up over his head. When I rolled him over his helmet came off and his head bumped against my leg. His blood and brain tissue stained my boot and trousers. His eyes were already glassy, and I saw he had been hit in the forehead, the bullet exiting the back of his head.

Right about then the CO, Captain Gerald Dillon, came down the trail wanting to know what had happened. I told him we had one wounded and one killed. He told me to leave Kentucky's body in place because he had called in an air strike to hit the area where the enemy fire had come from. We were too close to where the air strike would hit and, thinking of the safety of the rest of the company, he wanted us to move quickly out of the danger area. He said we would come back and recover Kentucky's body after the air strike, but I protested, and while two men helped Swede back up the trail, I convinced the captain to allow me to move Kentucky's body to a safer place. I remember telling the captain that he was in my squad, and I didn't want to leave him behind. The Captain told me to, "Grab him and hurry up."

Swede's injury was a very painful shoulder wound but not life threatening, so we were able to quickly move him and Kentucky up the trail out of immediate danger. I hadn't wanted to leave Kentucky's body behind because he was a member of my squad and I felt responsible for him. Two other men and I struggled to carry Kentucky's body back up the steep, muddy trail to the ridge top. I was amazed at how hard it was to move someone who was completely limp. We were exhausted by the time we reached the relative safety of the ridge top.

When we got to the top of the ridge, I looked at my watch and saw it wasn't even 1100 hours, so the cease-fire had still been in effect when the NVA killed Kentucky and wounded Swede.

Within twenty minutes of our reaching the top of the ridge with Kentucky's body, two F-4 Phantom fighters and a FAC came on station overhead. As they circled, I saw that the F-4s had United States Navy markings. The captain called on the UHF radio and gave the FAC his target information. I saw the FAC dive and mark the target area with a white phosphorus rocket. The F-4s dove, firing long bursts from their 20mm mini-guns into the valley below us.

The guns made a growling sound like a huge chain saw. The explosive 20mm shells burst in the dark trees below us, sparkling like hundreds of firecrackers. The jets made several passes, each time firing a long burst from those guns. The jets left after using all their 20mm ammo.

Right after the jets left, the dust-off helicopter arrived overhead and lowered the jungle penetrator so we could evacuate Swede and Kentucky. We lay Kentucky's limp body on one of the seats and strapped him in. Swede sat opposite him and helped hold him in place as they were hoisted up to the hovering helicopter. Although Swede's wound was painful, he had a wide smile on his face as he was hoisted up to the dust off. He knew he had received a **'million-dollar wound'** and would not be sent back to the field.

The strong down draft from the helicopter's rotors broke a big limb off one of the trees we were standing under, and the limb struck Sp4 Hippolito Morales and broke his collarbone. So, they lowered the penetrator back down and hauled him out, too.

After the dust-off left, we moved back down the trail, alert for more contact with the NVA. We drew no more fire and reached our old position without incident. We sent several patrols out but found only temporary NVA campsites. It appeared that the NVA unit we had run into had just been passing through.

More than thirty years later, while reading *Firebase Ripcord, Screaming Eagles Under Siege, Vietnam 1970* by Keith W. Nolan, and after reading an after-action report, I learned that many the enemy units we had engaged were passing through the area on their way to participate in the Ripcord battle. According to the after-action report for that period, the units we engaged were elements of the 29th NVA Regiment, mostly from the 7th, 8th, and 9th Battalions. The main battles around Ripcord did not take place until July 1970, but the NVA we fought were already moving into the area where Firebase Ripcord was being built.

We spent the night at YD512068 near the area where the ambush had occurred. As night fell, I was still in shock. Kentucky and I had become friends. He had befriended me when I first joined the company in January and we had shared a few foxholes. Only two days before, Kentucky had given me a pair of dry socks because I had a case of "immersion foot," a painful condition caused when your feet are constantly wet with no chance to dry them out. Dry socks are quite a luxury to an infantryman and it was the type of gesture that was typical of Kentucky.

That night, the NVA probed our perimeter. The man on guard at my position woke me and the others and whispered that he had heard regular movement in the brush in front of our position. I sent another man crawling to the CP to tell them what we were hearing. By then, I had heard it too, but we waited for instructions.

A man at the position next to us apparently decided not to wait and threw a frag toward the sounds. I heard the grenade strike something, probably a tree, with a sold **THUNK** before it exploded with a bright flash. I heard a loud gasp and then someone began to moan "I'm hit! Oh, fuck, I'm hit!"

After the grenade explosion, the sounds of movement outside the perimeter died away. We remained awake the rest of the night but for some reason the enemy did not attack us. It turned out that the man who had thrown the grenade had taken a chunk of shrapnel from his own grenade through one of his kneecaps. He was evacuated without incident the next morning.

It was a long night, and one that I've never forgotten.

Chapter 25

The Battle Winds Down

"Nothing except a battle lost can be half as melancholy as a battle won."
The Duke of Wellington, after the Battle of Waterloo, 1815

May 20–May 24, 1970

We kept moving down the steep slope into the valley between Dong A La (Hill 714) and Dong Kien Kien (Hill 882). Late in the afternoon we found six unoccupied enemy bunkers at YD506071 about six feet by six feet with two feet of overhead cover. A search of the bunkers revealed a cache of 60mm mortar rounds, AK-47 rounds, and some NVA uniforms. The bunkers had last been occupied three to four days ago.

We continued down, often sliding on our haunches because the angle of the slope was too steep for us to maintain our footing. As we neared the valley floor, I could hear the rush of water over rocks. The brush thickened as we got closer to the stream, and we struggled through it with our heavy rucksacks until we broke through onto the banks of a beautiful, clear stream running over rocks. We stopped so that everyone could fill their canteens. This stream was called the Khe Chi Chi and ran down a steep draw from the east side of Hill 882.

I filled all six of my one-quart canteens and, because I knew there would be no water on top of Hill 882, I filled my five-quart collapsible canteen. Water weighs about two pounds per quart, so I would be carrying about twenty-two pounds of water plus all my other gear.

After a short break, we crossed the stream and started up the steep slope on the southeast side of Hill 882. By this time, it was starting to get dark, so we set up our NDP at YD505054 about a hundred meters up the steep slope from the stream. I remember the hillside being so steep that I needed to straddle a small tree to keep from sliding down the slope while I tried to sleep.

May 21

The next morning, we continued toward the top of Hill 882 where we were to link up with Alpha Company and Recon. We climbed steadily for more than an hour before we took a break at YD499072. When we finally stopped, I collapsed with relief and shrugged out of my rucksack. My shoulders were numb, and I was soaked with sweat.

Although helicopters were used extensively in Vietnam for troop movement, line grunts still had to carry everything they needed to survive in a nylon rucksack mounted on an aluminum frame. Most of us were carrying full cases of C rations, six one-quart canteens, smoke grenades, signal flares, fragmentation grenades, at least twenty loaded M-16 magazines, a hundred-round belt of machine gun ammo, a machete, trip flares and claymore mines, a poncho and poncho liner, and our personal weapon (the M-16, M-60 machine gun, or the M-79 grenade launcher) as well as wearing a steel helmet; the average load was around seventy to eighty pounds. The machine gunners, assistant gunners, radio men, and medics carried even more.

A loaded M-16 rifle weighed about eight pounds and the M-79 grenade launcher about the same. A rifleman carried twenty to twenty-five magazines loaded with eighteen to twenty rounds each. The M-79 men wore a vest that held about twenty grenades in loops sewn to the front of the vest.

The M-60 machine gun weighed a whopping twenty-three pounds and was known as "the pig." The gunner carried one hundred rounds ready to fire and the A-gunner carried another four to six hundred rounds (at seven pounds per hundred), and they all had to carry their rucksacks and canteens as well. In addition, each platoon was assigned a medic, and these men carried two big canvas aid bags filled with medical supplies with which they could treat everything from headaches, blisters, and diarrhea to major gunshot wounds.

The radio men carried either the PRC-25 or the PRC-77 radio, which weighed in at about twenty-five pounds each. They carried extra batteries and had to keep the radio handset constantly pushed against their ears to hear any radio traffic to the company. These radios were called "prick-25s" from their initials PRC and for other reasons.

We were all well used up by the time we took our first break on the climb up Hill 882. For identification, otherwise nameless hills were known by their height in meters above sea level. In this case, at 2,894 feet, Hill 882 was a major challenge for an infantryman carrying seventy to eighty pounds of equipment in the heat and humidity of the jungle.

Only a few of the larger hills where big battles were fought had names. Dong Ap Bia (Hamburger Hill) is one. Bach Ma, the former French resort area, is another. The marines fought several large battles on and around the "Rock Pile," the "Razorback," and two hills called 881 North and 881 South near Khe Sanh Combat Base during the Tet offensive of 1968.

A few years later, I found out my brother-in-law had been at Dong Ap Bia, serving with Alpha 1st/506th Infantry, the "Currahees." I've known him for thirty years, but he still won't talk about it in any detail. He did tell me that the things that really bother him are remembering the sound of incoming RPGs and the screams of wounded men.

Right then, I wasn't really concerned whether 882 had a name or not—I just needed to make it to the LZ where Alpha and Recon waited. We finally reached the LZ (YD494069) just built by Alpha Company and Recon Platoon late that afternoon. The LZ had been built on one of the long, narrow finger ridges running northeast from the peak of Hill 882 with steep slopes on both sides. Fighting positions extended down the steep slopes on either side of the landing zone.

Both Alpha and Charlie Companies were shorthanded because of the casualties taken during the fights for 882 and 714. Charlie Company had sixty-three men and Alpha Company had even fewer. The Recon Platoon was working with Alpha Company, but their numbers were also seriously depleted because of casualties. It took both companies and Recon to fully man the perimeter surrounding the landing zone. The hillside was so steep there was no level place to sleep, so I had to scrape a flat spot into the side of the hill to have a place to lie down.

After preparing my position, I went over to the Alpha Company side of the hill to look for my friend Sgt. Mike Lucky. I found his platoon, where I was told that he had been shot in the throat during the fight for 882. He was thrown on a dust off and flown off the hill in critical condition. No one knew if he'd lived.

In the summer of 2001, I finally tracked down Mike Lucky and learned that he had survived relatively intact. I discovered that he had been evacuated for a serious knee injury rather than a gun-shot wound. Lucky was sent to a surgical hospital in Japan for treatment. When he recovered, they shipped him to Korea, where he served out his enlistment at the 'Peace Village' near Panmunjom on the Korean DMZ.

I was also able to locate Charles 'Swede' Swenson and learned that he had recovered from his shoulder wound with no serious complications.

The next morning, two other men and I were detailed to escort two staff officers to a location where a firefight for Hill 882 had been fought. We picked up the officers at the landing zone and walked along the knife-edged ridge into the jungle. Following a narrow trail through a bamboo thicket, we looked for the spot where the battle had taken place. The two officers ordered us to wait for them while they checked farther down the trail. I found a place with good concealment that also gave us a view for some distance down the trail. We stopped there, and the two officers went ahead without us. About fifteen minutes later, the officers returned and we all went back to the landing zone.

All that day, 8", 105mm, and 155mm artillery batteries fired continuously at the bunker complexes located all around the peak of Hill 882. The officers were probably identifying areas for Alpha and Charlie Companies to sweep, looking for NVA stragglers.

I guess they found what they were looking for, because almost as soon as we returned to the company, orders came down that both Alpha and Charlie were to leave 882 and search the hilly terrain down into the Rao La River valley to the north for more enemy camps.

In *West of Hue,* James Brinker describes a huge **TOT** (time- on-target) artillery barrage at that time lasting several hours. It's funny, but I have absolutely no memory of that event; I guess I was so beat up that I slept through the whole thing.

That afternoon, we packed up and began moving west, following the contours of the north slope of Hill 882. This part of the north side of the hill appeared to be unoccupied by the NVA. We found a relatively level area at YD491069 and set up our NDP. We sent out several ambush patrols around the NDP site, but the night passed quietly.

May 23

We remained in position at our NDP until late morning, when we received orders to move across the north slope of Hill 882 onto the west side looking for additional NVA bunker complexes.

As we moved out of the NDP, the point man for the lead platoon suddenly encountered a lone NVA on the trail about twenty meters out from the NDP. They exchanged fire and the NVA was hit but did not go down. The point team followed a blood trail but lost it about fifty meters down the trail from our NDP.

We split up into squads and began to search the heavily wooded slope around the site where our point man had encountered the NVA. We found several sites where NVA troops had apparently spent the night; there was evidence of someone sleeping in the brush and scraps of food and cigarette butts scattered around. We found no bunkers or any other NVA troops, and it was difficult to tell how old the sites were.

We spent the night at YD487066, about two hundred meters down the northern slope from the top of Hill 882. We again sent out several ambush patrols around the NDP site, but the night passed quietly.

May 24

At last we got orders to leave the area that had been such bad luck for our battalion. The five companies from our battalion (Alpha, Bravo, Charlie, Delta, and Echo) and the Recon Platoon would each have a turn serving as security for Firebase Bastogne, artillery base ten klicks east of Firebase Veghel.

About 0940 hours, Charlie Company was extracted by air from an LZ at YD487066. We were replaced by Charlie Company 1st/327th Infantry, a sister battalion in the 1st Brigade. We hopped aboard the same helicopters that brought C 1st/327th into the LZ and were flown to YD631083 at the base of Hill 342, aka **OP** Checkmate.

Authors Photo Album

Above: Greetings from the President of the United

States: my draft notice. Authors' Collection.

Sign on U.S. Highway 101 south of Santa Barbara, California honoring the 101st Airborne Division. Authors collection.

Left: Sergeant First Class Fletcher. **Right:** Staff Sergeant Salmon, also known as Sgt 'Fish'. D-1-3 Yearbook, Authors' collection.

SFC Fletcher counsels a trainee at the rifle range.
Authors collection

SSG Salmon coaches a trainee firing for record on the known
distance range. Authors collection.

In formation and ready for PT. Author is third from right looking to his right. Authors collection.

My AIT platoon at Fort Ord, California. The two soldiers wearing black helmet liners were "shake-n-bake" graduates of the NCOC School at Fort Benning. Author's collection.

75th Company Orderly Room and parade ground, Harmony Church, Fort Benning, Authors collection.

Barracks soda machine and water cooler, Fort Benning. Authors collection.

Sign outside headquarters building for the 7th Candidate Battalion, NCOC. Authors collection.

'Ranger Week' at NCOC. Author is at right with three buddies whose names I can't remember. Authors collection.

"FOLLOW ME"

NCOC 47-69, 75th Company
7th Student Battalion

Yearbook cover for Class 47-69, graduating 2 September 1969. Authors collection.

The author wearing camouflage paint with an M60 during 'Ranger Week' training. Authors collection.

NCOC Candidates Jerry Dyer (left) and Mike Lucky. Authors collection.

NCOC Candidates John Roberts (author, left) and Robert Wills. Authors collection.

Fort Ord in 1969. The fort was closed in 1994 and is now the *California State University, Monterey Bay*. Stillwell Hall is the building on the bluff at lower right.

Brand-new very young 'shake-n-bake' sergeant with 4th platoon, E/3-2, Fort Ord, September 1969. Authors collection.

The authors platoon at Fort Ord, November 1969. The author is at bottom row, third from right holding company guidon. Mike Lucky is bottom row, fourth from left. SGT Wilke, who served with the 101st in Vietnam, standing behind the 'Honor Platoon' guidon, told us stories about the famous 'fuck you' lizards. Authors Collection.

On the way to the Oakland Army Terminal and Vietnam on 2 January 1970. Authors collection.

John Roberts

UPLAND — Army Sgt. John G. Roberts, 21, son of Mr. and Mrs. John G. Roberts, 1064 E. 13th St., was assigned as a rifle squad leader with the 101st Airborne Division (Airmobile) in Vietnam, Jan. 24.

Article in authors hometown newspaper re: assignment to the 101st Airborne. Authors collection.

Above: Hue market place, heavily damaged during house-to-house fighting during Tet 1968. **Below:** Small Lambretta buses parked near destroyed market buildings. Authors collection.

Small boys selling cold soft drinks in the Hue market place. We were wary of them because their cases could contain explosives. Authors collection.

Command Sergeant Major Walter Sabalausky, wearing first Sergeant stripes. Photo by John Yeager.

Charley Company troopers move up the hill to 2-502 LZ at Camp Eagle. Buildings housing rear area for Bravo, Charley and Delta Companies are visible below. Author lived in the tent at left center while waiting to join Charley Company in the field.

The jungle near FSB Rifle and the author in his 'condo'. Authors collection.

NVA gold bullion captured from an NVA paymaster by Charley Two on 28 January 1970 near FSB Rifle. Photo courtesy Bruce Scott.

The author cutting an LZ, mugging for the camera and mail from home with a warm Coke. Authors collection.

Above: Some 1st Platoon guys on a firebase. **Top row L to R:** James "Bear" Pando; unknown; unknown; Charles "Swede" Swenson. **Center row L to R:** unknown; Vernon Okland; unknown; Terry Williams. Bottom row L to R: Wilbern "Ace" Marler; **Pete Ogo,** Philippine Scout; Gerald Kulm. Photo courtesy Terry Williams

View of the FSB Rifle TOC/COC. Photo courtesy Alpha Company 1-501 Infantry Association.

Luxury infantry accommodations on FSB Rifle. Photo courtesy Bruce Scott.

Aerial view of FSB Rifle. The author landed on the LZ on the ridge at right center on 25 January 1970.

Ch47 'Chinook' helicopters carrying 105's, ammo and the gun's crew approach a firebase during an artillery raid, March 1970. Authors collection.

SGT Mike Lucky at Camp Eagle shortly before he was wounded in operations near FSB Pistol in March 1970. Photo courtesy Mike Lucky.

The author at Eagle Beach with Terry 'Woodstock' Lowe celebrating my 22nd birthday. Authors collection.

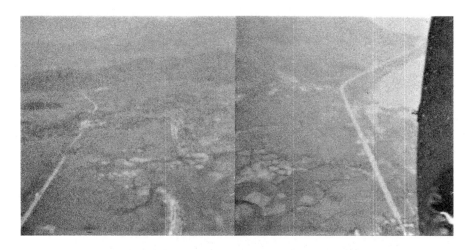

Aerial view of the Phu Loc district along QL-1. FSB Tomahawk was on the dark ridge at top left. C Company held the dark hill below ridge at left edge of photo. Authors collection.

The author at Camp Eagle at the start of Operation Texas Star, 1 April 1970. Authors Collection.

On the LZ near FSB Veghel at beginning of Operation Texas Star. **L:** Gerald Kulm, Charles 'Swede' Swenson and Tony Schweitzer. Authors collection.

Kit Carson Scout Hahn, a former NVA soldier who surrendered and became a scout for Charley One. Photo courtesy Lee Bartolotti.

Part of my squad at Camp Eagle: **L to R –** James 'Bear' Pando, Vern Okland, 'Ace' Marler and Frank Carvajal. Authors collection.

Captured NVA weapons. Photo courtesy Colonel (ret.) James Schonoover.

Bruce Scott. Photo courtesy Bruce Scott.

SGT Glen Witycyak. Photo courtesy Bruce Scott.

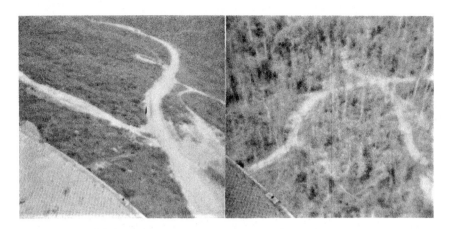

Left: Portion of QL=547, the 'Yellow Brick Road' running west from Camp Eagle to the A Shau Valley. **Right:** Trails used by woodcutters to harvest dead trees around FSB Bastogne. Authors collection.

Field of razor-edged 'elephant' grass near FSB Bastogne. Photo courtesy Lee Bartolotti.

The author enjoying a LRRP ration in the elephant grass near FSB Bastogne. Photo courtesy Lee Bartolotti.

From left: The author, Bill Hess and Roy Gordon at Camp Eagle before the A Shau Valley operation. Authors collection.

The author with a captured AK47 at Camp Eagle. Authors collection.

Clowning around with Roy Gordon at Camp Eagle during stand down of August 1970. Photo courtesy Lee Bartolotti.

Drinking Hamm's Beer with Lee Bartolotti. Photo courtesy of
Lee Bartolotti.

SBSD shoulder patch and my first badge, well-worn from
much polishing. Authors Collection.

1966 Dodge Power Wagon re-built by deputies for use by the West End Station Search and Rescue Team. Authors

Bottom Left: SBSD Bell B47G helicopter configured for rescue and patrol operations, circa 1972. Authors collection.

The author, Mike Lucky and Bruce Scott at the 502nd Infantry Vietnam memorial, Fort Campbell, KY. Authors collection.

Facing page, bottom: Veterans of Charley Company gather at The Wall in June 2015. **Top Row L to R:** Homer Hardy, Russ Funk, John Roberts, Hase Phillips, Bruce Scott, David McDonald. Bob Noffsinger, Doug Oswald and Bill Herrick. **Kneeling L to R:** Gerald Dillon, Richard Fulmer, Jim Hayes and Lee Bartolotti. Photo courtesy Shari Roberts.

Members of Charley One with memorial wreath at The Wall. **L to R:** Larry Kuss, John Roberts, Richard Fulmer, Gerald Dillon and Bob Noffsinger. Photo courtesy Shari Roberts.

The author at The Wall holding the memorial ribbon for Billy 'Kentucky' Lucas, KIA on 19 May 1970. Photo courtesy Shari Roberts.

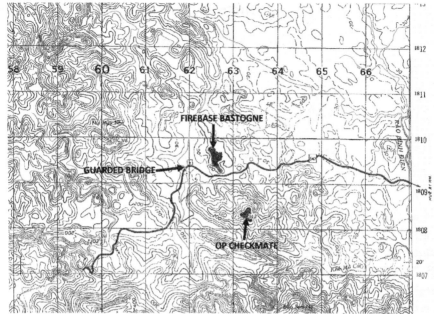

Firebase Bastogne AO from map series L-7014 sheet 6441-I
Ap Lai Bang District, Thua Thien Province. Authors' collection.

Chapter 26

Booby Traps in a New AO

May 25–June 7, 1970

During this time, Charlie Company was to operate south of FSB Bastogne in the hills and river valleys that bordered QL 547, the main route from the coastal areas around Hue/Phu Bai to the Laotian border. The area around FSB Bastogne was quite a bit different than the double-and triple-canopy jungle that covered Hills 714 and 882. The once heavily forested area had been defoliated with chemicals, among them Agent Orange. It was an eerie place: The defoliant had killed the tall jungle trees but had left them standing with bare branches resembling grotesque telephone poles. Because of the sunlight now able to reach the ground, heavy underbrush had grown, mostly bamboo and wait-a-minute bushes. We had to cut our way with machetes through the heaviest growth.

There were many dirt roads and paths running off QL 547 that were used by woodcutters. These people harvested the many dead trees to sell in the busy markets of Hue and Da Nang.

We were not used to being in an area with civilians around. It complicated matters because you had to take the time to make sure it was the NVA or Viet Cong and not a civilian before opening fire. If it was the enemy, that hesitation could be fatal.

Even with the problems they caused, having the woodcutters around made us feel a little more secure. Historically, they would not work in an area where the NVA and Viet Cong were active or getting ready to mount an attack. The downside was that the woodcutters informed the local Viet Cong where American units were operating to curry favor with the guerrillas.

The Veghel Operation had been costly for the O-Deuce. According to the "Daily Journal" dated May 31, 1970, the battalion had lost thirty-one killed in action and two hundred and ten wounded two hundred of them seriously enough to require helicopter evacuation from the field. Out of approximately four hundred and fifty field troops, we were left with only two hundred and nine men capable of operating in the field. This gave the line companies a more than 50 percent casualty rate.

The NVA losses were a hundred and eighty-five killed in action by actual body count. Since the enemy was very good at removing their wounded and dead from the battlefield, their losses were probably much higher.

Charlie Company had started the campaign with its company strength at about ninety men. At the end of May when we moved into the Bastogne area of operation, company strength had been reduced to about sixty men. Alpha and Bravo Companies had suffered more than 50 percent casualties and the Recon Platoon had been reduced to a single squad. Delta Company had suffered the least of the line companies, but that would change as the long summer wore on. The NVA were obviously building up their strength in western Thua Thien and Quang Tri Provinces, probably planning a big offensive before the monsoon started in late September.

We had been told that the 3rd Brigade had moved into the mountains on the east side of the A Shau Valley. They were attempting to build Firebase Ripcord to support operations into the valley itself. That area had long been a stronghold of the NVA and they would fight hard to protect it.

The high mountains that formed the eastern border of the A Shau Valley had been turned into a stronghold by the NVA. The slopes between Co Pung Mountain (Hill 1615) and Hill 1275 were known as the "warehouse area" and Ripcord was meant to support operations aimed at the destruction of this area.

I didn't know what the future held for us. The one thing an infantryman learned in a hurry was to take it one day at a time and grasp every opportunity to take it easy. Things could change dramatically within a single heartbeat, so we enjoyed the quiet new area as the battalion built up strength for another operation in the NVA's strongholds west of the Song Bo.

For four days, the O-Deuce continued operations in the Bastogne AO with absolutely no contact with enemy forces. I was hoping the area would stay quiet so we would have time to train any cherries who were sent to the field to replace those who weren't coming back.

May 29

About 0820 hours in the area around YD599102, 2nd Platoon, Delta Company was attacked by the enemy using RPGs. This attack left one US KIA and four WIA with one scout dog also losing his life. A stay-behind sniper team was put into the area at YD599119, and they were attacked by NVA troops tossing grenades into their position. The sniper team killed one NVA.

May 30

The O-Deuce was moved by air to patrol positions scattered all over the new AO. In the late evening of that day, 2nd Platoon was CA'd into a new patrol area near YD643060. As the ships approached the LZ, they began to draw heavy fire. Bruce Scott told me, "I do remember...one hot LZ. One was coming in and the bird was taking fire, and I was more or less pushed out, I guess, about six to eight feet off the ground. It's funny that I don't remember more about what happened next, I know it could have been about the same time that a new sergeant came down [and] a small tree stump went through his leg".

A hot LZ was one of the more serious things an infantryman had to deal with. Nowhere is a helicopter full of troops more vulnerable than on takeoff or landing at a jungle LZ. The NVA had a habit of keeping one or more soldiers at an often-used LZ. Sometimes they would set up command-detonated mines or fire up the troops as they scrambled off the slicks and tried to find cover.

June 1–8

In a letter home on June 1, I wrote: *"The Battalion Commander, LTC Shay, came out to see us yesterday. He said that there would be a battalion stand down on the 20th of this month...stand down will last about 10 days and then it will be time for my R&R....June is finally here and I'm starting my sixth month over here; I can't believe I've been gone that long."*

The new AO around Firebase Bastogne was nice and quiet compared to what we'd been through in April and May. On June 2, 2nd Platoon Charlie Company, while moving onto an LZ, detonated an antipersonnel mine left behind by the NVA. There were seven WIA.

The booby trap was a 60mm mortar round fitted with a pressure device which, when detonated, set off a Chicom claymore mine; the claymore caused all the casualties

Most of the contacts with the NVA were meeting engagements with only two or three men exchanging fire. On June 3 and 4, Alpha Company fired on two enemies; one escaped, and the other was killed and his AK50 captured. 1st Platoon Charlie Company continued to have no contact with the enemy.

There were mines and booby traps all over the place. A vehicle from the 327th Engineers detonated an anti-vehicle mine on QL 547, the main route from Hue and Camp Eagle to the firebases built west of the Song Bo River. No one was injured by the mines and traps, but Alpha Company received sniper fire with one WIA. Later that day, an Alpha Company trooper set off another booby trap and was wounded. The next day, Alpha Company found a small cache and again set off a booby trap, wounding one. The cache contained 1 RPD machine gun, 4 AK-47s, a P38 9mm pistol, 5 boxes of blasting caps and 100 ¼ pound demolition charges.

Another near-by bunker contained NVA entrenching tools, machetes, steel helmets, canteens, two US M-2 carbines and, of all things, an alarm clock.

In another letter home dated June 6, I described 1st Platoon's recent activities: "Right now, we are pulling ambushes on the road between Bastogne and Firebase Veghel. It's easy duty, hardly any walking, and there are streams where we can get freshwater…Well, they have moved the stand down to the 14th of this month instead of the 20th…and we are supposed to go to Firebase Bastogne on the 8th to secure it for about 6 or 7 days."

Some of the ambush locations were so close to Bastogne that we could hear the big generators and see the glow from the lights and hear, sometimes, men yelling back and forth.

Chapter 27

Firebase Bastogne: Watching the Woodcutters

June 8–June 30, 1970

On June 8, Charlie Company was assigned to secure the perimeter of Firebase Bastogne. First Platoon was so close to the big base that we simply walked down QL 547 and through the main gate. I don't remember which company was securing Bastogne, but there was some confusion as they moved out and we moved in. Never having been involved in firebase security before, I found it a strange environment.

The perimeter wire on Bastogne followed the shape and contour of the hill, wriggling around like a snake. The bunker I was assigned to over looked a depression and the PSP-covered LZ outside the wire. The base was surrounded by low hills covered with low brush and the trunks of dead trees sticking up like telephone poles.

Down in the depression was a big self-propelled artillery piece pointed west towards the A Shau Valley. I think it was an eight-inch howitzer because it had a short barrel. It had a large crew of "**gun bunnies**" (infantry slang for an artillery crew) to handle the big shells and powder bags.

The crew had fire missions at all hours of the day and night. I would watch, fascinated, as the crew worked to load the big gun; after each shot, it took between two and three minutes to reload the damn thing and get off another shot. The crew was very courteous; one of them would always call out in a loud voice, "Watch your ears" or "Cover your ears" before the gun was fired. The muzzle blast was ferocious, with a cloud of dust and loose debris flying into the air every time the gun was fired.

My squad had several duties other than perimeter security, shared with the other squads and platoons. On June 12, I wrote in a letter home: "We aren't doing much here. We pull guard duty at night and during the day we pull security for supply convoys running between Firebases Birmingham, Bastogne, and Veghel. Boy is that road dusty!"

On June 9th, Firebase Bastogne received a visit from an unusual VIP; Prince Lowenstein of Germany. The prince wanted a briefing and a tour of the firebase. His assimilated rank was that of a brigadier general. Lowenstein was a free-lance writer and lecturer in Germany. His visit was very brief because he did not have the proper clearances. I do remember a covey of officers escorting the prince around the firebase as he looked over the fighting positions and artillery emplacements. I wondered why the man had placed himself in such a dangerous position when he didn't have to be there.

My favorite duty was the bridge security detail. There was a stream a few hundred meters west of the firebase that had a metal culvert/bridge on QL 547 spanning the stream. I would take three or four guys with me to guard the bridge, and we would take turns bathing in the clear, cool water as the stream ran noisily over rocks. Right next to the bridge was a well-used dirt road leading up into the de-foliated hills north and west of Firebase Bastogne

While we were guarding the bridge, we had orders to "keep an eye" on the Vietnamese woodcutters who worked among the dead trees on the hills surrounding the bridge. They drove old trucks with flatbeds, booms, and cable-and-winches on the back. It was a family affair; the alpha male drove the truck with wives crammed into the cab, and the kids and old mama-and papa-sans rode on the bed.

None of us could speak any Vietnamese except to say hello. All we could do was watch the trucks pass by all day and return in the afternoon with a load of big logs secured on the bed of the truck. I learned that the logs were taken to saw mills in Hue and Da Nang to be cut into lumber.

On June 18, I sent a letter home: "*Well, pack your suitcase! My R&R starts on the 7th of July until the 13th of July. Hawaii, here I come...take a taxi to the R&R center where you can wait for me. I will arrive sometime in the afternoon of the 7th.*"

Another duty, which I didn't care for as much as bridge security, was escorting the engineers every morning as they swept QL 547 for mines. We rode on wooden seats in the bed of a three-quarter-ton truck. There were filled sandbags on the floor of the cab and in the truck bed, which were supposed to reduce the blast effects if we ran over a land mine. I doubted very much that the sandbags would have saved us.

We took turns walking along the edges of the road, acting as security for the sweepers who walked down the middle of the road, moving their mine detectors from side-to-side. Marching very rapidly, we would walk until we met the team coming west from Firebase Birmingham. We'd exchange some gossip and then jump on the truck for the dusty ride back to Bastogne.

On one occasion, while I was pulling guard duty on the bunker line during the day, I heard and then saw a slick hovering over the perimeter wire. The pilot moved the Huey along the wire and a man in the cargo area of the helicopter was spraying something from a big tank with a hose and nozzle. When they got to the wire in front of my position, I realized that they were spraying some type of herbicide onto the weeds growing among the wire strands. I felt something wet on my face and arms; the rotor wash was blowing the stuff all over the place. It got into my hair, eyes, nose, mouth and ears and on my fatigues. I had no way to wash it off because there wasn't enough water for bathing on Bastogne and I didn't have a set of clean fatigues. The poor guy sitting in the back had on a baseball cap and a scarf over his face; it was the only protection he had.

Some years later, I realized the stuff had been Agent Orange, Agent Purple, or some other defoliant agent. When I was diagnosed with type II diabetes in 1997, the VA told me the disease was most likely caused by prolonged and direct exposure to Agent Orange. The whole area around Firebase Bastogne had been defoliated and the chemicals had impregnated the soil and contaminated the water in the streams we used as a source of drinking water.

On the night of June 18-19 one of the sensor positions to the northeast of Firebase Bastogne registered significant movement at YD 637102. The map indicates an established trail running through that area and, when the sensors continued to register movement, 30 rounds of 81mm mortar fire was directed at the area. The next morning a patrol from Charlie Company investigated the area and found very large 'cat tracks'. It must have been a tiger moving through the area which set off the movement sensors.

Our stay on Bastogne ended on June 21st, and we were shipped to Camp Eagle riding in the long bed of a five-ton truck. On the way to Eagle, we passed a 'relocation village' occupied by Montagnards, the indigenous hill people of Vietnam. They had been moved from the western mountains along the Laotian border into a 'secure' area to keep them from being used as slave labor by the NVA.

We were all very happy about going to the rear for several days and some of the more irresponsible guys got carried away. As we passed the village, they threw smoke grenades and burning trip flares into the village. The 'yards' went nuts, running after the trucks, screaming and shaking their fists at us.

Thinking they had gotten away with it, they were still laughing when the trucks dropped us off at the O-Deuce. Not long after we got there, a division staff officer appeared and went into LTC Shay's office. A little while later, 1st Platoon's LT told us that we had to pay a fine even if we had not thrown anything, and I had to fork over $20 dollars in MPC. The LT gathered our money and took it into the headquarters building.

Apparently, the village chief had complained to the district chief who had in turn complained to the liaison officer at division headquarters. It wasn't hard to figure out who the culprits were, since Charlie Company was the only company being moved back to Camp Eagle by truck. For once, the wheels of military justice had moved quickly.

Chapter 28

Refresher Training: Beer, Mortars and Rockets

June 20–June 29, 1970

After the excitement from the incident at the Montagnard village had died down, we were told that we could take a shower and get clean uniforms. The engineers had set up a shower point not far from the headquarters building; this one had wooden floors to keep your feet out of the mud. Of course, my feet got dirty again when I stepped off the wood platform after my shower, but this was the first time I had felt clean in months, so I didn't mind too much.

Decked out in our clean fatigues, we made our way over the creek on the single plank bridge to Charlie Company's area. We drew army cots and set them up. We slept out in the open with no shelter; if it rained, you simply pulled your poncho up over you and the cot and went back to sleep.

In a letter dated June 24, I wrote: "We just got back from a day and a night at Eagle Beach. It was sure nice to sleep on a cot with a real mattress. I went for a dip in the China Sea and watched a couple of movies."

One night, we were watching a movie (I think it was _MASH_) at Sabo's outdoor theatre when I heard an explosion very close to us. I jumped up and looked toward the sound and I saw a series of mortar blasts 'walking' down the road toward the theatre. I remember seeing yellow and blue sparks when the shells went off. We had just started to run for cover when the mortar rounds stopped. When the gook gunner didn't drop any more rounds, we went back to the movie.

I remember a line from the movie where Hot Lips was complaining to the chaplain about Hawkeye's bizarre behavior and asked how he had obtained such a position of responsibility. The chaplain replied with a straight face, "He was drafted." This brought down the house because many of the men in Vietnam at that time were draftees. All we wanted was to do our job the best we could, survive, and go home.

On another night, the NVA dropped several 122mm rockets into another sector of Camp Eagle. We heard the awful noise as the big rockets came in but they exploded some distance away from the O-Deuce.

There was a lot of beer drinking during a stand down. Top Stanley would borrow our ration cards and go to the supply dump in a jeep pulling a trailer. After a while, he would come back with the trailer full of ice and beer. Sometimes he would get steaks and we would have a beer and steak BBQ. My personal favorite was Budweiser, but since it was a premium beer, we almost never got any—I think the REMFs got most of it. We usually drank Schlitz, Olympia, Pabst Blue Ribbon, Hamm's (from the Land of Clear Blue Waters) or a foul-tasting brew called Carling's Black Label.

Some guys chose another method of altering their consciousness that didn't involve beer. I remember that we used the words **'juicer'** and **'head'** to designate a man's choice of intoxicant; I was a juicer. I never saw drug use in the boonies; if anyone in 1st Platoon had brought dew or something else out to the field, he would have been dealt with quickly. We all wanted to survive and we couldn't take a chance on someone being stoned on guard duty.

While we were at Camp Eagle, we underwent some training where we re-zeroed our M-16s to make sure the bullet went where you wanted it to. We also practiced rappelling from a forty-foot tower. We were supposed to do an actual rappel from a helicopter, but the birds were unavailable, for which we were grateful. I never had to rappel during my time in the 'Nam, but the engineers and Recon did so under fire on a couple of occasions on 714 and 882.

On June 22, the day that the 1st platoon was undergoing training at the rappelling tower, a horrible accident occurred. I was on the platform at the top of the tower waiting my turn to slide down the rope when I heard a series of loud, rumbling explosions. Looking around, I saw a huge black mushroom cloud climbing rapidly into the sky. We all thought Camp Eagle was under attack, but we later learned that the ammunition dump at the 2nd/502nd had blown up, killing and wounding several men.

Item number 38 for the Daily Staff Journal for the 1st Brigade states that at 1430 hours, "2-502 ammo dump has blown up." An EOD team, graves registration, the Camp Eagle fire department and the MPs all responded to the scene. 6 men were treated for relatively minor injuries but three men were killed. One of these men was so badly injured that his body was not identified for several days.

The men killed by the explosion that day were: Sgt. Jimmy L. Chamblee, HHC, 2-502; Sgt. Ralph A. Gaddes, HHC, 2-502 and Sgt. William W. Morrow, HHC, 2-502. I don't know if the cause of the explosion was ever officially determined, but I have heard that the initial explosion was caused by a trip flare igniting which then cooked off more ammunition, resulting in a chain reaction of explosions.

Chapter 29

Waiting for R & R

On June 29, Charlie Company returned to the field and was moved by air to Hill 316 over-looking Firebase Bastogne and began operating in platoon-sized elements. The jungle was still thick in the areas that weren't close to QL 547. I remember one incident during a resupply when the helicopter couldn't land and had to kick out the cases of C rations from a hover about a hundred feet above the ground.

On June 30, 3rd Platoon sent a patrol to look for an LZ. While the patrol was moving down a trail, they noticed a lot of movement in the brush along their route of advance. They fired at the movement but received no return fire. When the squad checked the area where they had seen the movement, they found a large dead monkey, killed by rifle fire.

Also, on June 30, a truck convoy from 1st/83rd Artillery was fired upon while moving west on QL-547 about 4 klicks east of Bastogne. Trucks 3 and 5 were hit by small arms fire and an RPG was fired at the convoy. There were no casualties.

In a long letter home, I complained about the way the resupply was being handled: "*...there are no LZ's in the area, so all we get is kick outs. You should see a case of C-rations after it's [sic] fallen 100 feet from a helicopter! So bent up you can hardly open them.*"

In that same letter, I also complained about the mail delivery: "*And today they kicked out our mail to another platoon! Typical Army in-efficiency! But the [other] platoon is setting up not far from us tonight, and we'll send a patrol to police up the mail.*"

The mail was brought out to the field in big, bright-red, nylon bags. When the log birds came in on resupply missions, everybody looked anxiously for the red bags that were our only link with our families and the outside world.

We eventually moved out of the heavy jungle and into an area that had been worked over by the ARVN. They had built a lot of LZs, and one day a log bird came in carrying a new platoon leader for 1st Platoon. He scrambled off the helicopter and just stood there looking confused while the helicopter was quickly unloaded and took off.

Another man and I took mercy on him and we led him off the open LZ and into some cover. He was a scholarly-looking man, wearing a pair of army issue glasses. I quickly learned that the new LT was a recent graduate of **OCS** from the infantry school at Fort Benning. My first impression of him was that he was going to need some hand holding, but he surprised all of us by quickly taking over. He eventually became a good LT until he was wounded during the Firebase Barnett operation in August.

June passed into July, and on July 4, I was airlifted from the field to Bastogne and from there to Camp Eagle to get ready for my R&R. On that same day, 1st Platoon received small arms fire with no casualties. Also, on July 4, a convoy security vehicle drove over a land mine planted on QL 547, leaving one KIA and three WIA. The dead man was from the 2-17th Cavalry, a unit attached to the 101st. They were used for convoy security and for quick in-and-out missions such as securing a downed helicopter until it could be picked up.

Chapter 30

R & R: Fireworks, Waikiki Beach and Sunburn

Almost as soon as I reported to the company clerk in the Charlie Company orderly room, Top Stanley grabbed me and put me in charge of three other men who were in the rear and assigned us to bunker line guard duty. Even though I had just come from the field and deserved a rest, I was saddled with that duty. I guess the REMFs thought it was necessary so they would be free to party on the 4th of July. They had probably been planning it since my orders came down a few days before.

And so it was that during the early evening we were taken to the bunker line and dropped off at our assigned bunker. By this time in the war, the Camp Eagle bunker line was very formidable. In front of our position were rows of razor wire several feet high. Running inside the razor wire was a layer of tangle foot wire, designed to prevent sappers from crawling through the razor wire coil.

In addition to all this, chain-link fences stretched in front of each bunker that was supposed to detonate incoming RPG rounds before they could hit the bunker. There were permanently emplaced claymore mines, trip flares, and empty soda/beer cans with some gravel in them attached to the razor wire, all backed up by the four men in the bunker with M-16s or an M-60. Behind all this were spotlights that could be turned on if that sector was attacked.

It seemed to me that with all that security live bunker guards were hardly necessary; but, because of all these measures, Camp Eagle rarely received a ground attack. The **dink**s preferred to drop 82mm mortar rounds or big 122mm rockets on the camp.

Later that night, after it had gotten fully dark, I was taking my turn at guard on top of the bunker. The inside of the bunker was hot, stuffy and smelly, so we usually stood our guard on the roof. Anyway, I happened to be looking in the direction of Firebase Arsenal, a dark shape rising out of the rolling plain southwest of Eagle when I was startled by several signal flares rising into the sky. They were called star clusters, and I recall that they came in yellow, white, green and red and they were often used to indicate a ground attack on a position.

When I spotted some red star clusters, my first thought was that they were under attack, but the flares kept rising into the air until there were at least fifteen or twenty of them in the air at the same time. I figured out that they weren't under attack but were simply celebrating July 4th. Who knows how long they had hoarded those star clusters, just to be able to use them on Independence Day? I saw a lot of spectacular pyrotechnics during my tour in 'Nam, but that display remains clear in my mind even after forty-three years. To this day, I can't look at fireworks without feeling an urge to hide or remembering the 4th of July on Firebase Arsenal.

For the next two days, I managed to make myself scarce around Charlie Company, not wanting to get stuck with another shit detail before I left for Hawaii on July 7th.

That morning, I picked up my orders from the company clerk, and the company jeep driver, a guy named Granger, drove me to the main LZ to catch the shuttle. The shuttle was a CH-47 cargo helicopter that made a round-robin flight carrying passengers and cargo from Camp Eagle to Da Nang and points in between. Pilots flying those missions referred to them as 'ass and trash' missions.

When I landed at Da Nang, I reported to the R&R center, where they told me my flight didn't leave for a couple of hours more. I went to the big PX at Monkey Mountain hoping to find some civilian clothing for the trip. As usual, the selection of civvies was very poor. I found a pair of slacks in my waist size (29 inches!) but they were an inch short. I bought them anyway, along with a shirt.

We finally boarded a big Pan Am Boeing 707 and took off. I don't remember anything about the flight except that it was long and boring. We arrived sometime in the afternoon of July 7, Hawaiian time. We had been flying backwards in time because of the International Date Line. It was already July 8 back in the 'Nam.

We got off the plane and I saw the usual OD green army buses waiting for us. Someone checked off our names from a list as we boarded, and soon we were off through the streets of Honolulu. I experienced a kind of culture shock: no one was in uniform and I didn't see a single M-16, nor was there any barbed wire or sand-bagged bunkers in sight. I had been in the war zone for over six months and had gotten used to the sights and sounds of war.

After a short drive down Ala Moana Boulevard, we arrived at the R&R Center at Fort DeRussey. I spotted my mom right away as the bus stopped in front of the center. I got off the bus and stood right in front of her. She was looking all around me until I said, *"Hi, Mom."* Recognition dawned and she gave me a hug only a mother can give. Of course, I didn't look anything like I did the last time she had seen me. I'd lost weight, my hair had been bleached by the sun to a red-gold color, and I was very tan. My girlfriend then came up to me and we had a nice reunion right there in front of the R&R Center. My dad had rounded up a taxi and we were soon on our way to our hotel.

My mom later told me, *"I just didn't recognize you. All I saw was a great big guy who was blocking my view."*

My style was a little cramped by the presence of my parents. Dad told me that my girlfriend's mom and dad wouldn't have allowed her to come unless my parents came along and acted as chaperones. She was nineteen, but in those days you weren't considered an adult until you reached twenty-one.

Using my R&R discount, I rented a bright purple (the only car they had left) Dodge Charger. We tooled all over Oahu in that thing, getting a lot of strange looks as we drove around. I remember I found a beach on the north side of the island that was completely deserted. We were in the sun for several hours, talking and playing in the surf, and we both ended up with very painful sunburns.

During our conversations, I noticed a kind of coolness from her. Under my probing, she finally told me that while she was glad to see me, she was bored and lonely and she wanted to date other guys. There was nothing I could do about her change of attitude towards me, and later that summer I received the inevitable "Dear John" letter. It bothered me for a while, but I had more urgent things on my mind and I learned to live with it.

Of course, she wasn't entirely to blame; I was not the same person she'd known for the last two years. I was no longer a happy-go-lucky young man but a grim, nervous one always looking around and jumping at sudden loud noises. No wonder she wanted to be with 'normal' young men.

My departure was kind of an anticlimax; everything that needed to be said had been said. The long flight back to Vietnam was broken by a refueling stop at Anderson AFB on the island of Guam, where they let us get off the aircraft while it was being serviced. Looking around, I noticed a large group of **B-52** bombers on the other side of the airfield, affectionately called **BUFF**s by their crews.

I arrived back in Vietnam and was flown back to Camp Eagle via the ass and trash Chinook. I hitched a ride with some guy in a jeep who quickly drove me to the O-Deuce. Strangely, it felt as if I'd come home even though I hated the damn place.

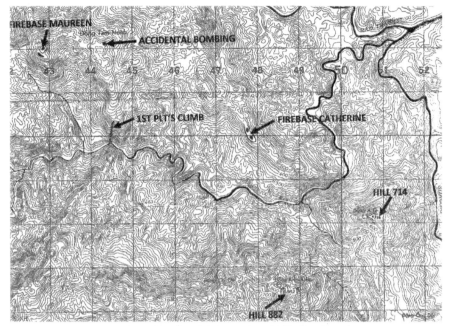

Firebase Maureen AO from map series L-7013, Sheet 6441-1 Ap Lai Bang District, Thua Thien Province. Author's collection.

Chapter 31

Firebase Maureen

While I was on R&R, the O-Deuce had been moved by air from Firebase Bastogne to Quang Tri City and then to Firebase Shepherd as part of frag order Clinch Valley. The firebase overlooked the Ben Hai River, part of the DMZ.

The battalion patrolled the area without any contact except for Bravo Company's 2nd Platoon, who spotted three NVA walking along QL 9 and called in mortar fire on them with unknown results.

On July 13, Alpha Company spotted lights near their NDP and heard movement along the trail. Artillery and mortars were called in and the lights went out. There was no further contact with the enemy.

When I reported in at the company orderly room, I was told that the battalion was coming back to Camp Eagle from Firebase Shepherd and would arrive sometime in the afternoon. I was put in charge of a detail moving dozens of folding cots from the back of a truck to the clear area below the battalion LZ. Working with other men in the hot sun helped get me over the bad mood I still carried from R&R.

Pretty soon a long string of loaded slicks began sitting down on the battalion LZ and Charlie Company was home. A little later, Top Stanley showed up with a trailer full of iced-down beer and even some steaks, so Charlie Company had a party. The steaks weren't very good cuts of meat, but there was plenty of cold beer to wash them down. To a boonie rat it all tasted wonderful.

On the sixteenth, the O-Deuce was inserted into an AO southwest of Firebase Veghel. One platoon engaged some enemy soldiers with no results. Alpha Company engaged three NVA with one US soldier wounded. There was no further contact and the O-Deuce returned to Camp Eagle on the twenty-first.

During the last part of July 3rd Brigade and elements of 2nd Brigade were busy trying to disengage from the enemy and close Firebase Ripcord. The units at Ripcord were the 1st/506th, 2nd/506th, and 2nd/501st, and they were facing NVA troops in division strength who were determined to drive the 101st from the immediate area of the A Shau Valley. The casualties were high and would only climb higher if the firebase remained occupied, so division and corps command decided to cut their losses and close Ripcord on July 23. They could not afford a media frenzy such as the one that had occurred after the battle of Dong Ap Bia the year before.

While all this was going on, the O-Deuce was designated as the division immediate reaction force. During the stand down we always had all our gear with us in case we were called to the Ripcord AO.

At one point on the afternoon of July 23, Charlie Company and the Recon Platoon were moved to the division LZ on 15-minute stand-by for movement to Firebase Ripcord. About an hour later, the alert status was lowered and we went back to 'regular' alert status.

Ripcord was successfully evacuated and all the units, operating in the jungle around Ripcord were extracted. The B-52s then bombed Ripcord out of existence.

July 25–August 12

So, on July 25, the O-Deuce moved by air to Firebase Maureen on Hill 980(YD429122) and opened the firebase under frag order Chicago Peak. The movement of the O-Deuce by air from Firebase Veghel to Firebase Maureen was routine except for Delta Company: they hit a hot LZ and the fourth slick into the LZ was hit but not disabled, and there were no US casualties. About twelve NVA were seen moving away from the LZ; artillery and an airstrike were employed with unknown results.

I remember a near tragedy occurring soon after Charlie Company was completely on the ground. We were still on our LZ getting organized when I heard a fighter bomber roaring in on a bomb run but I couldn't spot the aircraft. There was a lower hill next to the hill I was on. I happened to be looking in that direction when I heard a loud **WHUMP** and a dirty grey and brown cloud burst above the trees. I recall thinking, "Wow, that's pretty fucking close." Then I saw a group of men frantically run out of the dust cloud and down the hill. I could hear them yelling at each other but couldn't distinguish the words. I never learned what unit the men were from or if there were any casualties.

Years later, while doing research for this book, I found an entry on page 1 of the July 25 Daily Journal that reads: "*Regard received Air Strike in area near friendly elements. No contact with Bilk 16 to determine who requested strike.*" Bilk 16 was probably the Air Force FAC in charge of the fighter bombers operating in the area. Since battalion headquarters was unable to reach Bilk 16, no one knew why the air strike was targeted at that location. The Daily Journal says nothing about casualties so, hopefully, no one was hit.

Patrols from Recon and all four field companies were moving all over the new AO. We were finding small ammunition caches, many abandoned/unoccupied bunkers, booby traps, and enemy graves; two graves were found on Firebase Maureen itself. The 3rd Platoon Delta Company found more than fifty fighting positions, some with overhead cover. Alpha Company caught three NVA crossing a stream and called in artillery with unknown results. The enemy was moving all over the AO but no significant contact was made.

On July 27 at about 1935 hours, we began receiving what we thought were incoming .50 caliber machine gun rounds from the direction of the firebase. The sound of the big half-inch bullets thumping into the trees was chilling; there wasn't much that would stop a .50 caliber round. The incident was reported to battalion and the fire stopped. There were no casualties.

Sometime during this period, 3rd Squad was sent on a ridiculous mission. Charlie Company was on a high, narrow finger ridge that extended from a large hill mass. The slopes of the finger ridge were nearly perpendicular, falling into a small river valley. The squad's mission was to climb down into the valley and check it for NVA positions. The platoon LT was sent along to make sure we did what was ordered. We began the steep climb down, and after about two hundred meters, we came to a very steep place where we took a break. The LT radioed the CP that we needed ropes to continue the mission, but the captain replied, "You are to continue the mission, out" and nothing else.

The LT sat fuming for a few minutes and then ordered us to try to descend the cliff. We tried until one man lost his grip and slid about fifteen feet down before he was able to stop himself by grabbing a bush. We formed a human chain and dragged the man back up to a more level place.

As one of the old-timers in the squad, I told the LT that it was too dangerous to continue without ropes. The LT called the CP again and asked for ropes to be dropped to us. The request was again denied, so the LT asked permission to abort the mission. This request was also denied. The LT struggled with his decision whether to continue and finally decided we would stay where we were. This was the only time I saw a refusal to obey orders during my time with Charlie Company and the O-Deuce.

The squad remained there until late afternoon and then began the difficult climb back to the ridge top. We got to the top just before dark and collapsed at our positions, exhausted by the long day of slipping and sliding on the cliffs. If there were any problems from the LT's decision, I never heard about them.

In July, the weather was a big factor in how the troops in the field could conduct themselves. Much of the time, the temperature was over a hundred degrees with high humidity. We were **humping** the usual seventy to eighty-pound loads and we began to take heat casualties. The only breaks in the hundred-degree weather were the thunderstorms, which lowered the temperature slightly but increased the humidity.

I remember a miserably hot day when 1st and 3rd Platoons, along with the CP group, were working in a narrow valley with a creek running through it, just below Hill 980. I was carrying an M-79 that day because the gunner was in the rear for some reason. Sometime in the late afternoon, the column stopped and word was passed that a PFC named Smith had passed out from the heat. The medics had put him (PFC Curtis L. Smith) in the creek to try and cool him down.

The CP asked for a dust off and one soon arrived and lowered the jungle penetrator. The sick man was being pulled up to the medevac when an AK on full automatic fired on the hovering ship. When the helicopter left, the platoon sergeant told me to fire my M-79 at the area where he thought the AK fire had come from. I fired several rounds but we received no return fire.

A **pink team** arrived on station and received fire but was not hit. The gooks were all over the place but they had chosen not to fully engage us.

The next day we had another heat casualty (PFC Thomas E. Hughell), but he was evacuated without the dust off taking any fire.

While reading the Daily Journal for July 28, I came across an interesting comment: "*Reliable agent reports enemy forces equipped with individual weapons, 82 and 60mm mortars, 12.7mm heavy machine guns have moved vicinity Hill 900 YD415111…with mission to coordinate attacks by fire on friendly units in area.*"

It's not known who this "*reliable agent*" was or how he came by his information, but it does show that the enemy was in the AO, heavily armed and ready to fight the O-Deuce.

I found another interesting entry for July 28: a tally of the battalions' strength in the field. Alpha had a hundred men and Bravo and Charlie each had ninety-seven; for some reason, Delta's field strength was not listed. The total of the troops listed was only two hundred ninety-four; it seemed that the O-Deuce still hadn't fully recovered from the devastating casualties received at Hill 714 and Hill 882. Estimating Delta Company's strength at about a hundred gave the battalion strength in the field of about three hundred ninety-four men.

The mission continued with no contact with the enemy. The companies continued to find abandoned and unused bunker complexes scattered around the AO. Alpha Company found an extensive tunnel complex, and when they tried to destroy it by setting explosive charges, they set off twelve to fifteen secondary explosions that lasted about seven minutes.

August was slow also; we had no direct contact with the enemy. Charlie Company found a tunnel complex and some type of communications wire with insulators every few feet. Bruce Scott recalls that finding the wire made everyone nervous because the NVA usually did not go to that much trouble unless there was a major headquarters in the area.

On August 2, Charlie Company walked onto Firebase Maureen and took over firebase security from Bravo Company. On August 6, I sent word home: *"We are securing a firebase; it's called Maureen. There [is] nothing here, we are building it...digging bunkers, stringing barbed wire, filling sand bags and other fun jobs...but it beats humping the hills with a rucksack."* In a PS to that letter, I told them *"only 150 days! I'm getting short!"*

There was some civilian guy on the firebase representing a defense contractor back in the world. He was plugging a newfangled type of motion detector, telling us that motion sensors had to be planted around the perimeter you were defending. The men on guard around the perimeter would be issued the warning device, which was worn on the wrist and looked like a giant watch. If the sensor detected movement, it would send an electronic signal that would cause the wristwatch to vibrate sharply. Being line grunts, we looked at this thing with great skepticism but decided to try it out.

A couple of days later, I was on guard duty around midnight and things were quiet except for the ARVNs at the 155mm artillery battery next door when the thing on my wrist suddenly vibrated, shaking my whole arm. I checked the area in front of my position carefully but did not see anything. When the damn thing went off again about a minute later, I decided to throw a frag out into the wire to see if anything happened.

I didn't know that the ARVN artillerymen had established their unused gunpowder dump down in the gully to the right of my position.

I pulled the pin and threw the grenade out into the wire. I heard it clang against something metal and nothing happened for a couple seconds. Suddenly, with a bang and a **WHOOSH**, a huge fireball erupted from the gully. I was horrified because my grenade must have bounced into the powder dump and set it off. Luckily for me and everyone else in the area, loose powder does not explode but burns with a loud whooshing sound. I thought *"Oh, shit! If they find out who did that, I'll be on my way to the **LBJ**."*

I never heard a word about it; it was as if it had never happened. The sleeping men at my bunker didn't even wake up and the ARVNs made no outcry, so I relaxed.

A couple of days later, I was helping to unload heavy ammunition cases from the back of a mechanical mule. I lost my grip and the edge of the ammo case landed across the toes on my right foot. There was a lot of pain and I hopped on one leg for a bit. When the pain subsided, I went back to work.

One day, I was walking around the small knoll in the middle of the firebase when I ran into a small, erect man wearing starched fatigues. I saw the name Sutherland on his chest and three stars on his collar and I knew I was looking at the XXIV Corps commanding general.

I was not wearing a helmet or a shirt but I came to attention and waited. It was not the custom to salute officers when in the field. I had spent the morning digging a trench and filling sandbags and I was filthy, so when he looked me over he must have noticed the sweat cutting channels in the dirt on my chest and stomach. Finally, he asked the usual questions: "How do you like the army?" "Are you getting enough to eat?" "Are you getting your mail?" So, I gave the usual answers: "I like the army fine, sir" and "The chow is great, sir." He did not ask my name or rank for which I was grateful. He let me go and walked off to raise somebody else's morale.

I'm positive the general's intentions were good but his world was so far removed from the reality of trying to exist in the jungle or on a firebase that he had absolutely no idea of what a grunt or an artilleryman's life was like.

One day I walked over to the 105 battery on the south side of Maureen looking for a shovel I could borrow to fill sandbags with. I happened to be standing at just the right angle behind two of the guns during a fire mission so that when the guns were fired, I could see the projectiles for a second as they left the muzzle. Following the trajectory, I could see the shells bursting on the summit of Dong Ngai (Hill 1774) about 4 klicks southwest of the firebase.

During the early morning hours of August 7, my position and the position next to us had indications of movement in or near the barbed-wire perimeter. We didn't have a star light scope and using the Mark 1 eyeball didn't reveal anything. One guy in the adjacent position decided to fire an M-79 **HE** round into the wire to see if he got any reaction. He fired the shot and immediately the round exploded. The M-79 gunner let out a startled yell, grabbed his crotch, and took off running for the aid station on the other side of the firebase.

We found out later that the man had been hit by a fragment of his own HE round on a very delicate portion of his anatomy. He went out on a medevac at first light, along with an ARVN who had malaria. It seemed the grenade had traveled just far enough to arm itself when it hit something in the wire and exploded. Murphy's Law that "anything that **can** go wrong **will** go wrong" appeared to be in full effect on Firebase Maureen.

The man recovered and returned to 1st Platoon a few weeks later. He joked about his injury, calling himself "Iron Dick." I was glad he saw the humor in the incident; an injury like that would have depressed the hell out of me.

Out in the AO, Alpha, Bravo, and Delta Companies were uncovering big bunker complexes, fighting positions, weapon and ammunition caches, and a lot of tunnels. There was no hard contact; it was mostly sniper fire at troops on the ground and at passing aircraft.

While looking at the Daily Journal for August 8, I noticed an unusual entry: "(U) No white team for last light check. Aircraft has used all blade time allowable."

Curious, I did a little more research and found that "blade time" referred to the amount of time a helicopter spent in the air. It seems that at that time of the war, flight time for the division support helicopters was being rationed. It's a good thing that information wasn't generally known; it would have had a bad effect on troop morale.

During this time, my foot had become more and more painful and I finally went to the aid station on the firebase. The medic helped me take off my boot and sock and I saw that my right big toe was swollen and a bright red color with fluid running from it. The medic asked when I had hurt it, and when I said, "*Several days ago*" he scolded me and said he was going to send me to the rear for better treatment. He wrapped up the toe and told me to wear a sock only.

The next day was August 12, and the whole battalion was airlifted from the Maureen AO for an overnight stand down at Camp Eagle to get ready for the next operation.

When we arrived at the O-Deuce LZ I dropped off my rucksack and, worried about my toe, went right to the battalion aid station. The medics who were on duty said they'd have to get the infection under control before anything else could be done.

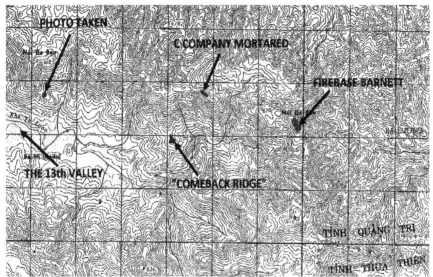

The Firebase Barnett AO from map series L-7014, sheet
6442-III, Ba Long District, Quang Tri Province. Authors'
collection.

Chapter 32

Firebase Barnett: In The Rear With The Gear

After a few days in the rear, the medics at the battalion aid station performed minor surgery on my toe. The swelling had gone down, and they could see that the impact from the heavy ammo box had driven a sliver from my toenail into the flesh beneath the nail that had become infected because of my neglect. The sliver was easily, although very painfully, removed and I was given light duty through August 20.

During this time, I tried to avoid the area around battalion headquarters, the lair of Sergeant Major Sabalauski and the new XO, Major Gunter Seibert. Late one afternoon, a man with an arm wound and I were walking past headquarters on the way to the battalion E-Club when we were challenged by Seibert. He wanted to know why we were in the rear, and before I could say anything, my friend loudly replied, "Wounded, sir!" His arm was bandaged and so was my foot, so Seibert turned and walked away without another word. I felt guilty for a while at being placed in the same category as the combat wounded, but I got over it.

August 13–September 5

We began to hear stories in the rear that the new Firebase Barnett AO had become what is known as a hot AO, meaning that there was almost constant contact with the enemy. The Veghel AO in April and May was a hot AO.

On August 13, the first day of the operation, Alpha Company found two dead NVA killed by artillery on their LZ and received incoming 60mm mortar fire while they were still on the LZ. The air support called in for Alpha Company received small arms fire. Alpha also discovered a bunker complex near their LZ.

In another part of the AO, Recon Platoon engaged an unknown number of NVA in a sharp firefight that resulted in four NVA killed with one O-Deuce trooper killed and three wounded. All this on the first day before the battalion even had a chance to spread out.

The next day was quiet, but the fifteenth started out with a bang: a white team took small arms fire and a crewman was wounded. Rumor had it that he was hit in the anus with a .51 caliber round and survived. A pink team spotted a group of bunkers with a lot of fighting positions and Bravo Company saw eight of the enemy at a distance moving away from them. Firebase Barnett received twelve incoming mortar rounds, six of which exploded inside the wire perimeter. Elements of Bravo and Delta Company received mortar fire resulting in five US wounded and one KCS wounded. It began to look as if the O-Deuce had kicked over an NVA anthill.

In the early morning hours of August 16, 2nd and 3rd Platoons Bravo Company and 3rd Platoon Delta Company were in their NDPs within sight of each other on a ridge at Hill 390 (YD 172319). A determined enemy launched three very strong ground attacks against the combined positions of Bravo and Delta Companies; all three assaults were driven back with heavy losses to the attacking NVA. The O-Deuce troopers named the place "Comeback Ridge" because the NVA came at them the same way all three times, getting their asses kicked each time. The results of that bitter fight were one US killed and eleven wounded, while the NVA lost fourteen killed in the assaults and twenty killed by the heavy artillery support.

That same day, Charlie Company landed at a hot LZ, coming under RPG, small arms, grenade, and satchel charge fire. Charlie lost two wounded while the NVA lost one killed and one POW. After driving the enemy off, Charlie discovered a lot of ammo and weapons abandoned by the fleeing NVA soldiers.

After a couple of quiet days, August 19 saw heavy combat with the enemy, again on Comeback Ridge. Bravo Company encountered an NVA company-sized element and pushed them back off the ridge. During this fight, Bravo had one killed and five wounded while the NVA lost fifteen killed by small arms fire, ten killed by artillery, and one POW captured. It seemed like the NVA just couldn't learn their lesson about Bravo Company and Comeback Ridge.

On August 19, Charlie Company had been humping hard all day down a long ridge looking for and finding bunker complexes, all abandoned. Bruce Scott remembers that day and the early morning hours of August 20. In an e-mail dated May 25, 2012, he wrote: *"I was a short timer and had only two weeks left to go home. At that time, the 101st would not take people out of the field until they had four days left. We had been humping on a ridgeline for a while and it was starting to get dark. We had passed one LZ and were trying to make it to another. It was getting [very] dark so the decision was made to back track to the last LZ....I woke up Dave Kingery at 11:00 pm for his guard duty. I gave him my watch. I think it was about midnight [when] I heard three large explosions. I later learned [that there] were three 81mm mortar fins [that] were found the next day. I got up and expecting an attack tried to fire off the claymore mines. I remember clicking them, but nothing seemed to happen. I suddenly realized that I could not breathe very well. I had a sucking chest wound and from shrapnel and [sic] which I still have pieces in my body today. I remember going towards a bright light [and] I thought I was dieing [sic] and was going to heaven but the light turned out to be a medivac helicopter."* The sudden attack killed two and wounded seventeen troops from Charlie Company.

Bob Noffsinger said he was walking point for the company on August 19 and the KCS called Hien was his slack man. They were moving very cautiously because evidence of the NVA's presence was everywhere: wide, well-worn trails, tree markings, abandoned campsites. They were relieved from point because they were being too cautious and not moving fast enough to suit the company commander. They stopped at an LZ for a quick resupply and then moved on.

Charlie Company had been ordered to set up their NDP at a certain terrain feature, but in the late afternoon it was realized that they weren't going to make it before dark. Noff said that they backtracked and set up their NDP in the trees near an LZ (YD 177328) they had recently passed. Noffsinger says he recalls there were foxholes already dug around the edges of the LZ.

He remembers that the attack came with no warning because mortar rounds, unlike artillery, make very little sound as they drop toward the ground. He told me that all three rounds were "tree bursts," meaning that the explosions were in the tops of the trees above the NDP so the shrapnel exploded downward, hitting men who were asleep on the ground under the trees. Noffsinger said he received a very small wound to the back of his head but no other injury.

He also remembers that there was complete pandemonium on the ground while they figured out if they were under ground attack or not. The wounded were screaming for help and the survivors had to look for them in nearly complete darkness under the trees. Bob says that it seemed to take the dust-off helicopters a very long time to reach them.

For some reason, the dust offs would not land on the LZ but chose to hover over the NDP. The strong rotor wash began to set off trip flares, which led to a tragedy. A seriously wounded man was on the hoist being pulled up to the helicopter when one or two trip flares ignited. The pilot either thought they were coming under ground attack or lost his night vision, but someone aboard the medevac ship cut the cable with the wounded man still suspended in the air and the man fell to the ground. Noffsinger says there was a rumor that the man died because of the fall when he otherwise would have survived. He doesn't know for sure if the incident just described occurred but he believes it did. Too many other men said they saw it for it to be completely unfounded.

The story about survivors finding three 81mm mortar fins the next day started a rumor that persists to this day that Charlie had been hit by shells fired from US mortars on Firebase Barnett. We heard the rumor back at Camp Eagle, and most of us believed it to be true. A man from another company, while in his NDP near Charlie Company, says he heard three shots fired from a mortar tube on a hill not near Firebase Barnett but that information is not well known. There were some hard feelings towards Echo Company's mortar platoon but I don't think anything ever came of it.

However, Noffsinger says he personally saw the three mortar fin assemblies the next day, and they had markings on them that led him to believe they were of US manufacture. He brought up the point that the NVA mortar tubes were 82mm, allowing them to fire 81mm ammunition, which they often did using captured US rounds.

In an e-mail dated November 7, 2012, James Brinker said he remembers *"Some Charlie guys came to the Echo company bar to confront Echo mortar 'forkers' about the incident. Denials were made and no fights took place."*

During a phone conversation in November 2012, Tom Boyce, a member of Recon Platoon, told me he heard the NVA fire the three mortar rounds and that he had a good idea where the rounds came from. Another man in Recon had the radio but wouldn't relinquish it so Boyce could call in the information about the NVA mortar position.

I came back to the field the next day on a log bird headed to Firebase Barnett. It was a long flight, as Barnett was in Quang Tri Province, a good distance northwest (66 kilometers) from Camp Eagle. As we approached the Barnett LZ, the pilot suddenly turned away and I could see explosions on the firebase itself. It seems the NVA were paying their respects to the troops on Barnett with 82mm calling cards. When the explosions stopped, the bird darted in and had barely touched down before I was out the door and running towards some sand bags piled at the edge of the LZ.

As I stood there, I could smell high explosives mixed in with helicopter exhaust, just like I remembered from that first day on Hill 714. The **pathfinder** in charge of the LZ told me to get ready to dash because another helicopter was coming in to carry me and some others out to Charlie Company's position. The bird didn't really land but stayed 'light on the skids' until we got aboard, and I didn't even have time to plant my butt on the deck before the pilot jerked the bird into the air, put the nose down, and hauled ass. Apparently, that pilot had come under mortar fire before.

I got off the helicopter at Charlie Company's LZ and went to find 1st Platoon. Almost immediately, I noticed a change in the way the men were behaving. First Platoon was normally very alert, with good dispersal and noise discipline. However, on that day they were sitting in groups in the open talking among themselves, and I saw several men just staring off into space. Evidently, the mortar attack had done great damage to 1st Platoon's morale.

For the next few days, Charlie Company moved short distances and did not patrol aggressively: they just didn't seem to care. We gradually moved from the area of the mortar attack into the low foothills overlooking the Khe Ta Laou river valley from the south. It's a good thing the NVA didn't follow up the mortar attack with a ground attack because they might have done a great deal of damage to Charley Company in its demoralized state.

The NVA continued pounding away at Firebase Barnett and the other companies of the O-Deuce. On August 22, Barnett received eleven rounds of 60mm mortar fire. LTC Shay, moving around the AO in his **Charlie-Charlie bird** spotted four NVA in the open. He called 155mm artillery fire from Company B, 2nd Battalion, 11th Artillery. The fire was accurate and killed two of the NVA.

Alpha Company engaged six or seven enemy soldiers with six US wounded. D company was in contact with an NVA force of unknown size off and on for three hours, leaving one US wounded. The first medevac to respond to Delta's location was heavily damaged by small arms fire and had to sit down on Firebase Barnett.

The next day saw Delta Company pelted with thirty to fifty rounds of mortar and RPG fire; two men received very minor wounds. Alpha Company fired at eight NVA at two-hundred-fifty-meter range with no results.

Firebase Barnett took another beating on August 29 when they received ten rounds of direct fire from a 75mm recoilless rifle. Delta Company had one man wounded by friendly fire while on an OP, and they also engaged an enemy squad with five US wounded and one NVA killed.

On August 30, the O-Deuce turned the Firebase Barnett AO over to the 4th Battalion 3rd ARVN Regiment and returned to Camp Eagle for a training stand down. On that day, while the rest of Charlie Company was being extracted, they came up one helicopter short of enough to extract the whole company. Five other men and I were stuck on an LZ by ourselves with no help anywhere close while we waited for a bird to come and get us. One of the other men left behind was a staff sergeant who had come to the O-Deuce from the LRRPs. He told me he thought he heard movement on our back trail and began to fire M-79 rounds down the hillside. Pretty soon I also heard movement; it seemed like the sounds were coming up the trail toward us. I began to fire my M-16 down the hillside toward the sounds. The other four men were on the other side of the LZ; they didn't seem interested in what was going on.

Finally, we heard the thudding sound of big rotors as the bird approached the LZ. Someone threw a smoke grenade and the helicopter came right on in. The staff sergeant and I fired down the hill until the last minute, then we dashed across the LZ and threw ourselves onto the cargo deck and the pilot immediately took to the air. I have a photo of myself sitting in the helicopter with an ear-to-ear grin right after we left that LZ; it's overexposed though, so I couldn't use it in this manuscript.

I didn't know it at the time, but a US Army journalist named John Del Vecchio was traveling with the O-Deuce during the Barnett Operation. Del Vecchio later wrote a great novel called *The 13th Valley*, using the O-Deuce and the Barnett Operation as the basis for the story.

All in all, the 5-O-Deuce did very well during the Barnett Operation. We fought against the 9th NVA Regiment's 1st, 2nd, and 3rd Battalions and left the enemy with about a hundred and thirty casualties while the O-Deuce's total casualties were only sixty-nine. We destroyed or captured many weapons, ammo, grenades, and satchel charges and quite a few bunkers and crew served weapons positions.

Operation Texas Star officially ended on September 5 while the O-Deuce was at Camp Eagle. The results for Operation Texas Star were thirty-seven US killed, two hundred and ninety wounded, and two hundred eighty-eight medevac'd. The NVA losses were two hundred twenty-eight killed, sixty-one killed by artillery, and two POWs captured. Since I don't believe body counts should be used to measure the progress of a war, I include them only to show the ferocity of the fighting endured by both the O-Deuce and the NVA.

The battalion was at Camp Eagle seven days for "refresher training. "I don't remember a whole lot of training going on, but I do recall a lot of partying. The juicers drank as much beer and whiskey as they could stand while the heads produced enough smoke from burning **dew** (marijuana) to create a light fog over the battalion area. I know I drank my share of cold and lukewarm beer and paid for it with a couple of mega hangovers. We were all glad to be alive, and this was the only way we had to celebrate.

One night during this stand down, the NVA attacked the O-Deuce battalion area with 122mm rockets. I had been drinking beer steadily since the training day ended and was well under the influence. When the first rocket came in, it didn't really register. The next one was closer, and this time I heard the awful screeching, whooshing sound the rockets made just before impact. I hit the ground and then crawled into a nearby tent as if the canvas roof would stop the rocket. By that time in my tour, I knew that if a rocket, bullet, or RPG had your name on it, it would kill you no matter what you did, so I just lay there under a cot. I don't remember how long the attack lasted.

The next morning, I found a huge crater only about twenty meters from where I had taken shelter in the tent. The rocket had severely damaged the four-hole latrine behind the Charlie Company dayroom/bar, so I had to go into the brushy gully behind the latrine to do my morning business.

In a letter written on September 3, I said: *"We will be back out in the field in about 3 days...will be in the area between Firebase Veghel and Firebase Bastogne...probably stay in that area during the monsoon season."*

Chapter 33

A September To Remember

September 6-September 27, 1970

On September 6, the battalion moved back into the field and Operation Jefferson Glen began. The O-Deuce was inserted into an AO around Firebase Normandy at YD690017, overlooking the Song (river) Huu Trach. The new AO proved to be pretty much a dry hole. First Platoon Bravo Company spotted four NVA in an open area probably taking a sun bath and trying to dry out. Bravo called artillery in on the poor guys, interrupting their sun bath and killing three of them.

There was no further contact, so on September 11 the battalion moved to Firebase Veghel. According to the 2nd/502nd Infantry Unit History for 1970, we went back to Veghel "with the mission of conducting saturation patrols in the area while closing the firebase for the monsoon season."

Also on the eleventh, I sent a short note home: "We are back in the field now. It's [sic] been raining every day. I guess the monsoons are not far off. I sure do dread all that rain." I also asked for more catsup and pudding cups in the next package. I was tired of Charlie rats and could hardly get them down. That would change in about three weeks, after we went into the A Shau Valley.

Sometime between the eleventh and the twenty-fifth, Charlie Company was moved to Veghel to secure it while it was being dismantled. During the spring and summer campaigns, Veghel had been developed into a formidable firebase. The 326th Engineers had used bulldozers to cut deep, wide trenches into the orange clay of the firebase. Using huge "flying cranes" and CH-47 Chinooks, the engineers had airlifted large prefabricated bunkers and placed them in the ditches. After waterproofing, the bunkers were covered with several feet of earth. Most of these bunkers had already been removed, but a couple remained, one of them in 1st Platoon's sector.

One day, it began pouring down rain, rapidly soaking us and everything we owned and turning the orange clay into orange mud. Leaving a couple of poor guys out in the rain on guard duty, the rest of us crowded into the one remaining bunker. It was not much better than being outside, but there were a few dry spots. It rained all that day and all through the night. When I woke up next morning I didn't hear any rain and, dragging my rucksack, I went outside. I was astonished; there was not a cloud in the sky and the sun was already hot.

September 25

The NVA avoided contact of any kind through September 25. On that day, Recon made a CA from LZ Anne to Firebase Tennessee to secure it so an artillery battery could be put in place. Recon was ordered to patrol down the long ridge finger on which the firebase was built to make sure it was secure enough for the artillery and a company from the 1/327th Infantry to be brought in. Delta Company and Bravo Company also made CAs that day. The weather continued to be cool, wet, and foggy.

Later that afternoon, 1st Platoon moved to grid square YD532087, setting up our NDP at the head of a shallow gully running down to the Song Bo. In the "Daily Journal" for that day, 1st Platoon's field strength was listed as thirty-three grunts, one FO, and one sniper.

After dark, the antipersonnel radar on Veghel picked up movement from two or more NVA about four hundred meters out from the wire perimeter. Mortars were dropped in the area with unknown results. A few weeks later, 1st Platoon would be tasked with securing a similar radar unit on a rain-soaked, leech-covered hill near Firebase Strike.

The Strike Force, as of September 25, had four hundred twenty-two men present for duty in the field with an additional strength of seventy-eight men from the additional units (B 1st/327th Infantry and B 1st/501st Infantry) that were OPCON to our battalion.

September 26

On September 26, Charlie Company moved to YD532024 at the site of closed Firebase Blaze. There is a large field about three kilometers square just across the Rao Nai River from Blaze. Division had designated this place as the jumping-off point for operation Apache Snow back on May 10, 1969. This was a large operation with the entire 3rd Brigade (3rd-187th, 2nd-501st, and 1st-506th) CA'd into the A Shau Valley in one giant air movement. Third Brigade was reinforced by the 2nd-1st and 4th-1st ARVN Regiments. All this led to the famous (infamous?) battle of Dong Ap Bia (Hill 937) with all three battalions participating in the pitched battle to overrun the hill.

I didn't know it then but my future brother-in-law was in Alpha Company 1st-506th and participated in the fight to take Hill 937. Even today, forty-three years after the battle, he prefers not to talk about it.

Anyway, we were still fighting the weather. The weather report (item #28 in the "Daily Journal") for September 26 read: "Visibility less than one mile, ceiling less than 500 feet with heavy rains." I already knew about the rain; I'd been wet and cold for the past two or three days.

Item #13 in the same document says: "LTC Shay Bn CO conducted conference with company Commanders and Staff on move for today and tomorrow. All Units will receive rations for a four-day supply today. A decision will be made on the 30 [sic] if we are going to remain at FSB Whip and be resupplied on the 1st of October."

Also, on the twenty-sixth, the engineer mine sweep team found three Chicom claymores equipped with pressure devices on QL 547 between Veghel and Bastogne. They were blown in place.

On September 26, I explained about the coming monsoon season to my folks: "The reason I write so much about the monsoons is that military operations slow down a great deal during the rains. It's impossible to use any of the dirt roads and a few of the paved ones; and it's also hard for birds [helicopters] to fly."

I also mentioned that I only had a hundred days left on my twelve-month tour and told my mother to start crossing off the days on the short-timers' calendar I had sent her.

September 27

On the twenty-seventh, the cold, wet, miserable weather continued. Entry #4 in the "Daily Journal" states: "I H hour 1000H, another weather decision will be made within the next hour." Battalion evidently checked with the Air Force's weather service because entry #5 reads: "Operations on a 24-hour hold. All units will remain in place and establish local security."

The next entry, #6, was a message from Battalion to units: "*Maj. Kite Bn S-3 to all units: we have a 24-hour delay, remain in place, keep all traffic down radios and don't say anything about the operation on clear transmission.*"

Of course, the brass changed their mind and sent all three of Charlie Company's platoons to different locations. It was creepy humping through the rain and low fog, but we only had to move about a klick to our new positions. We made no contact, and I thought: "The NVA aren't as dumb as we are; they aren't out walking around in the rain and mud like us."

A photo mission was run over the area of the A Shau where we were to assault if the weather ever cleared (I hoped it never did). The photo recon showed two large fields under cultivation, one with a fence around it; another cleared area with at least one bunker visible; a north-south trail with several camouflaged bunkers; and, the most dangerous, a 12.7mm (.51 caliber) machine gun in a camouflaged position. Air strikes were ordered on these targets. The brass did not tell us about any of this; I guess it was just too secret for the guys actually going into the area to know about.

We all sat waiting, in various stages of discomfort, for the weather too clear. None of us wanted to go on this operation; some of us had vague premonitions that something would go wrong.

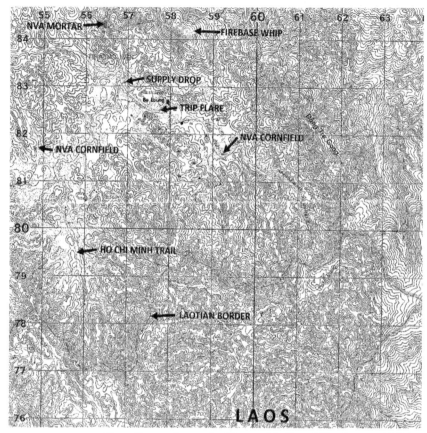

Southeastern A Shau Valley/Firebase Whip AO on the border with Laos and Vietnam from map series L-7014 sheet 6441-II, A Sap District, Thua Thien Province. Author's collection.

Chapter 34

The A Shau Valley: And The Rain Came

September 28–October 4, 1970

On the morning of the twenty-eighth, I crawled out of my wet poncho liner and saw that it was not raining and the low ceiling had lifted a little. As I ate my C-ration breakfast, I noticed that the food we had received on the 26th was already half gone. Word eventually came down to platoon level that the move would go as scheduled and we all packed our rucksacks carefully. I filled all six of my canteens from a nearby stream. I didn't have any iodine pills to sanitize the water and I drank it just as it came from the stream. In a few weeks, I would become very sick from drinking water from a polluted stream.

At about 1130 hours, the slicks came for us and we got aboard as quickly as we could. After we took off, we flew directly west down the Rao (river) Nho Valley and passed over abandoned Firebase Canon. There are several different words in the Vietnamese language describing the type/size of a water feature. Among them are Khe, Ngoc, Ngon, Rach, Rao, and Song describing everything from a rivulet to a major river.

The slicks then gained altitude to clear some medium-sized hills, flying just under the grey cloud ceiling. The birds made a couple of slow turns and we seemed to be heading back to the east.

I was at my usual spot in the doorway, so I could see that we were flying low over a narrow, elephant-grass-covered valley. The grass was an incredible bright green color and covered the whole valley floor. Looking to the front, I didn't see the right door gunner unlimber his M-60 and aim it forward. He began to fire and I jumped as if I'd received an electric shock and the hearing in my right ear disappeared instantly. I mean I could hear absolutely no sound from that side. It was as if the ear wasn't there. Looking out the door, I saw that the muzzle of the machine gun was about two feet from my right ear.

Right about then, an AH-1G Cobra gunship pulled up beside my slick. He was fully equipped with a 40mm automatic grenade launcher, 7.62mm mini-gun, and rocket pods full of 2.75-inch rockets painted white. He kept station with us about a hundred feet away, and I could clearly see the pilot and the gunner sitting in tandem inside the narrow fuselage. As I watched, he began firing rockets from both pods. Each time a rocket was launched, a bright red puff of smoke shot out from the rocket pod. Seeing this, I got the door gunner's attention and asked if we had a hot LZ. He shook his head and shouted that the red smoke meant the gunner was firing rockets containing flechette rounds.

According to Webster's Collegiate Dictionary, *flechette* is a French word meaning 'arrow'. It is also defined as a "dart-shaped projectile that is clustered in an explosive warhead, fired as a missile from an airplane." Whatever the definition, it's a scary and very deadly weapon. I have heard grunts tell stories of finding gooks literally nailed to trees by the little darts. I never saw anything like that, but I guess it could have happened.

The slick started to slow, and soon the nose came up and we made a light landing on the skids. As soon as the six men were out of the aircraft, it roared away into the grey sky. I saw that the LZ was a thousand-pound bomb crater that had blown down the elephant grass to a radius of about a hundred feet from the center of the crater.

The crater was nine or ten feet deep and twenty to twenty-five feet wide. It was already partly filled with water even though the B-52s had dropped their bombs only yesterday afternoon.

On a side note, I believe I have located that very same crater on Google Earth. It is now filled with water and being used as a duck or fish pond by the local Montagnards. I found the crater by locating the grid square where we landed on the tactical map for that area. I then compared the terrain features on the map with the same terrain features on the Google Earth satellite photo and there it was. I have used tactical maps and satellite photos to locate many of the places the O-Deuce occupied during 1970.

Each time a slick landed, the men would move to the edge of the blasted area until a complete perimeter was formed. This caused some confusion because the randomly scattered men had to be reorganized back into their squads and platoons.

First Platoon was ordered to move in a southeasterly direction toward some low hills rising out of the sea of elephant grass. Grunts hated to move through elephant grass; it was full of bugs and snakes and you couldn't see more than a few feet around you. The worst thing about contact with the grass was the little, razor-sharp silicone teeth that grow on the edges of the big leaves. Point men dreaded walking through the stuff because they had to break trail and if they didn't roll their sleeves down and wear gloves, they would be sliced to pieces.

As we pushed through the grass, I noticed that the stuff was disappearing, replaced by shorter grass and low scrub brush. We suddenly stopped and word filtered down the file that the point had found a large dead animal. We started moving again and I passed the animal. It had grayish-brown hair and looked like an elk or a very large deer with big ears like a mule. There was no way to tell how it was killed without moving the damn thing and we didn't have time.

As I walked away, it began to rain. At first it was just a few scattered drops that became big, fat raindrops that made a *splat* when they hit the top of my steel pot. Now that the slicks and Cobras had all left, it was very quiet except for the falling rain.

There was no contact with the enemy that day, but Delta Company found two small bunkers containing NVA uniforms, ammo, and food. Next to the bunkers was a cultivated field with corn growing two to five feet tall and not ready for harvest. When Delta approached the area, they saw ten to fifteen enemy troops running in all directions. No fire was exchanged with the fleeing enemy.

Alpha Company spotted a lone NVA about six hundred meters away, wearing a dark uniform and carrying a rucksack. He was traveling from east to west coming from a wood line.

Charlie Company climbed the low hill next to the dead animal and set up an NDP at YC574824, overlooking the sea of elephant grass on the valley floor. It was still raining like hell when I rolled up in my poncho and poncho liner and tried to go to sleep.

September 29

When I woke up on the twenty-ninth, I faced more of the same: rain, cold, fog, and growing hunger. We were almost out of food and it didn't look like any log birds would be able to fly anytime soon.

At about 0700 hours that morning, the NVA pelted Firebase Whip with twenty-six rounds of 60mm mortar fire. The attack resulted in four US wounded and one ARVN wounded. The 81mm mortars on Firebase Whip tried counter-battery fire but couldn't stop the barrage. Finally, a pink team managed to get into the area under the clouds and locate the mortar position. The Cobra fired it up, killing one NVA and destroying the mortar.

We moved off the hill, passing the dead deer (which was now giving off a foul odor) to YC577821 without incident. We saw absolutely no sign of the enemy, although elements from other companies were finding bunkers, corn fields, and some supplies and ammo.

The weather was so bad that the FAC had to cancel a scheduled airstrike by fighter-bombers. Recon Platoon reported that the dog from their scout dog team set off a booby-trapped claymore mine and was killed. Ranger Team Orlando, an LRRP team from Lima Company 75th Rangers, found a cultivated cornfield and one NVA plus two 60mm booby traps. In the most unusual contact of the day, Team Orlando spotted an unidentified helicopter landing in an area known to be occupied by the NVA. There were four other Ranger Teams in the area, but they reported nothing like that.

We had all heard the rumors about NVA helicopters in the **A Shau Valley**, but I had never seen one and I didn't know anyone who had. The helicopters sighted by other units were of Russian make; they didn't look like an UH-1 Huey helicopter in any way. The NVA had their huge Base Area 611 on the west side of the A Shau just over the Laotian border; anything was possible in the "Aw Shit" Valley.

In the afternoon, Delta Company found eight small bunkers with reinforced overhead cover. A bamboo footbridge was located next to the bunkers, spanning a small stream. The bunkers and bridge were all destroyed.

In the late afternoon, 1st and 2nd platoons and the company CP were ordered to move to YC577825, about a six hundred-meter march through the rain and fog. I just couldn't believe it; I had never seen so much rain in my life. Everything was flooded: the trails, the small creeks, even the hilltops. If this was indeed the monsoon, I could see why it was dreaded by everyone, especially line grunts. We had to live in it for however long it lasted.

When we arrived at our new location, I saw that the NDP's perimeter would span a large trail or primitive road heading northeast out of the valley. I went out with two other guys to set up a trip flare across the trail. It was almost fully dark and we had to hurry. I found a place to tie off the trip wire and string it across the trail. I strung it about a foot above the ground and found a small tree stump to secure the flare. One of the guys had gone down trail from me for security, and he began to move back towards the NDP just as I was setting the pin on the flare. Because of the fading light, I had my face close to the top of the flare and was just letting go of the pin when he backed into the wire, pulling out the pin.

The flare went off with a popping sound, and the top of the flare hit me right between the eyes. The magnesium went off just as I jerked my face away. I smelled my eyebrows and lashes burning, so I ran straight into a bomb crater filled chest-high with water and ducked my head under water. My eyes were swollen almost shut and someone came into the crater, pulled me out, and led me back to the perimeter. By this time, I could not see.

The CO, who was really pissed off, came up to see why the flare had gone off. I could hear someone explaining that somebody had accidentally tripped the wire just as I was setting the pin. The CO was concerned because the burning flare had given away our position to any NVA who happened to be watching.

The CP medic came up and led me to a tree which was sheltering the CP group and sat me down. He said there was nothing he could do until daylight. Believe me, it was a very long night, sitting there under the tree in total darkness; I didn't know if my eyes were permanently damaged or not. And so, I sat there listening to the rain tapping on my steel pot, wondering if I was blind.

September 30

Next morning, I realized that I could see the dark grey turning to a lighter grey and I knew my eyes were going to be all right. The medic came to check and told me that the hair around my eyes was all burnt off and the skin was blistered by my eyes and forehead. While the medic was looking me over, the CO walked by and gave me a dirty look but didn't say anything.

The CP's RTO was a friend of mine, and we stood talking for a few minutes while everyone got ready for the first move of the day. The RTO told me that between 0030 and 0130 hours, he had lost all contact by radio with the battalion TOC on Firebase Whip. Later I found out that the TOC had lost commo with all the line company's in the battalion.

I didn't worry about breakfast because I was out of food except for a couple of cans of peanut butter, jelly, and C-ration crackers. No one else had any food, either.

The battalion TOC on Firebase Whip received a weather warning from 1st Brigade: "thunder storms ceiling 300 scattered, 500 ft broken, 1000 ft overcast, visibility ½ mile winds 15 to 35 knots."

It was more of the same and I was starting to get hungry.

Battalion sent an air request to 1st Brigade for extraction of the O-Deuce and supporting units, but with the weather the way it was, that was more of a wish than reality. There was no contact with the enemy that day. Alpha Company found some hooches containing one dead NVA; Delta Company found a cornfield with a one-meter high fence around the field, with rodent traps around the perimeter of the field. Charlie Company found some sticks to the side of a trail arranged in a way that suggested it was a signal for the NVA. We moved to three different locations that day but did not find any enemy troops. We returned to the NDP where we'd spent a night before. This was dangerous because the NVA like to set booby traps or set an ambush at old NDPs. We checked this one carefully and, finding it clear, set up for the night.

However, the NVA were obviously smarter than us: they were not running around in the rain and mud with no food. I was starting to run out of water, too. The streams were overflowing and very muddy so we didn't want to drink that water. That night we set up our poncho shelters in a way that would allow us to catch rainwater. It was a little dirty but not nearly as bad as getting water from a stream.

A request was put in for three log birds to be on standby at the O-Deuce pad at 0800 hours just in case the weather cleared enough for a resupply.

October 1

Early on the morning of October 1, I woke up and saw that it was still raining. I began to scrounge around in my empty rucksack hoping to find an overlooked can of food. Looking around, I saw everyone else doing the same. I managed to find a packet of instant hot chocolate, instant coffee, and two packets of coffee creamer. We had an abundance of water now, so I heated a canteen cup full on my C-ration can stove and stirred in all the ingredients for boonie rat hot chocolate.

Taking the first swallow, I felt the hot drink trickle down my throat into my empty stomach. It felt and tasted good and I shared the drink with the other men at my position. We all stood around sipping from the cup and waiting for orders.

Word was passed to take down our poncho hooches and get ready to move out. We began to move slowly, passing through the thick vegetation on a narrow trail. I remember listening to the billions of raindrops falling on billions of leaves. Close by, you could hear the rain hitting individual leaves with a splat, all of it blending together into a dull roar.

We moved up a slope for two or three hundred meters as the rain slowed and finally quit. The file came to a halt just short of a small knoll (YC 579819), and we took up defensive positions along the trail. I knelt in the brush facing away from the trail and waited. The news was passed from man to man that we were waiting for a log bird attempting to penetrate the thick clouds and fog covering the mountaintops. I could hear the roar of a river down in the steep-walled valley to my front, but there were no other sounds and it was eerily quiet.

I tried not to dwell on my growling stomach or the thought of the food carried in the belly of the helicopter, but I couldn't. After an endless wait the bad news came: there would be no resupply today. The helicopters could not safely break through the clouds to get to us, and we'd have to go hungry for another night. We simply did an about face and went back down the hill into a wide gully, crossed a small stream, and went up the opposite hillside to our NDP just southwest of the peak of Hill 606.

It was quiet all night except for the rain pounding down on our poncho shelters. The summary from the "Daily Journal" for that day stated: "I 2-502 Infantry continued operations vic. FSB Whip with no enemy contact. Resupply missions are unable to reach the units due to bad weather, and supplies are running low. Plains [sic] are being made to extract the battalion when the weather clears."

October 2

The next morning, we immediately moved from the NDP site to a position at YC 570827. When we arrived, we set up our DDP and wondered what was going on. Very suddenly, the clouds opened and sunlight poured through. All of us unrolled our bedrolls and spread our poncho liners any place we could to catch the sun. I took off my shirt and draped it over a bush, watching as steam began to rise from the soggy garment.

The guy next to me had his transistor tuned to AFVN radio at a low volume. I could not believe my ears when I heard the Beatles' hit song "Here Comes the Sun" pouring from the small radio speaker. I sat there and grinned, enjoying the music and the sunshine hitting my bare chest.

Right about then, I heard the thudding roar of a Huey's big rotor blades beating the air. Jumping to my feet, I craned my neck looking for the helicopter, thinking we were going to be resupplied. Then I heard what sounded like loud speakers broadcasting a message in the Vietnamese language. The Huey passed almost directly over us and I realized it was a "psyops" (psychological operations) bird and not a log bird.

I was very disappointed, but then I thought: "If a psyops bird can get through the clouds, then so can a resupply bird." I mentioned this to the guys at my position and we all felt a little better, but unfortunately, it didn't happen. Shortly after that, the clouds closed in again and the sunlight disappeared.

During my research, I noted the weather report for October 2: "(U) Weather I Corps 020900-030900, thunder storms 500 feet overcast, visibility ½ mile, winds is to 35 knots (about 53 MPH), from NE 2"-4" rain."

Another message regarding the coming resupply drop on October 3 states: "Message from the Bde S-3 (operations), the rations drop has been approved, load is 1,000 lbs. and will be coming down at 35 miles and hr. Want to know if there is any other place than FSB Whip to drop rations? Maj. Kite will call Bde back."

It rained on and off all through the day, and Charlie Company changed positions twice, humping hungrily through the rain. We reached our NDP site at YC 574824. It was a hill we had stayed on before overlooking the elephant grass valley. The information that we were to be resupplied by parachute drop from an Air Force C-130 was passed down from the platoon CP.

We all went to our guard positions in anticipation of getting something to eat the next day.

At the end of the "Daily Journal" for that day, I found this entry: "From Bde: reference air drop: Zone A TOT (time on target) 0815H, YC 57008272 approaching from 270 degrees (west), will make two passes, dropping out 2 containers on each pass. Zone B TOT 0845H at YC 59258771 approach from 290 (northwest) degrees making 3 passes, dropping 2 containers on each pass except last pass which only 1 container will drop. Call sign Terry 804."

The above message was copied from the "Daily Journal" intact including all grammar and spelling errors.

October 3

During the early morning hours of the third, the NVA began heavy jamming of the battalion radio net. After the jamming stopped, Battalion received word from the Air Force that the parachute drops were going to be delayed because of radar problems aboard the C-130 making the drops.

The first parachute drop was made at 0900 and that bundle plus another one was recovered by Alpha Company. The rest of the resupply did not come in until 1545, and again Alpha Company recovered both bundles from that drop. There is no mention in the "Daily Journal" of any companies receiving resupply on that day except for Alpha; Bravo Company, securing Firebase Whip, received their resupply from Pony 74, a regular log bird.

In fact, my memory of that day is that Charlie Company did not receive resupply until the next day, October 4. One of my letters home says we received our air dropped rations on the fourth, the same day we were extracted to Camp Eagle.

I also found an entry stating that the brigade commander had notified LTC Shay that he was considering bringing the O-Deuce back to Camp Eagle for a twenty-four to forty-eight-hour rest. LTC Shay replied that the stand down would be necessary because the battalion was in bad shape physically.

Late that afternoon, Charlie Company moved to YC 578826 and set up an NDP between a small river and a trail leading to the abandoned village of Be Luong. The area was covered with short grass and low brush, so the captain said we couldn't put up poncho hooches to sleep under. His reasoning was that the bushes were not tall enough to conceal the ponchos from any passing NVA, but he later relented when it began pouring down rain. I don't remember who I shared my hooch with, but we slept back to back under our poncho liners, hoping the shared body heat would dry us out a little.

October 4

When I woke up on the fourth, I realized that it wasn't raining and my fatigues were half dry; my boots and socks were still soaking wet, though. When I stood up and tried to walk my feet were so sore that it was difficult to walk without limping.

Anyway, I gingerly walked over to some bushes near my sleeping hooch to relieve myself. When I looked down and began to unbutton my fatigue pants, I saw fresh blood stains on the crotch. I remember thinking "What the fuck is this?! I hope a fuckin' leech didn't get me." When I pulled myself out, I saw two little bite marks on the end of my penis, still bleeding a little. I knew they were bites from a land leech, so I finished my business, went back to the hooch, and got a canteen. I walked back into the bushes and washed myself very thoroughly. I didn't tell anyone about my "wounds" because I would have never heard the end of it.

A little later that morning, we were told that supplies were to be air-dropped to us and that the weather showed signs of clearing up. This cheered us up considerably because we were going to get to eat and we might be extracted from the 'Aw Shit' Valley.

At around 0900 hours, we were told that the Air Force C-130 was inbound and to try and spot the parachutes as they broke through the clouds. A few minutes later, I heard the peculiar sound of turbo-prop engines droning away above the clouds. The company RTO suddenly shouted, *"Load dropped, they've dropped the load."* Anxiously, I scanned the sky looking for the pallet. I heard a faint whistling sound that quickly grew louder and became a loud screech.

Suddenly the pallet broke out of the low clouds, and I saw what was causing the sound. There were two parachutes, both with broken shroud lines that had caused the canopies to collapse. The pallet was dropping very quickly, but I followed it all the way to the ground, where it hit with a loud "whump."

I told the LT that I would lead a patrol to recover the food before the gooks got to it. I took off and several men followed me including Bob Noffsinger who had returned to the field after recovering from his wounds. We quickly found the pallet buried about a foot into the mud on a small sandbar in the middle of a stream.

The impact had jarred a few cases of LRRPs loose and we all grabbed as many as we could carry and started back. In this case, LRRPs were the rations the patrol teams (in our case, the 75th Ranger Regiment) carried; they were dehydrated and very light.

On the way back, we met a patrol from another platoon on their way to the pallet. I told them to just follow our trail and they would find the rations within thirty meters. We brought back seven or eight cases and dropped them in a pile. I quickly cut one open with my knife, grabbed the first two packets I could reach, and got the hell out of the way.

I was lucky: I had managed to grab chili and beans and chicken and rice, my favorite LRRP meals. It seemed to take an eternity for the water to boil. When it finally did, I broke open the chili and beans, poured in the water, and resealed the pouch. It normally took about five minutes for an LRRP ration to absorb all the water, but I was **HUNGRY!** and I couldn't wait that long: I opened the pouch after about three minutes, so the beans were still crunchy as I gobbled it down. After four days without food, it tasted like a filet mignon steak dinner with all the trimmings.

Looking around, I saw that most of the men were also engaged in stuffing their faces with the LRRPs. I had thought I'd be able to eat both pouches, but I found I was full after eating only one. I guess my stomach had shrunk.

Soon the word was passed that we needed to pack our gear quickly because a flight of slicks was in-bound to pick us up. I hadn't heard such good news since we'd been extracted from the Firebase Veghel AO back on May 24.

I heard a muttering sound in the distance that quickly turned into a loud roar as the slicks approached our LZ. We had already divided ourselves into six-man groups, a full combat load for a helicopter of the Vietnam era because each man weighed over two hundred pounds when he carried a full rucksack and a weapon. So, it took at least six helicopters to carry one platoon, and we waited as each slick approached and set down. All of us were grinning at each other like a pack of fools because we were so glad to be getting out of the infamous A Shau Valley in one piece.

The flight to the site of Firebase Veghel was routine and we were off-loaded into a big cleared area at the bottom of the Veghel hill. The place was a sea of ankle-deep orange mud, and I saw two huge 175mm self-propelled guns half-mired in the mud. They were attended by a large group of mud-covered artillerymen. I wondered how they were going to get back to Camp Eagle because QL-547 was covered with mud and probably wouldn't support the guns' weight. They were way too heavy to be lifted by even the largest helicopter the division had, and they seemed destined to be stuck in the orange mud until the road dried out a little.

I admired the gun crews; they worked day and night in all kinds of weather. They manned their guns and shot back even when they were under fire. Their lives were only a little bit better than the infantry because they were usually on a "secure" firebase and had a dry place to sleep. I have a picture in my mind of a 105mm gun crew I saw on Firebase Arsenal. They had received a fire mission, and they were firing in just about a minute after the call came in.

It was a battery fire mission with all six guns firing, and the gunners scrambled around in what appeared to be mass confusion but was really a carefully choreographed mission. When they completed that fire mission, they had to turn the guns and fire in another direction, and they made the change in direction and were firing in less than five minutes.

The guns were very loud, and the sound thumped against your eardrums every time one was fired. There is a scene in the movie *Good Morning, Vietnam* where an artilleryman calls in a song request to AFVN disc jockey Adrian Cronauer, played by Robin Williams. Cronauer asked the gunner what song he wanted to hear. I understood what the artilleryman meant when he replied in a shout, *"I don't care, as long as it's **LOUD**."*

Soon Charlie Company was picked up by three huge Chinook helicopters and flown to the O-Deuce LZ on the hill. The whole battalion had immersion foot, called trench foot in WWI, because everyone's feet, boots, and socks had been soaking wet for many days. The bottoms of my feet were burning as if they were on fire and I was limping heavily, and a lot of the other men were in the same condition.

There were no tents set up at any of the company areas and there weren't enough hooch's to shelter all the O-Deuce, so we were directed toward the 1st-327th battalion area where there were plenty of empty hooch's. I don't know where the 327th was but we moved right into their barracks and made ourselves at home.

After we had moved in, I picked a cot and put my gear down. Sitting on the cot, I pulled my boots and socks off and had a look at my feet. The bottoms of my feet and toes were dead white and deeply wrinkled. Some of the wrinkles had cracked open, showing raw flesh at the bottom of the crack. Most of the men were taking their boots and socks off, and I saw many feet that were as bad as mine or worse.

Orders from the battalion surgeon came down: we were to take off our boots and wet socks and leave them off until further notice. The surgeon wanted us to wear socks only but nobody had any dry socks. The supply sergeant was directed (grumbling about issuing so much equipment at once as supply sergeants do in all armies) to give each man clean, dry socks. Just sliding the warm, dry socks onto my feet made them feel better, and with the pain diminished, I went to sleep on my cot.

October 5–October 31

The remainder of October is a big blur of rain, flooded roads with washed out bridges, and short periods of sunlight in between typhoons. We remained confined to the 327th hooches, waiting for our feet to heal.

As many veterans know, the time spent recovering from a wound or an injury quickly becomes boring. It rained hard every day for several days. I remember a time when someone had acquired a bag of dew and those inclined to use it had quickly become high. I watched with great amusement the antics of some of the guys who were under the influence of the stuff. I remember one man who grabbed a machete from a rucksack and began waving it threateningly at others who were high; the closer the blade came to their faces, the harder they laughed. I laughed too, but having never tried dew, I didn't really understand what the deal was. Someone tried to explain what was happening, but he was so high himself that he didn't make much sense.

There was a man there who had a guitar, and I watched him fingering the chords as he played. He saw me watching and asked me if I played. When I said no, he offered to show me the chords to some popular songs of the day.

I learned to play the opening chords to Johnny Cash's "*Folsom Prison Blues*" and the beginning music from Eric Burden and the Animal's "*House of the Rising Sun*." It was a way to pass the time and I enjoyed it, but I never followed up on guitar lessons when I got home.

On October 7, the battalion was inserted into the area north of Firebase Bastogne to conduct search and clear operations. The battalion forward CP was at OP Checkmate on Hill 342. There was absolutely no contact with the enemy, although signs of his presence were found all over the place. We had been told that the O-Deuce would be brought back to Camp Eagle later in the month for a stand down. We all looked forward to that as we struggled with the rain, mud, and leeches of the monsoon season.

In a letter home dated October 9, I explained: "We've had a let up in the rain for a couple of days. Boy, does that ol' sun ever feel good! As long as we have these little breaks, I guess I can stand the monsoon."

We dealt with two typhoons (hurricanes) that parked themselves off the coast of central Vietnam. It rained constantly and heavily for several days during each typhoon. Throw in very high winds and maybe you can imagine what it was like to be living in the jungle with no protection from the weather except for a poncho. Again, we dealt with hunger because the bad weather prevented resupply.

In a message to my family dated October 15, I related: *"We've had pretty good weather for the last 3 days...right now, we are sitting on top of Strike, an old abandoned firebase. We (1st Platoon) are securing a [portable] radar unit that is supposed to detect enemy incoming [mortar] fire. Anyway, it is good goof-off time."*

It wasn't really goof-off time because, before the mission was completed, one of the typhoons mentioned above struck the area with heavy rains and high winds. The hilltop was completely devoid of vegetation, so we spent most of our time huddled under our ponchos trying to keep dry. I was very sick during this time. Just before we were flown to the hill, I had refilled my canteens from a flooded stream, and evidently the water had been polluted because I soon developed a severe case of dysentery. The platoon medic treated me with the medication he had in his aid bag, but I only got worse. It got so bad that I couldn't eat, and I got so weak that I had to crawl through the mud when I had to dig a cat hole.

Finally, on October 23, the battalion was airlifted to Camp Eagle for the promised stand down. I went to the battalion aid station to explain my problem. They sent me to the 326th Medical Battalion where they performed the usual tests, coming back with a diagnosis of amoebic dysentery. I was given an antibiotic and other meds and sent back to the company with a light duty order.

The rest of the stand down was a fog of illness and rain. Still unable to eat very much, I lost weight steadily. Camp Eagle was socked in by another typhoon stalled off the coast of Vietnam. I told my folks that: *"The temperature drops down into the 60's, but after 100+ temperatures, that feels pretty cold."*

It was still raining four days later, and the O-Deuce was unable to return to the field. When the weather finally cleared on November 1, the battalion was airlifted to Firebase Bastogne. They were put to work expanding the perimeter defense while I remained at Camp Eagle for a few more days.

Chapter 35

Waiting To Go Home

November 1970

On November 9, I went by truck to Bastogne and from there to the company in the field. By now, I was a short-timer and very interested in the many rumors about "early outs." At that time, President Nixon was under a lot of pressure to further reduce US troop strength in Vietnam. The way the army chose to do that was by sending men home early, before their full year in the 'Nam was completed. Eligibility for a drop was determined by how much time was left on your tour and by how much time you had to serve once you returned to the CONUS. Nothing was clear cut, so we short-timers waited anxiously for news.

Getting short or not, I was still in the field and subject to anything that might occur during combat operations around Bastogne. We were still working in platoon and squad-sized elements, conducting search and clear operations. The army had changed the phrase from "search and destroy" because of the outcries from the antiwar camp protesting such explicit language as "destroy." I was amused that the conduct of the war had come down to the language being used to describe field operations. Men were still fighting and dying but the antiwar people were raising an outcry over the use of one word.

There was little contact with the enemy but we knew they were still there. By this time, I had been demoted from squad leader to fire team leader because of my long absence while dealing with amoebic dysentery. One day, my fire team had the point. We were following a well-used trail that followed the contours of a steep jungle-covered ridge. We came to a fork in the trail with the left fork continuing along the ridge and the right fork zigzagging up the steep hillside. While waiting for the LT to decide which trail to take, I watched the trail going up the hill when I saw movement; three NVA soldiers suddenly jumped out of a clump of brush and hauled ass up the hill. I hollered "gooks" and fired at them. Others followed suit and we fired until the gooks disappeared over the top of the ridge. We chased them, finding a small blood trail but no bodies.

This incident made me nervous because I noticed I was developing a bad case of '**short-timers fever.**' This was a common affliction in men who were nearing the end of their combat tour. You might become overly cautious and hesitate to move when you should, and this inaction could get you killed.

The weather alternated between rain and sun and my feet were again showing symptoms of immersion foot. One day after a long march, my feet were giving me a lot of trouble. When we reached our NDP site, I took off my boots and socks to have a look at my feet, and they showed definite signs of immersion foot. I sat massaging them when I had an idea. I got out my C-ration can stove and a heat tab. I held a sock over the blue flame and watched the steam rising from the sock as it dried out. I put the dried sock on and held the other one to the flame until it also dried. With warm, dry socks on, I felt a lot better. Lighting another heat tab, I held my boots over the flame. They didn't dry as well as my socks, but they got nice and warm. I put them on and I resolved to try and do this every day.

On November 15, I had forty-nine days left on my full tour. Rumors about early outs abounded and we short-timers were getting anxious. In a hopeful letter home, I said: *"They are up to the 31st of December now. The man who would ordinarily leave on Dec. 31st will leave on November 26th. That's about a 35-day drop! I should find out very soon about my drop. I'll let you know as soon as I do."* I did not write any more letters home.

There was still a war going on; Delta Company had a hard contact on November 14 with a small unit of NVA sappers. The attack was repulsed with unknown enemy casualties. Delta Company lost two KIA and eleven wounded.

The battalion history for 1970 states: "The foul weather continued to affect tactical operations adversely. There were no significant firefights during the rest of the month as the Battalion relentlessly searched for the enemy. The Battalion rotated each of its companies for a 24-hour Thanksgiving stand down on FSB Bastogne and OP Checkmate. Operations were hampered severely by the weather as poor visibility hindered air support."

I don't remember the exact date, but around November 23 or 24, 1st Platoon was set up in a perimeter while small patrols were run in the area. I was sitting in the weak sunlight trying to dry out when the RTO called me and another man to the CP. He told us that we were being sent to the rear to begin the processing necessary before going home. I was afraid to be happy, thinking it still might not happen. The LT said that the platoon wasn't moving, so if we wanted to go we'd have to cut an LZ ourselves.

Hearing this, the other man and I wasted no time in getting to our rucksacks and machetes. Luckily, the platoon was set up in a relatively clear area, so all we had to do was clear some brush and small saplings to make an LZ. After about an hour of hard work, the LT came to inspect our efforts. We had cleared enough brush to allow one helicopter to approach and land. However, the LT pointed at two large trees at the other end of the LZ that would prevent a helicopter from leaving. The LZ was too narrow for a ship to turn around and exit the way it had come in, so those trees had to go.

I must have looked disappointed at the thought of felling the big trees with a machete or an ax because the LT told us that a log bird was inbound with a kick-out of dynamite, **det cord,** fuse, and blasting caps. When the log bird arrived overhead and kicked out the material, I immediately went to work. Back in January and February, I had been instructed by SSG Gibbons in the techniques used to knock down trees with dynamite or C-4. With the other man's help (I wish I could remember his name), I quickly rigged a charge around the base of the smaller tree and lit the fuse. The fuse was set for one minute, so I took my time finding shelter. The dynamite exploded right on time and the tree fell right where I wanted it to.

The other tree was a bit bigger, so I rigged three charges around the base of the tree connected to each other by det cord and blasting caps. I put a good-sized "kicker" charge as high as I could reach above the main charge, connecting it with det cord and a blasting cap. A kicker charge was supposed to push the tree in the direction you wanted it to fall. I lit a little longer fuse and took shelter behind a big log at the edge of the LZ.

I waited, but the charge did not go off when it should have. I remember thinking, *"Ah, fuck! I've got a hang fire."* That meant the fuse wasn't burning properly. I waited another couple of minutes, peering intently over the top of the big log. Having no desire to blow myself up on my last day in the field, I reluctantly got up and cautiously walked toward the big tree, watching the fuse as I went. When I got about twenty-five feet from the tree, I saw a sudden puff of grey smoke come from the fuse. Instantly, I turned and ran toward the big log, but I didn't make it; the concussion from the exploding charge knocked me head over heels and I landed face down in a mud puddle with debris falling all around me.

I managed to sit up and clear the mud from my eyes, and I saw that the charge had knocked the tree down in addition to scaring the living shit out of me. There were a few small trees still standing that the other guy and I quickly knocked down, and the LZ was ready.

While waiting for the log bird to return, men began coming up and asking for this or that piece of my equipment. I gladly let them have it as I had no use for it any more. I passed out all my rations plus three of my six canteens. I would later have trouble from the supply sergeant because I didn't turn in everything I had been issued back in January. I simply told him, "*I lost it in combat, sergeant*" and that was that.

The flight back to Camp Eagle and the O-Deuce LZ seemed to take forever. Looking out the door at the lengthening shadows of the jungle passing underneath, I rejoiced that I would never have to walk through shit like that ever again. I was nervous, hoping we wouldn't be shot down with a lucky shot from "Luke the gook" on my last helicopter flight from the boondocks.

As the helicopter approached the O-Deuce LZ and flared for landing, I saw Major Gunter Seibert, the battalion XO, waiting at the edge of the LZ. As the helicopter lifted off, he began walking toward us. As he drew near, I came to a loose position of attention. He stopped in front of us and looked us over. He then, in his strong German accent, demanded to know why we were in the rear. You're not supposed to look a superior officer in the eye when he speaks to you, but I did and replied, *"I'm here for ETS, sir."* He looked at me for a few seconds, then turned on his heel and walked quickly away.

I walked off the hill and reported to the company clerk in the orderly room. The first sergeant heard me speaking and came out of his office to look me over. Top Stanley was long gone and the new man was a younger, more gung-ho version of 'Top' Stanley. He told me to shave off my mustache, get a haircut, and find a bunk in the company hooch next to the orderly room.

I found an empty bunk and sat on the edge of the cot wondering what was next. The company clerk brought me a food package from home, but no mail. I opened the package and found several cans of my favorite brand of chili con carne inside. The clerk told me that I would be taken to Camp Hochmuth the next day for the rest of my out-processing. Camp Hochmuth was the administrative center for the 101st, and I would receive orders discharging me from the division there.

The company clerk also advised me to get a haircut and to shave off my mustache, saying the first sergeant had a thing about clean-shaven troops. He didn't give a shit if you were going home or not, he wanted his troops to be shaved. He told me it wasn't above the Top to delay a man's orders until the man complied with Top's tonsorial standards. Taking the clerk's advice, I hunted down the battalion barber and had the deed done. When I returned to the company hooch, I didn't recognize myself. It had been months since I'd had a regulation haircut, and my mustache had been growing since February.

Chapter 36

Trying To Go Home

November 25–28, 1970

The next morning, I turned in what was left of my field equipment, dealing with the usual load of bullshit from the supply sergeant over my missing 'lost in combat' equipment. I then boarded a waiting deuce and a half along with several other men from the different companies of the O-Deuce for the short ride to Camp Hochmuth. This admin center was located on QL1, west of Phu Bai Airbase.

This small base had originally been built by the marines as the headquarters of the 3rd Marine Division. When the 3rd Marine Division left Vietnam, the base had been taken over by the 101st Airborne Division in April 1970. It now served as administrative headquarters for the 101st. The camp had barracks for troops entering and leaving Vietnam and several huge buildings holding personnel files and all of the 'clerks, jerks and spoons' (cooks) necessary to keep REMF's fed and the paperwork flowing smoothly.

We were dropped off in front of an office where a clerk checked off our names from a list. He pointed to a barrack and told us to wait there and someone would come and get us when our orders were ready. There were stateside double-deck bunks with real mattresses, but the wooden floors were covered in dried mud, cigarette butts, and other trash. An unlucky PFC was appointed every morning and evening to sweep out the place.

That evening, I went to the mess hall for chow but I could hardly get the rich-tasting food down. I was used to eating out of a can or a plastic bag. I should have been ravenous after losing so much weight, but I just wasn't hungry.

Right after chow, a clerk came to the barracks and called out several names, some of them men I had just come in with. The clerk said that the next day was Thanksgiving and no more orders would be cut until Friday, November 27. Terribly disappointed, I went to a bunk and tried to go to sleep to make the time pass more quickly. I couldn't sleep because I was used to sleeping on the ground and the soft mattress felt strange.

On Thanksgiving Day, everyone went to the mess hall for the noon meal. The army always did its best to serve a good dinner on Thanksgiving, even sending a turkey dinner to the troops in the field, flown out to them by helicopter. Everything was there: turkey, potatoes and gravy, veggies and cranberry sauce, dinner rolls, and the traditional pumpkin pie. I managed to get most of this down and felt pretty good afterward.

That evening, they showed a movie in the mess hall; it was something about the Civil War but I can't remember the title. There was a group of guys from the South in the audience, and every time the rebel flag was shown on the screen, they would erupt into rebel yells and catcalls. Soon, men from the north and mid-west began answering their yells. Luckily, it was all good natured and no trouble developed. Since I was a westerner, I considered myself neutral and did not join in the yelling being traded back and forth.

It rained hard that night and I had to wade through soupy, ankle-deep mud to get to the three-hole latrine and take care of business. Right after breakfast, another clerk appeared and called out several names, but again not mine and the same thing happened after noon chow. I was very angry by this time; I was sure that Murphy's Law was again in effect and this time it involved me.

I waited a while and when no more clerks appeared with orders, I decided to find out what was going on. I trudged through the mud to the big metal shed where the personnel records were kept. I walked in and saw an obese E-7 wearing starched jungle fatigues, sitting behind a plywood counter reading a *Playboy* magazine. I stood in front of the counter waiting for him to acknowledge me. When he didn't I asked, *"Excuse me, Sergeant. May I speak to you?"* He reluctantly put the Playboy down and said, *"Yeah, whad'd'ya want?"* I remember thinking, *"This isn't going be easy; this guy's an asshole."*

I explained my problem in as few words as possible while he looked bored, and then he said, *"That's tough, there's nothin' I can do about it now. Come back tomorrow."* He was senior to me by two pay grades, so I had to do as he said. I was just turning to walk away when I heard a voice say, *"Is that you, Sergeant Roberts?"* Surprised, I quickly turned around and saw a young soldier wearing starched fatigues. He looked vaguely familiar and then he said, *"I was one of your trainees at Fort Ord. Do you remember me?"* When he said that, I **did** remember him. He motioned me forward and said, *"Don't pay no attention to that guy; he don't do any work or nothin'."*

I told him about my problem and he picked up a clipboard from a desk and looked at a list. He told me that my file was one of several that were missing. Then he told me that he could make up a temporary file based on my affidavit that would be sufficient to get my orders typed up.

Luckily, I had a good memory for places, dates, and times (I still do), so I was able to supply the information he needed. He told me to go back to my barrack and wait. I did and sure enough, that evening my name was called and I boarded a truck for the short trip to Phu Bai Airbase. I can't remember that trooper's name, but he is pictured in the Fort Ord group photo in the first row standing on the bleachers, second from the left. I owe him a lot.

We arrived at the Phu Bai passenger terminal after dark, so I couldn't see if the sign claiming "Phu Bai Is All Right" was still hanging from the control tower. After waiting for a while, we finally boarded a big Air Force C-130 turbo-prop cargo aircraft. As I climbed up the ramp, I saw that the cargo bay was configured for cargo, with metal pallets on little wheels on the deck. There were no seats for passengers. After everyone had boarded, the crew chief told us all to have a seat on the cargo pallets. There were no seat belts available.

The taxi to the runway and the takeoff was smooth. I was happy to finally be on my way, so I didn't much care about the travel accommodations, but that soon changed as we flew south. We ran into some bumpy weather that had the aircraft moving up and down and the pallets moving from side to side. I don't normally suffer from motion sickness but after a while, I became very nauseated. Luckily, we landed before anything got out of hand.

We climbed aboard the usual green bus for the trip to the barracks, where clerks collected our orders and told us we would be processed the next day. We put our luggage in a locked chain-link enclosure because thievery was a big problem at Cam Ranh Bay and the 22nd Replacement Battalion where we were staying.

Bob Noffsinger has an interesting story to tell about his experience at the 22nd when he passed through there a little later then I did. If you'll recall, in Chapter 16, Bob describes how he came to have a souvenir sniper rifle. In an e-mail dated May 11, 2012, he relates: "*I had the sniper rifle with me with all the correct paper work when I was leaving VN in Dec 1970, a clerk in the rear lied and said the paper work was not in order so I could not take it with me but he would buy it off me. What a jerk! I didn't have time to go above him to straighten it out and still catch my flight out so I found a privy barrel where they burn the poop by mixing it with diesel fuel and threw it in there rather than leave it for somebody who never got out of the rear with the gear.*" No wonder combat infantrymen hated the REMFs to a man.

According to Mike Lucky, a Veterans Affairs employee, many men who were REMFs are now claiming they suffer from latent PTSD when they never heard a shot fired in anger during their entire tour. VA has lowered its standards to the point that all they must do is claim they were in fear for their life at one time or another to receive benefits.

The next day, I got my first look at the huge base at Cam Ranh Bay. The 22nd was built on a sandy slope with a long road leading downward to the bay where big ships were at anchor in the sparkling water. After a terrible breakfast, we were issued short-sleeved khaki uniforms and low quarter dress shoes to go with them. While I was having E-5 stripes sewn on, I heard someone talking about a snack bar farther down the road toward the bay where they sold cheeseburgers. I hadn't tasted a cheeseburger for nearly a year, so I made a beeline for the snack bar. Murphy's Law struck again: they were out of cheeseburgers and would not have any for several days.

Thoroughly disappointed, I went back to the PX to buy ribbons for my uniform. Of course, they were out of the devices that hold the ribbons in one unit, so I pinned the ribbons on as best I could. They were also out of '**CIBs**,' the most important qualification badge of them all. Without my CIB, I looked like an REMF and I was ashamed.

Most of us sat around the barracks for the rest of the afternoon and into the evening, trying to find ways to pass the time. Finally, I gave up and went to sleep, so I didn't hear them the first time they called my name. Lucky for me, they checked the barracks for any stragglers. Someone shook me awake and asked my name then checked his list. He said, *"You better get your ass out there; they're loadin' the bus."* I jumped up and ran outside; luckily the chain link cage securing the luggage was still open and I was able to grab my suitcase. I was the last one to board the bus, but it didn't really matter: I was finally on my way back to the world.

Chapter 37

The Army Won't Let Me Go

Fort Lewis, Washington

When we arrived at the airfield I saw my **freedom bird** sitting on the ramp: a Flying Tiger Lines stretch DC-8. I wondered if it was the same aircraft that had brought me to Vietnam nearly a year ago. Shining in the spotlights, it was the most beautiful sight I had seen since coming in-country in January.

After the usual delays, we began boarding the airliner; it even smelled like home. Soon, the plane began to taxi and turned onto the runway. As the landing gear left the earth of Vietnam, a huge cheer went up from the men, celebrating having survived their tour in the 'Nam.

After several hours in the air, we landed at Yokota Air Base, Japan. Having several hundred dollars with me, I went to the PX and bought a new 35mm camera.

I don't remember anything at all about the flight from Japan to the United States. I do remember waking up when the pilot announced over the cabin loudspeaker that we had just crossed the coastline of Washington state, USA. A short time later, we touched down at McChord Air Force Base, adjacent to Fort Lewis. I was a little confused about the date, but, because of the International Date Line, I thought we arrived at McChord on the same day we left Vietnam. Now I know that we landed in the early morning hours of November 29, 1970.

We filed off the plane into the cold November air; in fact, I think it was snowing lightly, a big contrast to the hundred-degree heat and humidity of Cam Ranh Bay. We collected our luggage and filed into the customs shed for inspection. I laid my small suitcase on the counter in front of a customs agent who asked me to open it. All it contained was a set of jungle fatigues and boots, toilet articles, and several tactical maps I had managed to save. He thumbed through the stack of maps and asked me if I had anything to declare. When I said no, he looked at the maps again and finally said, "OK, you can go. Welcome home." Those words sounded good, but I didn't hear them again from anyone other than my family for more than thirty years.

By the way, I still have the maps and boots.

After a big steak-and-egg breakfast with gallons of real stateside coffee, we boarded buses for the trip to Fort Lewis. We found bunks in the transient barracks, and it was a real luxury to sleep under clean sheets and a wool blanket again.

That morning, I began the waiting game again. We were issued winter-weight Class A uniforms, and I was occupied for a while buying the stripes, ribbons, brass, and badges for the uniform, which I still have. I waited all day as men who had been on the same freedom bird as I were called to begin the discharge process. After a restless night, I waited all morning and into the afternoon of November 30 before I got pissed off again and went to the office where the paperwork was processed.

I waited at the counter, trying to get the attention of one of the scurrying clerks. Then I saw a man wearing the uniform of a command sergeant major come into the room; he had a 101st Airborne patch on his sleeve. I got his attention and he came to the counter. I explained what had happened to me in Vietnam and that my orders sending me to Fort Lewis were based on my affidavit. He told me, *"No problem, sergeant, I'll call [Fort] Benjamin Harrison and get all your info. I think you'll be out of here before midnight tonight."* He wrote down my name and social security number and told me to go back to the barracks.

After thanking him, I went back to the barracks to wait some more. True to the sergeant major's word, I was called early that evening and taken to a group of buildings to begin the process of being discharged from the army.

The actual discharge process remains a blur. There were clerks to talk to, forms to fill out and sign, a brief physical exam and a lecture urging us to behave ourselves with an admonition not to try to drink the whole day's output of beer from the Olympia Brewery just up the road. I was given my back pay and that was it: I was again a PFC, a 'proud fucking civilian'.

Chapter 38

Back In The World: Learning To Live With PTSD

Out in front of the discharge section, I climbed aboard another army bus (the last one, I hoped) for the trip to Seattle-Tacoma Airport and a quick trip home. We poured off the bus and nearly ran into the terminal, we were so anxious to get home. I gave the honor of transporting me home to the now-defunct Western Airlines. I bought a ticket to San Francisco and then on to Los Angeles International, about fifty miles west of my parents' house in Upland.

The flight was scheduled to leave at 11:00 p.m. Pacific time, so I found a bank of phones. I had not written to tell my family that I was on the way home, so I knew this call would be a big surprise. The phone rang for a long time before my mother finally answered. I said: *"Mom, guess where I am?"* There was no answer for a long time and I thought she might have passed out. Finally, she asked, *"Where*?" I told her I was in Seattle on my way home, and I could hear her yelling, *"Glen, Glen (my father) get up! He's in Seattle on the way home."*

I finally got my mother calmed down enough to give her the airline, flight number, and my arrival time.

After hanging up, I went into a nearby restroom and saw a man in the process of stripping off his dress greens and stuffing them into a trash can. He had civilian clothes in a paper bag, and I turned away laughing as he hurriedly began dressing himself.

We boarded the aircraft and I saw it was snowing hard. There was a long delay while the wings were de-iced before we left the ground. After another long delay at San Francisco, we finally arrived at LAX about two hours late. I got off the plane and there they were: the family I hadn't seen since July. Often, I had thought that I would never see them again at all. I asked my dad where my brother was and he pointed toward the wall. I found my tall, skinny brother stretched on his back asleep with his knees draped over an armrest. I woke him up by pushing his feet to the floor and we had a great reunion.

It was a long drive home and I got sleepy. I went to bed in my old bedroom but I couldn't sleep. The bed was too soft and it was way too quiet. After a couple of hours, I gave up and went to the kitchen to have coffee with my brother before he left for classes at the University of California, Riverside, where he was a full-time student.

After the Christmas and New Year holidays, I went back to school myself. My classes were aimed at a career in law enforcement because I had applied for a position as a deputy sheriff with the San Bernardino County Sheriff's Department. The sheriff, a former WWII marine and FBI agent, had a policy that gave preference to returning veterans and I was hired very quickly.

While waiting for the next academy to begin, I remained in school. Early one morning in February 1971, I heard a very loud rumbling and the house began to shake. Instantly, I rolled off the bed into a ball on the bedroom floor, thinking it was a mortar or rocket attack. My dad came in and his eyes widened comically as he took in the sight of his grown son rolled up into a little ball on the floor. I told him why I was on the floor, but I know he didn't understand.

The epicenter of the earthquake was in Sylmar, northeast of downtown Los Angeles. There was a veteran's hospital in Sylmar, and the quake was so powerful that the entire building collapsed, killing and injuring many vets who were hospitalized there. The hospital was never rebuilt.

I did not like going back to school very much but I knew it was necessary to finish my education. I didn't fit in with the other students, who all seemed like a bunch of silly kids. In my classes, I always sat in the back row as close to the door as I could manage. Most of the other students avoided me; I imagine they all thought I was crazy.

One day, I bumped into my former track and field coach. He remembered me and stopped to chat. He asked where I had been and I told him I had just returned from Vietnam. He looked at me strangely then said: *"Oh, really? Well, I've got to run; I've got a class to teach."* He never spoke to me again although I saw him all the time.

After my experience with the coach, I did not tell anyone else that I had served in Vietnam with one exception. My anthropology professor was taking the class on an overnight field trip to an early man archeological site affiliated with Dr. Louis Leakey in the Calico Mountains northeast of Barstow, California. Leakey had discovered and developed several early man sites in the Olduvai Gorge in East Africa. The professor explained that she liked to use veterans to drive the vehicles when the class went on field trips because they were more mature than the rest of the students.

I was having bad dreams at night, but they were only about vague things; they weren't yet the horrible, detailed, realistic nightmares I would suffer through later. I was living alone in a one-bedroom apartment so I didn't bother anyone, but neither did I have anyone to comfort me after a bad dream.

On July 4th that year, I took a girl to Disneyland to see Herman's Hermits (a sixties rock band) perform. I should have known they would have a firework display after the show, but I didn't even think about it. We were still standing in front of the outdoor stage when I heard the first whistle and boom. Startled, I looked at the sky and saw several bursts of yellow and blue sparks spread across the sky. They looked just like mortar rounds exploding at night, and I began pushing my way through the crowd, trying to get away. My date managed to keep up with me until I found shelter beneath an awning where I couldn't see the sky. I was trembling and very embarrassed by my behavior. My date was very understanding and asked if I wanted to leave. I told her no, and we waited until the fireworks display ended and we could get on some rides.

Three days later, I started the thirteen-week, seven-day-a-week sheriff's academy. I got through that all right, although the pistol range and explosives training did bother me a little. There were other veterans from the air force, army, and Marine Corps attending the academy, and we all hung around together and helped each other.

I graduated in September 1971 and was assigned to the jail system. Every new deputy sheriff in San Bernardino County worked in the jail until he passed a year-long probation period. During that year, I lobbied hard for an assignment to the sheriff's station nearest my apartment, and in January 1973, I was posted there.

■ ■ ■

My field training officer was a big man whose nickname was 'Moon Fox' because he loved to work the midnight to 8:00 a.m. shift. He was a former army Ranger who had gone to Lebanon when President Eisenhower sent troops there on a peacekeeping mission in the late 50's. We got along well, and he taught me a lot of things about surviving on the streets as a patrol deputy.

In 1974, I became a member of the mountain search and rescue team based at that station. It gave me a chance to spend time in the San Gabriel mountains rising above the valley in the west end of San Bernardino County. We used helicopters from the sheriff's department aviation division in a lot of our search operations. They were army surplus B-model Hueys, Hughes Aircraft LOH's and Bell-47G's of the type used during the Korean War as medevac helicopters, converted for civilian use. I felt comfortable working with the helicopters; I found that I had missed being around helicopters and my experience was useful in training the other members of the team.

Southern California Edison donated a used Dodge Power Wagon four-wheel drive truck to the search and rescue team. With other team members, I spent a lot of off-duty time converting the old truck for use as a search and rescue vehicle.

■ ■ ■

Things went smoothly until June 1976, when I was helped handle an officer-involved shooting. Another deputy and I responded to a call reporting a man firing shots from a freeway overpass at traffic passing on the freeway. Additional radio reports told us he had broken into an apartment and was holding the residents' hostage at gunpoint. My partner took position on a freeway bridge overlooking the apartment.

A local police officer and I went into the apartment building's parking lot looking for another vantage point. I heard two shots, and when I looked across the parking lot, the police officer was down and not moving. Keeping under cover, I got to him and saw he had been shot at least once in the head. Another officer came up and we managed to get him out of the kill zone, but he was already dead.

The portion of the freeway that runs adjacent to the apartment complex where he was killed is now named in his memory.

Shortly after this incident, I began having detailed nightmares about the death of Billy 'Kentucky' Lucas, the point man who had been killed in an ambush back in May 1970 during what was supposed to be a cease-fire. The dreams were repetitive; I always stood there watching helplessly as Billy obeyed my order and walked into the ambush. There were some variations: sometimes he got to his feet and grinned at me with blood running down his face from a bullet hole in his forehead, and, in other dreams, he lay there like a puddle of Jell-O; I couldn't move him or pick him up.

I didn't know what to do; there was nobody to talk to and the VA hadn't yet recognized post-traumatic stress disorder or developed a treatment. Another deputy assigned to that station had been involved in the fighting around Firebase Ripcord and had been wounded by grenade fragments. We talked to each other about what had happened to us, and it helped a little.

So, I began drinking beer after my shift ended, hoping I could get drunk enough to pass out and get some sleep. The beer didn't help much, so I became a gin drinker; I drank a fifth every two days, but that didn't help very much either. I found a doctor who was willing to give me some Valium. That helped for a while but as my body grew accustomed to the effects of the drug, the stuff worked less and less effectively.

During this troubled time in my life, I met a wonderful woman named Shari and we married. Her older brother is the man I referred to above when I talked about the Battle of Dong Ap Bia (Hamburger Hill), so she was used to dealing with a former combat vet suffering from PTSD-induced nightmares.

I carried on this way for several years, until 1982. I was home recovering from an on-the-job injury when I began to write in detail about the things that bothered me. I wrote about the dreams and about the actual occurrences that now fueled them. This seemed to help get it out of my mind, and my wife encouraged me and listened to me when I needed to talk.

I stopped drinking and gradually got things under a certain amount of control. I had an exaggerated startle reflex (I still do), I was always on guard, checking to make sure the doors and windows were locked several times a night, and I couldn't resist looking up when I heard a helicopter passing over. Certain odors triggered memories and I was constantly aware of places that might hold an ambush. Things went along in this semi-peaceful way until September 11, 2001.

The sight of the twin towers collapsing and the troops (including the 101st Airborne) being sent to Afghanistan brought everything roaring back. The nightmares began all over again, and I must have driven my wife and kids crazy.

My wife put up with it for a while as I sank into a major depression, but one day after several months of my crazy behavior, she called me and told me she had made an appointment for me with the behavioral health clinic at Kaiser Permanente. She ordered me to get my butt to that appointment and if I didn't go, I'd have to deal with her. After many years of marriage, I had a healthy respect for my wife's ability to get her way, so I kept the appointment.

It was a good thing I did, for I met an amazing woman named Dr. Belen. She is a tiny person, less than five feet tall, but she is a powerhouse of knowledge regarding the treatment of PTSD. She prescribed combinations of medication, changing them until she found a formula that seemed to work. Gradually the depression lifted, and the nightmares came less frequently.

I saw Dr. Belen for nearly two years, until she told me there was nothing more she could do for me. She told me to contact the Veterans Affairs hospital in Loma Linda, California, for individual and group therapy. My brother-in-law had been receiving help from the VA for several years. I talked to him about it, and he said that the treatment he'd received at the Loma Linda VA had helped him a great deal: he urged me to get over there and get help.

I have been in therapy with the VA for several years. At first, I saw someone every week, but now it's down to once a month. I feel pretty good, and I'm now about to graduate seeing someone every three months. The symptoms of PTSD will be with me for the rest of my life, but they're under control right now, and I have never met a more caring and professional group of people than the staff at Loma Linda VA.

Thanks to them, I'm living a normal life with my wife, my children, and my eight wonderful grandchildren. I still have bad dreams, especially on the anniversary dates of the incidents that are the main cause of my trouble, but I've found I can deal with it.

In August of 2012 I attended, along with Mike Lucky, the 70th Anniversary Reunion for the 101st Airborne Division in Nashville, Tennessee. I met some men I hadn't seen for 42 years as well as making new friends. I was amazed at the strong feelings of comradeship which developed, even though I hadn't seen or talked to some of these men in four decades. It was a true healing experience. Being in phone and e-mail contact with fellow veterans of Operation Texas Star helps a lot and I thank them for their friendship.

Chapter 39

Mighty Men Of Valor Meet Again

We few, we happy few, we band of brothers;
For he today that sheds his blood with me
Shall be my brother.

-Shakespeare, H*enry V,* Act IV, Scene 3

In January of 2015, Bob Noffsinger put together and posted a Facebook page honoring the men who fought and died on Hill 714. It's a place where the survivors can leave messages and photos for each other and just talk about what's going on in their lives. Someone, I don't remember who, proposed a reunion of Charley Company men in Washington DC in the spring of 2015. The response was immediate and enthusiastic and planning proceeded for the reunion, scheduled for late June.

Several of us began to search for 'missing' men from Charley Company so they could be invited to the reunion. It took a while, but we located several men that no one who fought on Hill 714 had heard from or spoken to in over 40 years. Plans were finalized for everyone to meet on June 26, 2015 at the Quincy Hotel in downtown Washington DC.

My wife and I flew to DC the day before and met with several of the men and their wives who had done the same thing. The 'official' reunion did not begin until the next day when Bruce Scott, working through his congressman, had arranged a tour of the White House. Most of us decided to walk the few blocks to the tour entrance for the White House. We had been told not to bring any cameras on the tour because photographing the interior of the White House was prohibited. Ironically, just a few days later, the Secret Service lifted the ban on cameras inside the White House.

Most of us wore the special T-shirts that had been designed for the reunion, so the Secret Service, recognizing us as a group of veterans, treated us with respect during the screening process prior to entering the White House.

One of the things my wife and I immediately noticed was that the interior of "The House" seemed a lot smaller and more confined then it looked when viewed in movies or on television. It was still very interesting, though, to walk through the rooms where distinguished presidents such as Abraham Lincoln, Theodore and Franklin Roosevelt, John Kennedy and Ronald Reagan had walked.

My wife and I were on the second floor looking out the windows overlooking the south lawn when a member of the Secret Service uniform division approached us. He told us that the President and Michele Obama were leaving very shortly for a speaking engagement and that, if we remained at the window, we'd be able to watch the big Sikorsky helicopter known as Marine One land on the south lawn.

Very shortly, we saw the big helicopter glide into view and slowly settle down onto the lawn. It was odd not to hear the considerable noise from the helicopters big rotors, but the thick bullet-resistant glass shut out almost all outside noise. As the rotors slowly ground to a halt a Marine sergeant, wearing dress blues, exited the helicopter through the door just behind the pilot and stood at attention at the bottom of the steps, waiting for the president.

Soon, President Obama and the First Lady appeared walking across the lawn toward the helicopter. As the president neared the stairs, the marine sergeant snapped off a crisp salute, which the president casually returned as be began to climb the steps into the helicopter. The door closed, the big rotors began to turn and Marine One lifted off and flew away to the south, disappearing beyond the trees.

As the tour ended, just about everyone returned to the hotel for a rest. Late that afternoon, Bruce Scott called our room and said that it had been decided to hold the ceremony at The Wall, scheduled for the next day, that evening because a storm front was due to pass through the DC area, with heavy rain forecast for the next day. It was only about a mile from the hotel to The Wall, so most of us decided to walk.

When we arrived at The Wall, we met up with those who had taken taxis from the hotel. Richard Fulmer, a former machine gunner had several ribbons with the names of those men killed on Hill 714 printed on them. There was also a large bouquet of flowers on a tripod which we placed in front of the wall panel on which the names of those we had lost were engraved.

Colonel (ret.) Gerald Dillon, who had been our platoon leader and then company commander during most of the action on Hill 714, read the names of the casualties. As he read each name, the corresponding ribbon was placed on the flower display. Colonel Dillon then recited from a poem called 'We've Drunk From The Same Canteen:'

'We've shared our blankets and tents together,
And marched and fought in all kinds of weather.
And hungry and full we've been;
Had days of battle and days of rest,
But this memory I cling to and love the best:
We've drunk from the same canteen.
The same canteen, my soldier friend,
The same canteen;
There's never a bond like this:
We have drunk from the same canteen!

The original poem was written by a civil war soldier, Private Miles O'Reily from the 47th New York Volunteer Infantry. By the time Colonel Dillon had finished his recital, there probably wasn't a dry eye among the veterans of Hill 714 gathered at The Wall 45 years later. Our little ceremony had attracted quite a few on-lookers and I noticed a lot of them were recording the ceremony on their phones.

We broke up into smaller groups then and we began to look for the names of those we were there to remember. I had a list of the panel and line numbers where the names could be found, and some of the men made tracings of the names on The Wall as they were located.

Later that evening, in the hospitality room set aside for us by the hotel, we met to tell war stories. Some of these were (actually) true while others, in the manner of combat veterans everywhere, were (only slightly) exaggerated. In those stories, the hills were always steeper, the loads heavier and the rain wetter than it was in reality.

Our wives were there too, and I'm sure they told their own war stories about living with their war veteran husbands. We all had a pretty good time of fellowship, tears and laughter and we promised to get together again soon.

Chapter 40

PTSD: A Wife's Perspective

In thy faint slumbers I by thee have watched and heard thee murmur tales of iron wars. . .
William Shakespeare, *Henry IV, Part One, Act II, Scene 3*

The following chapter was written by my wife Shari after she read my manuscript and asked to add her own story:

No person who is not a veteran can ever understand the horrors our husbands, brothers, and fathers experienced in war. It has always been hard for me to understand the mental anguish my older brothers experienced in Vietnam when I was a young girl. When I married my husband, John, those memories came back again with a vengeance.

My father was a Marine who fought in the invasion of Guam. When my father was 16, he was living in Hawaii with his parents while his father was employed at the Pearl Harbor Navy Base. On December 7, 1941, my father was awakened by the bombs falling on the ships in Battleship Row. When his father responded to the call for everyone to report to their stations at Pearl Harbor, my dad followed and ended up helping a Marine machine gun crew fire at the attacking Japanese planes. He carried ammunition and brought water for the water-cooled machine guns.

It was only recently I heard part of his story. He never talked about his war-time experiences. He had me help him write an article that was submitted to his high school newsletter about anyone's experiences in the Pearl Harbor attack. My heart sank when I heard his story, and I felt ashamed I never knew about it. My father never talked about Pearl Harbor except in the short story I helped write which we submitted together to the Roosevelt High School Reunion paper in Honolulu, Hawaii, which was printed, along with other stories about Pearl Harbor, shortly after we submitted the article.

My father lives in Florida today and I only talk to him on the phone. While doing this article and contacting him on the phone about his story I heard his voice crack and heard short silences while he corrected any mistakes I might have made typing his story. It is shameful that only now can I understand his pain and silence. I felt like I never knew him and felt ashamed that I did not understand what made him the man he was while we grew up. I never even knew he was a veteran.

On occasion, when we were young, he would take me, my brothers and sister with him to the VFW hall to eat with other men his age. I did not realize then the meaning this had for my father. I just knew that the VFW hall was a special place to him. He was always stand-offish to us as children and not loving to any of us. Our life growing up with him was harsh and hollow. I always thought of him as a man of steel. None of us ever understood any torment he might have gone through in war. It was only through my experience with my brothers and husband that I grew to understand his solitude and introspection.

I was eleven years old when my oldest brother, Michael, entered the Army in 1967. Both Michael and my second oldest brother, Stephen, were not drafted but joined the Army instead.

My oldest brother, Michael, was in the 1st/506th Infantry with the 101st Airborne Division and was a grunt. Stephen entered the Army a year later in 1968. He was in an attack helicopter squadron as a crew chief/door gunner on a Huey helicopter, also in Vietnam.

I remember the grief and terror on my mother's face as she saw them both off when they first left home. I remember very vividly the time my oldest brother first came home on a furlough from Vietnam. The look on his face (I now hear it is called the 'thousand-yard stare') and the way he would act at dinner time. He would sit sideways in his chair and constantly move his head around to look behind him swiftly, being disturbed at the slightest sound from the kitchen. He would eat like it was his last supper, rapidly downing his food.

After dinner, when we had moved into the living room, he would sit and stare off into space for long periods, silent and withdrawn. The slightest sound would bother him greatly, and in fact, neither one of them could tolerate the sound of any type of cooling fan. I believe it reminded them of the sound of helicopter rotors. Only now do I understand why they always hated the Fourth of July. How can you help someone deal with these torments, were the only questions my mom and I discussed? Nothing we ever did helped in any way.

Any conversations we had with him were short and precise; he had no small talk. I also could never understand why Michael would never sleep in his bed when he came home, instead lying on the floor and staring off into space; no amount of comfort we tried to give could console him.

I remember, on one outing I had with my mother in town, someone was talking to her about my brother's service in Vietnam. Someone close-by called out "he's a baby-killer" from the crowd in the store. We did not know who said this, and my mother whisked me out of the store after it was said. I saw my mother cry on the bus ride home and I asked her why a person would say such a thing and she just told me it was 'ignorance', and to forget it was said and never to repeat what was said to my brother. I never understood why he was called that and the incident was never spoken of again.

After my brothers came home on furlough and returned to Vietnam, my mother would stay in her bedroom and cry for days after they returned to duty. My dad would sit for hours in his lazy chair in the living room and not speak. My youngest brother Greg and my older sister never understood the long periods of silence from our parents, the many desperate, lonely hours in withdrawal from the family, nor how any of us could help them with their sadness. We just went about our daily activities, keeping our own fears inside, and finding comfort from each other.

I also remember one time my brother Michael came home on furlough. He took my mother aside and told her he came home as a special request he made to go to the family of a fallen soldier, a good friend he considered his brother. He was going to make a trip to the family of his fallen friend. He wanted to tell them in his own words what special friends they had been and how their son had died with honor fighting for his country. My brother never spoke of this again after that. I can only imagine what my brother must have gone through during this time. I know he has often wondered why he survived when so many of his 'brothers' had fallen. But I know God has a reason and a destiny for all of us.

The letters we received from my brothers, who were in Vietnam at the same time, were much anticipated and eagerly received. We knew the letters left out what was really going on with their lives, but even so, their experience changed our family forever.

My parents were outraged at the comments being made regarding the men serving over there. In response, they wrote many letters to the editor expressing their anger about the way the vets were treated on their return from Vietnam. We watched television in horror when Walter Cronkite and Dan Rather gave reports from Vietnam. None of the visions we saw fit the easy-going letters we received from my brothers. It was horrifying. I remember watching television when the Kent State University, Ohio shooting happened. Many people were shot protesting over Vietnam. For so long there was nothing shown on Vietnam, now it was inundated on television. Our fears for my bothers increased and we started fearing seeing the government show up at our house for notification. Luckily, that never happened.

When Michael returned from Vietnam, I remember going to the bus station with my parents. I barely recognized him getting off the bus. He immediately rushed into the restroom and changed out of his uniform. I asked him why he changed, and he said, "no one wants to see me in that uniform." I asked "Why not? You fought for your country; they should not say mean things to you." He just stood quietly and did not answer.

It amazed me that there were **NO** parades and "welcome home" greetings for any Vietnam men when they returned home; they only received contempt and name calling. I never understood this as a young girl. My brothers had risked their lives for this country in a war with no meaning and no end. After their service, it was hard for them to even get a job; no one wanted to help a Vietnam vet. They struggled alone with their demons for years.

Today I think of them as heroes, someone to be held high and praised for what they have been through. They risked their lives for our freedom to no purpose. What was the reason for their being over there? It is still disputed to this day. All the horrors brought to so many by this war were purposely forgotten, and so were the men who fought it. They were abandoned by their country.

I'm including an excerpt from a letter to the editor my Mother wrote one Christmas:

"I get very upset when I hear anyone trying to degrade those who went to Vietnam to fight for something that only Washington knew the reasoning behind. Put the blame where it belongs!

If you know a Vietnam combat vet, shake his hand and welcome him home. Though belated, it will be tremendously appreciated in this season when love abounds and wish him a sincere Merry Christmas-a truly priceless and deserving gift which will come from the heart."

Years later, who would have guessed I would meet my soul mate, my husband, John? He had served in the 2nd/502nd Infantry in the same 101st Airborne Division as my brother Michael.

When my husband and I were first married, he had many nightmares about the time he served in Vietnam. Night time became a terror for us both. Often, we avoided going to bed as long as we could.

My husband suffered what I called 'survivors guilt', often talking about his fallen comrades and why they had to die while he survived. He thought it was his fault that they were killed and he was not. He would feel guilty about being alive because of his fallen friends not being able to be with their families any longer. Night time became our enemy!!

I used to get stressed out when it was time to go to bed. Most of our nights, my husband would thrash about in the bed, and I was often hit by his waving arms. He would wake up in a heavy cold sweat, shivering and shaking, often calling out men's names that were in 'Nam with him. He would cry out blood curdling screams in his sleep and all I could do was hold him and try to calm him.

I had no friends whose husbands or boyfriends were in Vietnam, so my experience with my husband's terror was suffered in silence. I had only brief memories of what my brother's actions had been when I was small. There was no help for them, either. They were just expected to 'suck it up' and move on.

I rarely shared any of my fears with my family – it was just left private. Only those who 'have been there' truly know how hard life can be when your loved one comes back from war and is not the same person you knew before you said "goodbye." Even the government does not consider giving any healing time or counseling to these men. It is just expected that they will go on with their life as it was before they went to war.

During this time my husband became a heavy drinker. He would come home from his shift as a deputy sheriff with the San Bernardino County Sheriff's Department and would immediately make himself several strong drinks. I discovered that many of the things he was experiencing as a patrol deputy and later, a detective, would bring back memories of what had happened to him in Vietnam. He tried to subdue his demons with drink but, of course, it didn't work.

He would get drunk and rant and rave, slamming doors and kicking the walls. Our children were young and were very frightened of him. Finally, in desperation, I took him aside and told him his drunken behavior was badly affecting them and that they were afraid of him and did not want him around. A look of shock came on to his face and from that moment forward, he began to make a real effort to control his drinking. The first thing he did after I told him how his drunken behavior was affecting the kids was to pour the rest of his alcohol into the kitchen sink.

His nightmares and violent behavior went on for many years until I made him go to counseling at the VA hospital near our home. He was found to have PTSD, the first time a diagnosis was made for his ailment. Prior to this time, we never received any material from the military or VA advising us that we might be eligible to receive counseling should we encounter any problems related to my husband's service. We never heard the term 'Post Traumatic Stress Disorder.' We were left in the dark and had to figure things out on our own.

Through years of counseling, he has come to grips with his experience; finally realizing he was not to blame for surviving when so many of his friends perished. They are not forgotten; in his mind, they are still fighting beside him. He sees them as they were; strong young men doing their best under very difficult conditions. I have much admiration and love for this man who, like my brothers, suffered in silence for so many years. I am grateful my husband and brothers survived, for they are heroes in my eyes. They are men to be greatly honored.

For the last fifteen years, my husband has suffered from type II diabetes mellitus that the VA says is directly related to prolonged exposure to Agent Orange. He was diagnosed with a pituitary tumor, also related to direct exposure to defoliants. These diseases have left me paranoid, afraid that I will lose him before his time.

Today, society thanks them for their service. But only a few years ago, it was still considered shameful to have fought in Vietnam. My husband wears his Vietnam Veterans hat like a badge of honor. He is the strongest and best man I have ever known, a man of honor who loves and protects his family, and who fought for his country with pride and dignity.

Our children (2 sons and a daughter) are proud of him and talk often of his accomplishments during one of the most desperate wars of modern history. Growing up, they thought of him as one would think of General Patton. He didn't have the stars on his shoulders as Patton did, but he has the pride and honor of one who did his best. We have all grown stronger through his struggle to come to grips with his PTSD. It was, to say the least, a tearful and painful journey for our family. At times we thought we would not survive, but in the end we became a stronger, more loving family.

There are no doubts in my mind that other families have suffered through the same experiences. Silence is terrible and can take a family down. I have realized that to survive any hurt you must find inner strength and reach out for help. This is the first step to recovery. Anything can be overcome if you fight your strongest for what you believe in and want out of life.

Writing this book has been good for my husband. It has caused him to reach out to his past and deal with his trauma. Through his research efforts, he has located quite a few of the surviving veterans who served with him in Vietnam. Their information and support made the writing of this memoir much easier.

I keep my husband's photo, taken when he was in AIT at Fort Ord, California, on my desk at work. Looking at the picture, you can see what was stolen from us — the youth of his yesterdays. But we are grateful he survived those days and the long battle it took to bring his mind and soul back to us. He is our family hero, and what a legacy he is passing on to his children and grandchildren!

Shari   Roberts   -   December,   2012

Soldiers of the 2/502 Infantry Killed in Action, 1970. Listed by Operation Name and Date of Casualty

OERATION RANDOLPH GLEN

Operation Randolph Glen began in 1969; those names are not listed.

NAME	RANK	UNIT	DATE
Ronald L. Hag	E-5	HHC	11 February
John J. Burns, Jr.	E-4	HHC	11 February
Robert Davis	E-5	Co E	11 February
Morgan L. Canon	E-3	Co E	11 February
Raymond R. Moon	E-4	Co E	11 February
Marlin T. Petersen	E-3	Co E	11 February
Harold W. Schuller	E-3	Co E	11 February
Timothy C. Farrell	E-3	Co B	11 February

Vincent M. LaRocca	E-4	Co B	
11 February			
Pastor Ruiz	E-5	Co C	
16 February			
McArthur Johnson	E-4	Co B	
18 March			
Phillip G. Knieper, Jr.	E-3	Co B	
20 March			
Rudolph D. Lovato	E-4	Co A	
20 March			
Stephen A. Golsh	E-4	Co A	
21 March			
Louis J. Barbaria	E-4	Co C	
21 March			
John T. Gutekunst	E-4	Co A	
21 March			
Sidney Rohler ##	E-3	Co B	
28 March			

OPERATION TEXAS STAR

James A. Tyner	E-4	Co D	
15 April			
Robert A. Wall	E-3	Co D	
18 April			
Samuel E. Asher	O-3	Co E	
26 April			
Charles R. King	E-3	Co B	
26 April			
Delbert E. Hall ##	E-4	Co E	
27 April			
Steve Sandlin	E-3	Co E	
27 April			
Robert E. Backman	E-3	Co B	28
April			
Fernando Rios-Maldonado	E-3	Co B	28
April			
William J. Stieve	E-4	Co D	
28 April			

Name	Rank	Unit	Date
Donnie Horton	E-4	Co A	30 April
Leo J. Ludvigsen	E-5	Co B	2 May
Harold G. Graft	E-4	Co B	2 May
Glen Witycyak	E-5	Co C	3 May
Green Miller ##	E-5	Co A	5 May
Ivory L. McKinney	E-3	Co A	5 May
Francisco T. Carvajal	E-5	Co C	5 May
Gerald A. Kulm ++ ##	E-4	Co C	5 May
William E. Malcolm	E-7	Co C	5 May
Vernon L. Okland	E-4	Co C	5 May
Phillip R. Warfield	E-3	Co C	6 May
Kenneth L. Foutz	E-6	Co B	6 May
Wayne K. Smith	E-4	Co A	8 May
Peter F. Nolan	E-5	Co A	8 May
Roy L. Richardson @@ ##	O-2	Co A	9 May
Ronald E. Schmidt	E-5	Co C	14 May
Billy R. McCullough	E-4	Co A	16 May
David Christopherson	E-3	Co A	16 May
David L. Jones	E-6	Co A	16 May
John R. Mariani	E-3	HHC	16 May
Billy R. Lucas	E-4	Co C	19 May
Gary W. Gear	E-4	Co E	20 May

Name	Rank	Unit	Date
John A. Claggett ##	E-3	Co E	20 May
Robert E. Cain	E-3	Co E	20 May
Lawrence Bierbaum	E-6	Co D	29 May
John L. Davis	E-3	Co C	2 June
William W. Morrow	E-5	Co C	22 June
Jimmie L. Chamblee	E-5	HHC	22 June
Ralph A. Gaddis	E-4	HHC	22 June
Newton S. Clement	E-5	HHC	22 June
Russell Bahrke	E-3	Co E	13 August
Gary Washenick ++	E-5	HHC	16 August
Frederick E. Huttie	E-5	Co D	16 August
Frank Fratellenico **	E-3	Co B	19 August
Paul Miller	E-4	Co C	20 August
Marshall K. Jones	E-4	Co C	20 August
Ben O. Johnson	E-4	HHC	21 August
Sheldon Silverman	E-6	Co A	24 August

OPERATION JEFFERSON GLEN

Operation Jefferson Glen continued into 1971; those names are not listed.

Name	Rank	Unit	Date
William E. Johnston	E-4	Co E	9 October

Allen J. Smith	E-3	Co	A
14 October			
Michael C. Jensen	E-3	Co D	14
November			
Val C. Robertson	E-4	Co D	
5 December			

** Medal of Honor
@@ Distinguished Service Cross
++ Silver Star
Bronze Star with "V" Device

SOURCES OF INFORMATION

1. Company D, 1st Battalion, 3rd Training Brigade year book Fort Ord, 1969.

2. NCOC class 47-69 75th Company year book US Army Infantry School, Fort Benning, 1969.

3. 101st Airborne Yearbook Vietnam 1969.

4. "Where We Were in Vietnam" Michael P. Kelley; Hell Gate Press
Copyright 2002 by Michael P. Kelley

5. Combat Operations After Action Feeder Report Operation Randolph Glen December 7, 1969 through February 10, 1970

6. Combat Operations After Action Feeder Report Operation Randolph Glen February 15 through March 30, 1970

7. Combat After Action Feeder Report Operation Texas Star April
1 through April 30, 1970

8. Combat After Action Feeder Report Operation Texas Star May 1
through May 31, 1970

9. Combat After Action Feeder Report Operation Texas Star June 1
through June 30, 1970

10. Combat After Action Feeder Report Operation Texas Star July 1 through July 31, 1970

11. Combat After Action Feeder Report Operation Texas Star August 1 through August 31, 1970

12. After Action Report Come Back Ridge dated November 3, 1970

13. Combat After Action Interview Report Hill 882 June 1, 1970

14. Combat After Action Interview Report Firebase Veghel Mortar
Attack (April 26, 1970) Report dated May 28, 1970

15. Combat After Action Interview Report Ambush of Recon Platoon
Hill 714 April 27, 1970

16. Combat After Action Interview Report April 28, 1970 NVA Attack On Bravo Company's NDP. Report dated May 9, 1970

17. 2nd Battalion 502nd Infantry "Unit History of the Strike Force" Vietnam, 1970

18. S2/S3 Daily Staff Journal March 19 through March 23, 1970

19. S2/S3 Daily Staff Journal April 19 through April 30, 1970

20. S2/S3 Daily Staff Journal May 1 through May 31, 1970

21. S2/S3 Daily Staff Journal July 1 through July 31, 1970

22. S2/S3 Daily Staff Journal August 2 through August 31, 1970

23. S2/S3 Daily Staff Journal September 25 through September 30, 1970

24. S2/S3 Daily Staff Journal October 1 through October 4, 1970

25. Personal e-mail from Robert Noffsinger 1st Platoon C Co May 11, 2012

26. Citation for Award of the Bronze Star Medal with "V" Device,
Jesse Gomez, 2nd Platoon C Co

27. Letter from Daniel Kulm May 25, 2012; includes personal letters to his family from Gerald Kulm 1st Platoon C Co KIA May 5, 1970

28. Letter and photo of gold bullion on page 54; photo of Firebase Rifle bunker on page 60 courtesy Bruce Scott 2nd Platoon C Co 2/502 Infantry May 25, 2012

29. Telephone conversations with Harold Carstens 2nd Platoon C
Co May through July 2012

30. Telephone conversations with James Brinker Recon Platoon E Co May through August 2012

31. Telephone conversations with Robert Noffsinger 1st Platoon C Co March through June 2012

32. Telephone and personal conversations with Larry Kuss 1st Platoon C Co August through September 2012

33. Telephone conversations with Eraldo Lucero 1st Platoon A Co March through August 2012

34. Telephone conversations with Charles Swenson 1st Platoon C Co July through August 2012

35. Telephone conversations with Terry Lowe 1st Platoon C Co August 2012

36. E-mail on 11/7/12 from James Brinker about confrontation between Charlie Company troops and Echo Company mortar platoon re: mortar attack on Charlie Company, August 19-20, 1970.

37. Tactical Maps of Vietnam, US Army Topographic Command, 1970:
Map Sheets 6441 I, 6441 IV, 6442 III, 6541 I, and 6541 IV.

38. Authors personal letters to family January 16, 1969 through November 15, 1970.

39. Excerpt from the poem "The Battle of Blenheim" by Robert Southey 1774-1843

40. Information re: NVA units on Hills 714 and 882 taken from "Ripcord-Screaming Eagles Under Siege-Vietnam 1970" by Keith W. Nolan, Presidio Press, Copyright 2000 by Keith William Nolan.

41. Group photo on page 57 courtesy Terry L. Williams, C Company 2/502 Infantry.

42. Telephone conversations with Tom Boyce, Recon Platoon 2/502 Infantry, November and December 2012 re: mortar attack on Charlie Company on August 19-20, 1970.

43. Photos on pages 81, 87, 103, 148, 177 and 178 courtesy of Lee Bartolotti, Charlie Company 1st Platoon 2/502 Infantry.

44. Photo on page 66 courtesy of Mike Lucky, 3rd platoon Alpha Company 2/502 Infantry.

45. Photo of Firebase Rifle on page 60 courtesy of Alpha Company 1/501 Infantry.

46. Photo of Walter J. 'Sabo' Sabalausky wearing 1st Sergeant stripes in Chapter 10 by John Yeager, Jr.

Glossary of Military Terms and 'Boonie Rat' Slang

A-Gunner. The assistant machine gunner.

Airmobile. A technique for mass movement of troops using helicopters; a unit using this technique.

artillery raid. An artillery battery moved by helicopter with a basic load of ammo to a position secured by the infantry to fire at selected targets.

AK-47. The *Avtomat Kalashnikova* type 47, caliber 7.62mm by 39mm assault rifle. Can be fired either semi or fully automatic.

AK-50. Same as above but with folding stock; favored by NVA sappers because of its compact size.

air medal. A medal awarded to helicopter crewmen and airmobile infantrymen after a certain number of combat assaults.

arc light. Term used to describe a carpet-bombing mission by B-52 high-altitude bombers.

APC. Armored personnel carrier. A thinly armored, tracked vehicle used to transport infantry.

A Shau Valley. A forty-kilometer-long valley on the western border of Vietnam and Laos. A main branch of the Ho Chi Minh trail ran through the valley. In G.I. slang, 'Aw Shit Valley.' The scene of many serious firefights.

AIT. Advanced Individual Training or Advanced Infantry Training.

B-52. A large, high-altitude bomber used in saturation bombing. Slang for a beer can opener.

basic training. Training a soldier receives just after entering the army.

bird. A helicopter.

blue line. Code used for a river or stream as shown on a tactical map.

blue team. A squad-sized team of men, usually from a troop (company) of the 2nd battalion, 17th Cavalry Regiment used as a quick response team to asses a tactical situation before a larger unit responded.

booby trap. A concealed explosive device set to explode by stepping on a pressure device or by pulling a trip wire. Can also be electrically command-detonated by a trail watcher.

boonies. Slang for the jungle.

boonie hat. A soft hat with a full brim worn to break up the outline of the human head.

boonie rat. Slang for an infantryman operating in the jungle.

boonie spoon. Slang for the white plastic spoon packed in every box of C rations.

brown line. Code for the brown contour lines defining a terrain feature on a tactical map.

buck sergeant. Lowest ranking NCO. Often used as a fire team leader or squad leader.

BUFF. Big Ugly Fat Fucker. Air crew slang for a B-52.

Bug juice. Army-issue insect repellent in a squeeze bottle. It was so strong, it could damage the crystal on a wrist watch or melt a hole in a plastic poncho.

bunker. A fortified fighting position.

bunker complex. A mutually supporting group of bunkers sometimes connected to each other by tunnels.

bunker line. Individual bunkers placed around the perimeter of a firebase or base camp.

'butter bar'. Derogatory slang for a second lieutenant because of the dull gold color of his rank insignia, a single gold bar.

C-4. Plastic explosive. Can be used to destroy bunkers, knock down trees, or cook your C rations.

C rations. Canned rations that served as boonie rats' primary source of food. Twelve meals came in a case, a four-day supply of food. Also called '*Charlie rats.*'

CA. Combat Assault. The movement of troops by helicopter into territory controlled by the enemy.

canopy. The layers of jungle foliage, such as single, double or triple canopy.

charlie oscar. Slang for commanding officer of a unit.

Charlie or Charlie Cong. Slang for a Vietnamese guerrilla soldier.

Charlie-Charlie bird. Command and control helicopter. Used by commanders to control combat assaults or troop movement on the ground.

cherry. A soldier newly assigned to the field or boonies.

chieu hoi. Vietnamese for "open arms." Used to describe an enemy soldier who has surrendered to the allies.

chao co. Vietnamese greeting to adult females.

chao ong. Vietnamese greeting to adult males.

CIB. Combat infantry badge. Highly prized; awarded only to soldiers who have been under fire in actual combat.

claymore. A command-detonated antipersonnel mine named after a Scottish broadsword. Contains about seven hundred .32 caliber steel balls embedded in C-4 plastic explosive. Used for ambushes and perimeter security.

click. See *klick.*

co dep. Vietnamese for "beautiful girl."

Cobra. Nickname for an AH-1G assault helicopter usually armed with a 7.62mm mini-gun, 40mm automatic grenade launcher, and 2.75-inch rockets.

cong. Vietnamese for "red" or communist.

CONUS. Continental United States.

CP. Command post. The position within a perimeter occupied by the platoon leader/company commander, medic, RTOs, and the artillery forward observer.

dancing. Moving from one position to another, such as "dancing along the blue line."

DDP. Daylight defensive position. Used as a base for patrols searching for the enemy's presence.

DEROS. Date estimated rotation overseas. The day a soldier left Vietnam and returned to the United States.

det cord. Hollow cord filled with C-4 used to connect separate explosive charges to be fired all at once.

deuce and a half. An all-wheel drive, two-and-a-half-ton truck capable of traveling almost anywhere.

dew. O-Deuce slang for marijuana.

dink. Derogatory term for a Vietnamese person, usually an enemy soldier.

DMZ. Demilitarized zone. During the Vietnam War, the border between North and South Vietnam.

Doc. Slang for the platoon's medic, as in, "Doc Jones" or "Doc Smith."

drag. Rear security. The last man in a file of moving troops.

dust off. An unarmed Huey helicopter equipped to evacuate wounded troops from the field.

E-Club. Club where the lower four enlisted ranks party.

eagle dust off. Call sign used by medevac helicopters based at the 326th Medical Evacuation Hospital at Camp Eagle.

ETS. Estimated time of separation. The date a soldier is discharged from the service.

FAC. Forward air controller. Pilot serving as liaison between ground units and fighter-bombers. Pronounced 'fak.'

Fast mover. A jet–powered fighter bomber.

FDC. Fire direction control. The unit that controls the aiming and accuracy of artillery fire.

firebase. Fire support base; also FSB. A semi-permanent artillery or mortar position within a barbed wire perimeter containing an FDC bunker and TOC bunker secured by an infantry unit.

FNG. Fucking New Guy. A soldier just assigned to the field. See '*cherry.*'

FO. Forward Observer. An artilleryman attached to an infantry unit to control called for artillery or mortar fire. Pronounced 'foe.'

frag. A fragmentation grenade. Pineapple or baseball grenades.

freedom bird. Any aircraft used to fly a soldier home from Vietnam, usually a chartered airliner.

freeway. Slang for a wide, well-worn trail in the jungle. Also called '*high-speed trail.*'

FTA. Fuck the army. Slang used to sum up some soldiers' feelings about the army.

gook. Slang for an Asian, usually used to refer to the enemy. Possibly derived from the Korean word *miguk* meaning "country" or "countryman." The term has been in use by US troops since the early twentieth century in the Philippines, Nicaragua, Korea, the South Pacific and Vietnam.

Green beanie. Slang for a member of the army's Special Forces who wear a green beret; also known as 'green berets.'

Grunt. Slang for a combat infantryman serving in the field.

gun bunny. Slang for an artillery crewman.

gunner. An M-60 machine gunner or an M-79 grenade launcher gunner.

H & I fire. Harassing and interdicting fire. Random artillery fire used to disrupt the enemy's night movements.

HE. High explosive. Used to describe an artillery or mortar round.

head. A person who prefers drugs to alcohol.

Hill xxx. Used to identify hills or other terrain features on military maps. The number comes from the height of the hill in meters above sea level. Hill 937 was the one known as Hamburger Hill.

hooch or hutch. A bamboo hut, poncho shelter, or barracks at a base camp.

horn. A radio. As in, "Get on the horn" ("make a call").

Hot LZ. A landing zone where the enemy is waiting to fire on the helicopters and troops as they land.

Huey. A utility helicopter, type 1, model D or H. Standard helicopter for carrying cargo and troops.

humping. Walking through the jungle carrying your rucksack.

in country. The state of having entered Vietnam to serve your tour of duty. As in, "How long you been in country?"

I & I. Intercourse and intoxication. Slang for R and R.

juicer. A person who prefers drinking alcohol to drugs.

jump pay. Extra pay received by a trained paratrooper.

jump school. The parachute school at Fort Benning, Georgia.

jump status. Whether or not a unit is parachute qualified and being used in that capacity.

KBA. Killed by artillery.

KCS. Kit Carson Scout. An enemy soldier who has surrendered to US troops and has volunteered to serve as scout for a US unit.

KIA or KBHA. Killed in action or killed by hostile action. Official status of a soldier who has died in combat.

kill zone. Area of an ambush where most of the fire is concentrated.

klick. Slang for kilometer (one thousand meters, .62 miles).

KP. 'Kitchen Police.' A detail of trainees selected each day to assist the regular mess hall staff in preparing meals and cleaning the mess hall.

LAW. light anti-tank weapon. Because there were no enemy tanks in the 101st AO, it was mostly used against bunkers. Like an RPG.

LBJ. Long Binh Jail. A military stockade where serious offenders were incarcerated.

light on the skids. Describes a helicopter that doesn't fully land, keeping the helicopter ready for instant takeoff.

log bird. A resupply helicopter.

LOH. Light observation helicopter. A Hughes Aircraft OH-6 Cayuse sometimes armed with a mini-gun.

LP. Listening post. A position, usually three men, taken up at night away from the main body to give early warning of approaching enemy.

LT. Slang for a second or first lieutenant. Pronounced 'ell-tee'.

LZ. Landing zone. A cleared space in the jungle large enough for one or more helicopters to land.

M-16. A light assault rifle, either semi or fully automatic, with a 5.56mm 20 round magazine. Carried by US armed forces and allies.

M-60. A 7.62 x 51mm belt-fed light machine gun modeled after the German MG-42 from WWII.

M-79. A 40mm grenade launcher. Fires HE, illumination or shot gun rounds.

mad minute. Firing all weapons in a unit on automatic for about a minute. A defensive action used by units that suspect enemy presence around a perimeter.

medic. A trained medical aid man at the platoon level. No infantryman ever wants to hear the cry, "Medic!"

meter. 39 inches or 3.28 feet.

Military crest. An area around the circumference of a hill far enough below the summit where positions are not silhouetted against the sky when viewed from the bottom of the hill.

Million-dollar wound. A wound that is not life-threatening but is serious enough that a soldier is not able to return to combat duty in the field.

Montagnard. A French word meaning 'mountain people;' The indigenous people of Vietnam. Also called 'yards'.

MOS. Military Occupational Specialty; Describes a soldier's job. An example is 11B40, a light weapons infantry sergeant.

MP. Military police; The army's police force.

MPC. Military Payment Certificate. Used in Vietnam in place of US currency.

NCO. A Non-commissioned Officer. A sergeant at pay grades E-5 to E-9.

NCO club. Where sergeants socialize.

NCOCS. Noncommissioned Officers Candidate School.

NDP. Night defensive position. A more or less circular formation used for security by an infantry unit at night.

NVA. North Vietnamese Army. The enemy, consisting of soldiers sent down the Ho Chi Minh trail into South Vietnam from the north.

O club. Where officers socialize.

OCS. Officer Candidate School at Fort Benning. Many platoon leaders in Vietnam were graduates of OCS.

Old man. Slang for the commanding officer of a unit.

one twenty-two. A 122mm Katyuska tripod-launched rocket with an effective range of eleven klicks, about seven miles.

OP. Observation Post; A position away from the main body taken up to give warning of approaching enemy.

OPCON. Operational Control. Control under or by a headquarters other than your parent battalion. Charlie Company was OPCON to the 2nd/327th in March 1970.

P-38. Slang for the small can opener packed in every box of C rations.

pathfinder. Soldier trained to control the flight of helicopters and other aircraft into and out of an LZ. Also called *black hats* because of the black baseball caps they wore.

PT. Physical training, consisting of a daily routine of calisthenics taken from "army drills;" each army drill was made up of 12 different exercises. The exercises were performed in unison to a shouted cadence.

PAVN. People's Army of Vietnam; the formal name of the NVA.

PFC. Private first class; also, 'Proud Fucking Civilian.'

penetrator. A torpedo-shaped device on the end of a cable that can be lowered through thick jungle canopy to evacuate the wounded. It can carry three troops.

pink team. Two helicopters, usually a Cobra and a LOH, used to scout out and destroy enemy positions.

PX. Post Exchange; The army department/grocery store.

PZ. Pickup Zone. A designated location for helicopters to pick up troops or cargo for movement by air.

Quoc Lo. Vietnamese for "highway," as in QL-1 or QL-547.

R&R. Rest and recreation. A soldier's seven-day vacation paid for by the army, usually taken after about six months in country.

red team. Two Cobras used in a ground support role.

RIF. Reconnaissance in force. A squad or larger patrol sent out from the main unit to scout terrain or locate the enemy.

ROTC. Reserve Officers Training Corps. A program of military instruction in which students receive a reserve commission upon graduation from college.

RPD. *Ruchnoy Pulemyot Degtyaryova*; a 7.62mm Russian-built light machine gun, using either an ammo belt or a hundred-round drum.

RPG. Rocket-propelled grenade. A shoulder–fired, tube launched, fin-stabilized rocket with an effective range of a hundred meters; also, B-40 rocket.

RTO. Radio telephone operator. The radio man.

sat cong. Vietnamese for "kill reds" or "kill communists."

SKS. *Samozaryadnj Karabin Sistemy-Simonova;* a semi-automatic carbine firing a 7.62x39mm round from a 10-round internal magazine reloaded with a stripper clip. Sometimes used as a sniper rifle by the NVA.

shake-n-bake. Slang for a graduate of NCO school at Fort Benning or other military post, depending on the MOS.

slick. A UH-1D helicopter without machine gun or rocket pods attached to the fuselage; A log bird or a troop transport.

slope. A derogatory term for a Vietnamese person.

snake. Slang for an AH1-G Cobra gunship.

SOS. Shit on a shingle. Creamed beef served over toast.

Spec. 4. Specialist fourth class. Equivalent to a corporal.

straight leg. A derisive term used by paratroopers to describe a non-jumper; supposedly because the non-jumper had never broken his leg in a bad parachute landing, and thus had a 'straight leg'.

terrain feature. A significant piece of ground or a hill on a military map. Hill 714 is a terrain feature.

TOC. Tactical Operations Center, usually a forward command post on a firebase manned by a battalion or brigade staff.

TOT. Time on target. An artillery mission where shells are fired so they will all hit the target at the same instant.

USA. United States Army. Also, **U**ncle **S**am **A**in't **R**eleased **M**e **Y**et.

Victor Charlie. VC. The Vietnamese communist guerilla fighters.

Viet Cong. "Red Vietnamese" or communist Vietnamese.

VOCO. Verbal order-commanding officer. I traveled VOCO when I left Phu Bai for Cam Ranh Bay.

wait-a-minute bush. A small to medium-sized bush with long, vine-like branches. The branches have long thorns growing in such a way as to stick in your clothes or flesh when brushed against, causing you to yell, "Wait a minute" while you untangled yourself.

white phosphorous. An artillery round or rocket producing bright white smoke, used to mark a target. Sometimes called 'Willie Pete.'

WIA or WBHA. Wounded in action or wounded by hostile action.

World. Any place outside of Vietnam but usually the USA. Troops rotating home said, "I'm headed back to the world."

XO. Executive officer; The second in command of a unit.

zipper head. A rarely used derogatory name for a Vietnamese person, most often the enemy.

INFANTRY WEAPONS of the VIETNAM WAR

UNITED STATES ARMY AND MARINE CORPS

The M14A1 was issued to the Army and Marine Corps in 1959. Caliber 7.62 x 51mm, it weighed nearly 11 pounds fully loaded. It was replaced by the M-16 in the mid-1960's. It was used in Vietnam as an accurized sniper weapon and is still in use as a ceremonial and competition weapon.

Standard infantry assault rifle during much of the Vietnam War was the M-16, caliber 5.56 x 45mm with a twenty-round magazine. The manufacturer overcame jamming in early models by providing a chrome-plated bolt and slowing the rate of fire.

The light weight (6 lbs.) compact version of the M-16 is known as the CAR-15 caliber 5.56 x 45mm with a twenty-round magazine. This weapon could be fired semi-automatic, a three-round burst or full automatic.

The M-79 40 x 46mm grenade launcher replaced the rifle-launched grenade after the Korean War and was used extensively in Vietnam. It fired an HE round, buck shot, illumination, WP and flechette rounds.

The M-60 gas operated machine gun, modeled after the German MG-42, is a 7.62 x 51mm belt-fed light machine gun. The weapon fires 100 round disintegrating link belts of ball, tracer and armor-piercing ammunition at a 650 round per minute rate of fire.

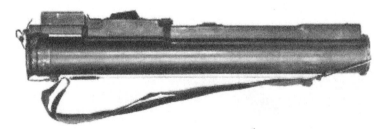

Facing page, Bottom: The M-72 Light Anti-Tank Weapon replaced the Bazooka of WW II and Korea. It is a shoulder fired 66mm fin stabilized rocket with a range of 200 meters that can penetrate up to 8 inches of armor plate. It is not reloadable in the field. It was used mainly against bunkers and entrenched troops.

The M-67 90mm recoilless rifles weighed 37.5 pounds and was most often used for perimeter defense using the M-590 flechette round. This weapon was used in the defense of Hill 805 by D/2-501 to great effect against NVA troops in the open.

The M1911A1 Automatic Pistol with a 7-round magazine fired a .45 caliber round at 852 feet per second. The weapon was carried extensively as a back-up weapon by medics, machine gunners, M-79 gunners and some officers.

PEOPLE'S ARMY OF VIETNAM – (NVA)

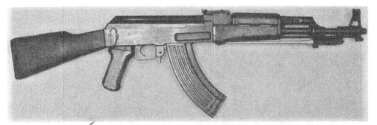

A very reliable weapon, the AK-47 assault rifle caliber 7.62 x 39mm with a 30-round detachable magazine was carried extensively by NVA and Viet Cong soldiers during the Vietnam War. Some models had a fold-down bayonet, shown above.

The AK-50 variant of the standard AK-47 had a fold-down wire stock but otherwise was the same weapon. Its compact size made it a favorite of the NVA's infamous sapper troops.

Facing page, bottom: This Russian-made RPD gas-operated light machine gun fires a 7.62 x 39mm cartridge from a non-disintegrating 100 round belt loaded into a drum magazine as shown with a 700 round per minute rate of fire.

The Russian-designed SKS semi-automatic carbine fired a 7.72 x 39mm cartridge from a 10-round internal box magazine loaded from a stripper clip. Some models were equipped with a fold-down bayonet. It was sometimes used as a sniper weapon.

The Russian-designed reloadable, shoulder-fired RPG 7 fired a 40mm fin- stabilized rocket grenade out to an effective range of 200 meters and a maximum range of 500 meters. It is deadly when used against hovering helicopters, bunkers and infantry that has not dug foxholes.

DEDICATION

This memoir is dedicated to the infantry, no matter what war, but especially to the men of the 2nd-502nd Infantry Battalion who fought in Operation Texas Star in the year 1970. When I remember the men who fought on Hill 714 and Hill 882, I see them as they were—determined young men who didn't want to be in Vietnam, but who were doing their duty just the same. When I think of the sacrifices made during the Vietnam War, an excerpt from the poem "The Battle of Blenheim" by Robert Southey (1774-1843) comes to mind:

"But what good came of it at last?"
Quoth little Peterkin.
"Why, that I cannot say," said he,
"But 'twas a famous victory"

Whether we 'won' the Vietnam War is not important. What matters is that we remember the valorous men who fought the battles of that ten-year struggle. Because of them, there were many famous victories.

STRIKE

DEDICATED
TO THE 2/502 TROOPERS
KILLED—IN—ACTION
VIETNAM
1965 — 1972

STRANGER, IF YOU GO TO THE LAND OF THE SPARTANS,
TELL THEM WE LIE HERE, OBEDIENT TO THEIR LAWS.

DO NOT FORGET US, FOR THEN,
WE TRULY WILL HAVE DIED.

MAY THE PRIDE, STRENGTH, AND COURAGE
OF THE STRIKE FORCE ENDURE FOREVER.

Made in the USA
Monee, IL
30 June 2022